A Concise Guide to Assessing Skill and Knowledge

with Music Achievement as a Model

Darrel Walters

GIA Publications, Inc.

GIA Publications, Inc.

A Concise Guide to Accessing Skill and Knowledge
with Music Achievement as a Model
Darrel Walters

G-7883

ISBN: 978-1-57999-811-0
7404 S. Mason Avenue, Chicago, IL 60638
www.giamusic.com
Printed in the United States of America.

Prologue

Imagine all teachers starting their education by learning basic principles of assessment. Maybe no other course has such a sensible argument for inclusion in the first year of the curriculum. During their next four years, while ruminating over teaching methods, techniques, objectives, lesson plans, and the other components of teacher preparation, prospective teachers would filter everything through concrete notions of how they might gauge progress—theirs and their students'. What a strategy! One might liken it to equipping hikers with compasses before sending them into the woods.

This book is a compilation of information about measurement, evaluation, test writing, and underlying statistical tools—interwoven with views I hold about their use. Music achievement is the model because of my background, but nearly all the content of this book can be applied directly to, or adapted to, disciplines engaged by others. A fringe benefit of using music achievement as the model is that it encompasses performance assessment, an important and sometimes mystifying aspect of such other disciplines as physical education, dance, art, medicine, dentistry, and various kinds of laboratory and action research.

My purpose is simple: to give faculty and students an unencumbered view of basic assessment information. I yield to others to claim a compre-hensive treatment of this subject. I claim only to (1) present information I know to be of use, (2) avoid false information to the best of my ability, and (3) be as clear as possible.

Darrel Walters

Contents

List of Figures

Chapter Three: Analyzing Statistics by Use of Microsoft® Excel

Chapter Four: Performance Testing for Instructional Improvement

Chapter Five: Performance Testing for Auditions and Other Comparison Tasks

Chapter Six: Knowledge Testing

Acknowledgements

Thanks are due the many Temple University students who contributed to the form and content of this book through their classroom interactions across the last two decades, and to two Temple University colleagues for their support and suggestions: Dr. Alison Reynolds and Dr. Debbie Lynn Wolf. Alison Reynolds began encouraging me to write this textbook many years ago, and without that encouragement I never would have begun. Debbie Lynn Wolf, who succeeded me in teaching the Temple course *Assessment of Music Learning*, used the original manuscript, met with me on numerous occasions to discuss the book, and has offered countless suggestions and unlimited encouragement along the way. Credit is due also to Dr. Edwin Gordon, who introduced me to some of the foundational material from which I developed the course over the years, and to Dr. Deborah Sheldon for her insight into the wisdom of placing undergraduate assessment instruction at the starting gate.

Another friend and colleague, Dr. Richard F. Grunow, of the Eastman School of Music, read the original manuscript thoroughly. He offered valuable suggestions and considerable encouragement, for which I am grateful. And Dr. Jennifer Bubser, a physical education specialist (and my daughter), offered her sharp eye along the way as one revision followed another. Finally, Kerry Robinson applied her considerable line editing skills to the final manuscript.

To all these fine people, and to my wife Carol—a constant source of support and inspiration—I owe more gratitude than I can show. Without them, *A Concise Guide to Assessing Skill and Knowledge* would not be in your hands today.

Introduction

Measuring human behavior is a tricky business. Some people—particularly musicians and other arts-related practitioners who teach, perform, and create—question whether it can be done at all. My view is pragmatic. Though my comfort level is highest when I am performing music, drawing pictures, writing poetry, or enjoying the arts as a consumer, I know my line of work carries me into the world of assessment through circumstance: auditions, lesson plans, grades, awards, etc. If I need to assess human behavior to do my job thoroughly—and apparently that is the case—why should I focus on difficulties? Why cry "Oh, isn't it awful," and claim that "I live by artistic standards that cannot be expressed in numbers"? Why not look for the most systematic, reliable, valid approaches by which to make those assessments?

One way to give an assessment book broad appeal on its face is to encompass a great amount of content across a great number of disciplines. I believe that approach makes a book difficult to use relative to any single discipline. I have chosen instead to combine broadly applicable assessment information with specific examples from a single discipline: music. The advantage to teachers of music is obvious. The advantage to others—teachers of virtually any subject matter—is that applying principles from the music content to their discipline may be less cumbersome than plowing through a more dense text designed to have something for everyone.

I have written this book to function as an orientation to quantitative assessment tools, a rigorous journey against the grain for most arts practitioners. I assure you, I have written this book as a musician, artist, poet, and mathephobe. Having trod difficult roads in my study of quantitative assessment and statistics, I believe I am now prepared to guide you along a path of minimal pain. Perhaps this book will open the door to a world that you can explore thoroughly with the help of persons more learned than I.

To prepare yourself to take the most from this book, assume that if you can conceive a desirable result for an endeavor, you can arrive at a best way to quantify (measure) it. Of course there are nuances beyond anything a quantitative measurement tool can account for. An artist's heart knows that intuitively. Still, by assuming that the job of assessment can be done quantitatively, you will come closest to doing it. After traveling the greatest distance you can manage into quantitative measurement, you will see clearly the point at which it cannot be done. Danger: if you assume that you know where that point is before becoming conversant with quantitative assessment tools, you will be the poorer for having neglected to probe the possibilities.

The content of this book is narrow by design. While qualitative evaluation—as by the assessment of portfolios and other means that do not call for calculations—is an important adjunct to quantitative measurement, I will let others offer advice for that arena. I do acknowledge that the full spectrum of assessment tools is important. Persons conversant with quantitative tools should not denigrate good, responsible qualitative assessment as soft and subjective, any more than persons practicing qualitative assessment should apply such terms as "authentic" to what they do, as if quantitative assessment is in some way artificial or counterfeit. To dismiss either type of assessment as irrelevant is shortsighted and irresponsible.

My goal in writing this guide is to give you quantitative tools that will help you identify the skills and knowledge your students have acquired, and the extent to which they have acquired them. I will leave advice about teaching methods, techniques, and objectives to other texts. In these six chapters you will find only bare bones quantitative information.

1. Foundational Components of Quantitative Assessment
2. Key Statistical Tools
3. Analyzing Statistics by Use of Microsoft® Excel
4. Performance Testing for Instructional Improvement
5. Performance Testing for Auditions and other Comparison Tasks
6. Knowledge Testing

A pocket on the inside back cover of this book contains a compact disc. On that disc are sound files useable for practicing performance assessment as described in Chapter Four. On that disc also are 15 PowerPoint sessions that your instructor is likely to use for classroom presentations. Each session is coordinated with specific pages of the book. You may want to use Appendix B in conjunction with those PowerPoint sessions. Appendix B contains a narrative for each PowerPoint session, complete with cues for slide advancement. The material in those narratives should help you seal in learning by reinforcing what you have heard in class and what you have read in the book.

I want to emphasize that my exclusion of qualitative assessment tools from this book does not imply that they are unimportant to the assessment of learning, any more than a book on framing a house would imply, by exclusion, that plumbing and electrical work are unimportant to building a house. This book is aimed at a very specific dimension of the assessment process. I have written it because quantitative assessment tools are important, because many teachers shy away from their use due to the difficulties they present, and because I believe that making quantitative tools easier to understand and use will constitute a service to the profession.

Chapter One

Note: terms in ***bold italics*** are defined at chapter's end
(in order of appearance), and in a glossary (alphabetically).

FOUNDATIONAL COMPONENTS OF
QUANTITATIVE ASSESSMENT

A Philosophy

At the heart of teaching are questions of WHAT to teach (curriculum) and HOW to teach (method). But no matter how well you master the WHAT and the HOW of teaching, eventually you will find yourself face to face with yet another question: TO WHAT EXTENT have my students actually learned? Teachers are likely to formulate that assessment-related question something like this: **How do I know they learned what <u>I think</u> I taught?**

The two underlined words are important. Without them, the question leaves room for the common misperception that to present material is to teach. That is not so. Just as meaningful broadcasting relies on performance from both a transmitter and a receiver, meaningful teaching relies on performance from both a teacher and a learner. You know the extent of your performance as the teacher/transmitter (with the help of self-study and external observation), but prior to assessing your students' learning you are in the dark about their performance as learners/receivers. A part of effective teaching is staying as familiar with their performance as you are with your own. Regular assessment is the tool by which you accomplish that. By making valid assessments of student output, you position yourself to make intelligent judgments about what to teach next. An assessment may tell you that students are ready to move ahead to new material, or that they need review. Or you may find that you need to re-transmit, in another way, all that you thought you taught! This array of potential outcomes implies a philosophy of assessment that, in explicit terms, is as follows: **the primary purpose of assessing student achievement is to improve instruction.** I use the term *instruction* to mean a process that encompasses both teaching and learning.

Think about what enables you to improve instruction. Some improvements grow simply from observing what works well and what flops, some from refining your sense of timing (when to teach or not teach a particular lesson), some from understanding students better over time, and some from learning ways to motivate them. All of these sources of improvement are important, but probably the most powerful tool for improving instruction is assessment of the extent to which your students have learned while under your tutelage.

When you make good use of information generated by high-quality assessment tools and post-assessment discussions with students, you reap two important benefits. First, you broaden your perspective on yourself as a transmitter: you discover what you taught most effectively and what you taught least effectively, and you hatch ideas and strategies to carry forward. Second, you find flaws in your assessment tools. By repairing those flaws for your next round of assessments, you keep these tools in a continuous state of improvement. Ever-better assessment tools feed ever-better instruction, which spurs you to construct still better assessment tools, etc., sending your entire instructional process into an upward spiral.

If all of this sounds foreign to the way you think about assessment, you might want to consider adjusting your perspective. Assessment's potential to enhance both the transmitting end and the receiving end of instruction is too powerful to ignore. My goal here is to give you information that will help you improve your assessment of learning. Once you have done that, you can use the results of your assessments to improve your teaching and your students' learning.

You will understand the information in all other chapters of this book best if you know some detail about several assessment-related terms. For learning efficiency, I will present key terms side by side, and then compare and contrast them. Those terms are as follows:

- Assessment, Measurement, and Evaluation
- Aptitude and Achievement
- Reliability and Validity
- Criterion-referenced Tests and Norm-referenced Tests

Assessment, Measurement, and Evaluation

These three terms are so close in meaning that I need to describe precisely how I am using them. To assess is to attach a value to something, so I use the term *assessment* broadly to mean the overall process of attaching a value. As a music teacher, you assess how well students sing, play, move, create, improvise, notate, understand, analyze, compare, and listen. Because of the wide range of assessment activities and approaches, you need to think of *assessment* as the broadest of these three terms. Assessment may entail measurement, evaluation, or both.

Measurement and evaluation describe two specific subsets of the overall assessment process. To use them interchangeably, as some do, is to cloud thinking and weaken communication. Think of *measurement* as the objective arm of assessment, and *evaluation* as the subjective arm. The two together inform you of the extent to which your students have acquired the skills and knowledge you are trying to impart.

If you were to take a tape measure into a classroom and find the room to be 36 feet long and 24 feet wide, you would have completed a *measurement*. Assuming an accurate tape measure, the results would be objective. Anyone else making the measurement would arrive at the same conclusion. In contrast, if you were to look into a classroom and say "this looks large enough for our ensemble rehearsal," that would be an *evaluation*. Your judgment would be subjective. Another person might judge differently.

Now assume that an out-of-town friend wants to know if you have a room in which a visiting ensemble might rehearse. Probably you would send a measurement to your friend (36 feet by 24 feet). Based on your measurement (objective), your friend would then make an evaluation (subjective) of the room's suitability as a place to rehearse the visiting ensemble. The two of you together, applying *measurement* followed by *evaluation*, would have made a comprehensive *assessment*.

That physical example can be used as a template for assessing learning. Responsible, comprehensive assessment commonly involves a partnership between measurement and evaluation. To assess learning comprehensively, you will construct measurement tools that yield numbers representative of your students' skill and knowledge, just as the tape measure yields numbers representative of the room's size. Using those measurements as a guide, you as the teacher will evaluate a student's suitability to proceed with a particular lesson or to assume a particular performance responsibility, just as your friend used the measurements of the room to evaluate its suitability to serve as a rehearsal space for his ensemble. In both cases, **accurate measurements increase the quality of subsequent evaluations.**

I need to make three important points before moving on from the topics of measurement and evaluation. First, measurements of achievement are used for two kinds of evaluation: formative and summative. *Formative evaluation* is aimed at guiding the next instructional step. *Summative evaluation* is aimed at making a summary statement of what has been learned, as in awarding grades. You will be required to award grades, but I will not delve into the details of grading. If you make good measurements and use them to make good judgments about teaching, you will have a wealth of information on which to base your grades.

Second, you should not think of objectivity in the measurement of human behavior as absolute. The tools by which you will measure learning will be much less precise and less consistent than the tape measure used in that classroom. You will do all you can to make your measurement tools optimally objective, but you will never duplicate the certainty of physical measurement. That being said, I will—as I write about measurement tools in subsequent chapters—refer to them as objective. Keep in mind that I use the term knowing that objectivity in this realm is relative. Imperfect as our "objective" measurement tools may be, they will enable us to learn more about our students than if we were to rely solely on off-the-cuff evaluations. They will not be the equivalent of measuring the room with a tape measure, but they will be closer to that than to guessing at the suitability of the room from afar with no guidance from measurement.

Finally, I need to admit that the line between measurement and evaluation is not clear-cut. I have encouraged you to think of the two terms in distinct ways and use them independently, because recognizing the separate functions of measurement and evaluation clarifies much about the assessment process. But in reality, the two sometimes bend in each other's direction. I will give an example of that bending in Chapter Four when I write about performance testing.

Aptitude and Achievement

Aptitude is the potential to learn. Achievement is learning already acquired. Using the terms *music aptitude* and *music achievement* to describe potential and acquired learning, respectively, is extremely helpful. Terms that involve both potential and acquired learning in unknown proportions, i.e., *talent* or *ability*, blur meaning and sacrifice precision.

Music Aptitude

The primary aim of this book is to present tools to help you assess achievement, but knowing the nature of aptitude and aptitude assessment will also be important to you. If you teach music, the information about music aptitude testing will be of specific interest. I will put into this section nearly all that I have to say about music aptitude and its assessment, leaving the remainder of the book to present statistical tools and means of assessing achievement of all kinds.

Music aptitude is less tangible than music achievement, and thus more complex to measure. A sculptor was once asked "how did you make that horse look so real?" He answered, "I took a big block of marble and knocked off everything that didn't look like a horse." The challenge is similar for one who would write a music aptitude test: knock off everything that does not look like aptitude—that is, everything that looks like achievement. Because the only way a test-taker can respond to aptitude test items is to perform a musical act of some kind, separation of achievement from aptitude is an enormous challenge. And of course the aptitude test's product (a representation of someone's music aptitude) is less-easily recognized and verified than is the sculptor's product (an accurate representation of a horse). Following is a brief account of some of the attempts made to measure music aptitude, along with information about current aptitude tests that you might consider using.

If there is such a person as the "father of music aptitude testing," that person would be Carl Seashore, author of *Seashore Measures of Musical Talent* (1919), a measure that he revised in 1939. Being a psychologist rather than a musician, Seashore wrote a test that was a measure more of aural acuity than of musicianship. Subsequently, test writers tried to write more music-oriented measures of music aptitude, but in some cases crossed the line into achievement by using established musical examples that were more familiar to some test takers than to others.

Edwin Gordon made a breakthrough in music aptitude measurement with his publication of the *Musical Aptitude Profile (MAP)* (1965), for which he wrote original musical material. John McLeish described *MAP* in Buros' *Seventh Mental Measurements Yearbook* (1972) as "the best test of its kind anywhere on the market" (p. 247). Since that time, Gordon's tools for measuring music aptitude have become dominant. The student population for which Gordon designed and normed *MAP* is grades 4 through 12.

MAP is comprehensive and of high quality. It consists of seven sub-tests, two for tonal aptitude (melody and harmony), two for rhythm aptitude (tempo and meter), and three for musical sensitivity (phrasing, balance, and style). Gordon refers to the tonal and rhythm subtests as *non-preference* tests, because each item has a correct answer. Listeners hear pairs of short items, and are asked to judge, for example, whether the second is a melodic variation of the first, or whether the second changes tempo or meter as compared to the first. By contrast, Gordon refers to the three musical sensitivity subtests as *preference* tests, because responses are technically matters of opinion. For those items, Gordon recruited professional musicians to offer opinions, used only items for which the professional musicians reached agreement at least 90 percent of the time, and keyed answers accordingly.

Two disadvantages of *MAP* are the administration time needed (three 50-minute sessions) and the cultural shift in perceptions of musicality since 1965. Many users of *MAP* omit the sensitivity battery, believing that today's test takers are insensitive to performances previously heard as having, for example, poorly turned phrases or ugly phrase endings. The other advantage of omitting that battery is reduction of administration time to two 50-minute sessions. Some consumers trim administration time to one 50-minute session by administering only one tonal subtest (T1) and one rhythm subtest (R2).

Gordon settled on grade 4 as the youngest students for whom *MAP* was suitable because all efforts failed to yield acceptable reliability for younger students. Gordon ultimately developed the theory of developmental verses stabilized music aptitude, contending that music aptitude did not stabilize until approximately age 9. Prior to that, he theorized, a child's lifelong capacity for learning music (aptitude) could be influenced, with the greatest influence occurring closest to birth and the window of opportunity gradually closing from birth to about age 9. That makes *MAP* a measure of stabilized music aptitude.

More than a decade later, Gordon published his first measure of developmental music aptitude. Designed and normed for students in grades K through 3, *The Primary Measures of Music Audiation (PMMA)* (1979) consists of two subtests: tonal and rhythm. Each subtest is administered in about 25 minutes and requires no literacy skills. After enriched musical experiences caused a ceiling effect (many students bunched at the top) for *PMMA*, Gordon created and published a slightly more rigorous version of *PMMA* and titled it *The Intermediate Measures of Music Audiation (IMMA)* (1982). He normed *IMMA* for children in grades 1 through 4.

Gordon stretched the boundaries of music aptitude testing each direction from his K through12 tests with publication of *Audie* (1989) for preschool children old enough to give verbal responses, and the *Advanced Measures of Music Audiation (AMMA)* (1989) for students beyond high-school age. The format of *Audie* differs from Gordon's other aptitude tests in that it is administered to individual children rather than groups, and responses are verbal rather than written. Time needed to administer *Audie*, which has separate subtests for the tonal and rhythm dimensions, is less than 15 minutes. The format of *AMMA* differs from Gordon's other aptitude tests in that he did not construct independent subtests for the dimensions of tonal aptitude and rhythm aptitude. Rather, test-takers hear a pair of items and then judge the second to compare to the first in one of three ways: identical, tonal change, or rhythm change. Administration time needed for *AMMA* is about 30 minutes.

Gordon has since renormed *IMMA* to extend upward and *AMMA* to extend downward to give consumers shorter alternatives to *MAP*. Whether the greater good is accomplished by administering *IMMA* and *AMMA* to populations for whom they were not originally designed, or by taking the time required to use the most rigorously constructed of Gordon's aptitude tests (*MAP*) is a matter of opinion. If you teach music, you will do well to study the manuals for Gordon's aptitude tests and listen to the test recordings. For more information about music aptitude and music aptitude testing, you might refer to *The Nature, Description, Measurement, and Evaluation of Music Aptitudes* (Gordon, 1986) or to "Edwin Gordon's Music Aptitude Work" (Walters, 1991).

Assuming you obtain music aptitude test results in which you have confidence, your knowledge of the extent to which given students are realizing their potentials will enable you to teach them more intelligently. The challenge of having aptitude scores is to use the information wisely. Like nitroglycerin, music aptitude scores handled carelessly can do a great amount of damage. The potential good is insight into what students need, what they might be able to accomplish, and what might be unfair to ask of them. A potential harm is the placement of artificial limitations on students capable of more.

One important principle to keep in mind when interpreting the results of a valid aptitude test is this: those who score high do have high aptitude, but those who score low do not necessarily have low aptitude. That is, if the aptitude test is of high quality and properly administered, a person lacking aptitude for music learning will not be able to "beat the test," i.e., register a spuriously high score. Conversely, a high-aptitude test-taker may score spuriously low for any number of reasons, including failure to understand directions; rebellion against doing well; distractions from sights, sounds, or thoughts; distress over personal problems; and physical illness. If you are a teacher who makes use of aptitude scores, you will do well to stay alert to signs of high-level musical behaviors on the part of students whose aptitude scores are low. Seeing such signs, you should have the student retake the aptitude test.

Music Achievement

A child's music achievement is simply the extent of that child's capability to sing, play an instrument, improvise on a musical theme, compose original music, or respond insightfully to music played or sung. Method and technique courses you take during your training to become a music educator, along with capabilities you acquire on the job, prepare you to teach such skills and knowledge. The primary purpose of this book is to prepare you to assess the extent to which your students have actually learned those skills and that knowledge. From this point on, all material in this book is aimed at the task of assessing music achievement. To be more precise, most of the material from this point on is aimed at the task of *measuring* music achievement, though evaluation will remain in the picture to some extent.

Reliability and Validity

An important aim in constructing tools to measure achievement is to make those tools optimally objective, i.e., to have them function as much as possible like a tape measure. Two characteristics important to achieving objectivity are reliability and validity.

Reliability is the consistency with which something is accomplished. A synonym is *dependability*. You may have a friend who, whenever you arrange to meet at 2:00, arrives at 2:15. You may be tempted to refer to that person as unreliable. That is not true. You can rely on your friend to be 15 minutes late. Your friend is consistent, and therefore reliable.

Validity is the extent to which something is accomplished as it is intended to be accomplished. A synonym is *accuracy*. If your friend were to meet you at 2:00 regularly, as planned, your meeting then would have been accomplished as it was intended to be accomplished. That would be an example of accuracy, or validity.

Figure 1 shows a physical comparison of reliability and validity. Assume that the person who shot at those targets intended to hit the bull's-eye. In that case, Target A is like the friend who shows up at 2:15. You see consistency—a pattern that says "you can depend on having the shots land in this area." That makes Target A a picture of reliability, but the shooting was not accomplished as intended. Therefore, Target A is not a picture of validity. For that, look at Target B. All the shots are in the bull's-eye. The task has been

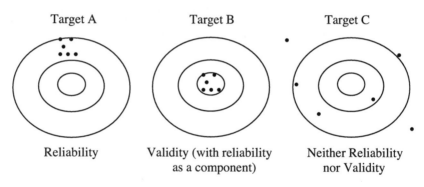

Target A	Target B	Target C
Reliability	Validity (with reliability as a component)	Neither Reliability nor Validity

Figure 1. Target Shooting as an Illustration of Reliability and Validity

accomplished as intended. It is accurate. Note that Target B is also an example of reliability, and necessarily so. If shots are scattered, as in Target C, the loss of reliability carries with it an unavoidable loss of validity. This will become an extremely important principle when the properties of reliability and validity are applied to tests: reliability is entirely possible without validity, but validity is not possible without reliability. Said another way, **reliability is a prerequisite for validity.** If you were to construct a test in such a way that student responses were unreliable (inconsistent; undependable), that test could not accomplish what you intend it to accomplish. Lack of reliability would necessarily cause the test to lack validity.

Reliability and validity are bedrocks of assessment. I have a great amount to share with you about them. Below I will elaborate on each in general terms. As I describe specific test formats later, I will write about reliability and validity more specifically.

Reliability

In the next chapter you will learn about a mathematical tool of measurement known as *correlation*, and more specifically, a statistic referred to as a *correlation coefficient*. To understand the rest of this chapter, you need to know only that such a coefficient exists, and that it shows the extent to which two entities are related, i.e., the degree of consistency from one to another.

You will estimate the reliability of your tests by calculating correlation coefficients. If I want to know whether student responses to a test I have written would be consistent enough with repetition for me to consider the test reliable, I could administer the test to the same students a second time. Then I could calculate a correlation coefficient between the two distributions of scores (results of the first testing and results of the second testing) to obtain a numerical indication of the strength of their relationship. A strong positive correlation between the two indicates that the test is high in what is called ***test–retest reliability***. When that is done, the correlation coefficient is given a specific name that indicates the purpose to which it was applied: it is called a *reliability coefficient* (and still more specifically, a *coefficient of stability*).

The test–retest reliability estimate is just one approach to estimating reliability. Some of the variations in approach are due to differences in test format, and some are due to computer programs that have opened up new possibilities in recent decades. In subsequent chapters you will read about more variations of reliability estimates in conjunction with specific testing formats.

Validity

Two over-arching kinds of test validity are *objective validity* and *subjective validity*. As you might guess after having read the early part of this chapter, objective validity involves measurement (numerical values) and subjective validity involves evaluation (judgment). In this case, I am referring to measurements and evaluations of the test itself—conducted to be sure the test helps you do a good job of measuring and evaluating student achievement.

Objective validity is almost exclusively the province of published, standardized tests. A validity coefficient shows the correlation between results of a test and results of a more comprehensive measure (criterion measure), something considered a benchmark for whatever skills or knowledge the test is designed to measure. Individual teachers generally cannot afford the extensive time and expense involved in "validating" a test by using such a thorough method. Generally, the best effort teachers can make toward the goal of objective validity for classroom tests is to measure reliability. Because validity is impossible in the absence of reliability, knowing that a test is reliable gives a teacher assurance that the test has at least achieved a major first step toward objective validity.

Subjective validity, on the other hand, is very much within a teacher's power to achieve, and is in fact a teacher's major responsibility in constructing a measurement tool. Think of subjective validity as judgment validity, or perhaps common-sense validity. Within that larger category of subjective validity are two subcategories: *content validity* and *process validity*.

Content validity is a matter of testing what you taught, and with emphasis roughly in proportion to the emphasis you gave while teaching. All of us have reacted to a test at one time or another with the question "where did that material come from? Why weren't we tested on the material that was emphasized in class?" I find no excuse for a test lacking content validity. In most cases, the cause is pure inattentiveness on the part of the teacher. Before you write any test, you should sketch out a taxonomy of the course content and note the material emphasized most, and then write test items that reflect that content. Some teachers do a content check when the test is new, but let the test lose content validity over time. That is, from semester to semester or year to year they alter their teaching (drop something out here, add something there), and when time comes to administer the test they fail to recheck the relationship between the test and what they actually taught. They administer a test that matches the course content as it was taught previously, but not as it was taught to the current group of students. That is unconscionable.

Process validity, the other primary subset of subjective validity, is a matter of ensuring that the only hurdles students have to clear are those related to the test content itself. Students should not have to overcome an illegible test copy; poor grammar or vague meaning written into test items; a room that is excessively warm, or cold, or noisy; verbal instructions difficult to hear or understand; or a poor-quality recording. In creating and administering a test, you are obligated to put students in clear, direct contact with the test's content, without distractions. Otherwise you will be measuring, along with test content, students' abilities to overcome your hurdles. That means the test grade will be influenced by factors other than the material the test was designed to measure. That is not accomplishing the task "as it was intended to be accomplished," the very definition of validity.

I am about to make a bold, sweeping statement, but one that I believe is warranted. In my opinion, **if teachers nationwide were to suddenly become conscientious about matters of subjective validity—does the content of my test reflect what I taught, and is my process for administering it free of artificial hurdles?—the quality of testing in this country would take such a dramatic leap upward that we would feel the effects from coast to coast**. You will read a great amount of advice in subsequent chapters about test construction, test administration, theoretical constructs, statistical analyses, interpretation of the analyses, etc. All of that is important, but perhaps the most important factors in assessment (and the easiest to monitor and improve) are those related to subjective validity.

Criterion-referenced Tests and Norm-referenced Tests

The terms in this heading do not describe types of tests, nor are they categories of tests. They are descriptions of how the results of a test are interpreted. Any test could instantly become either criterion-referenced or norm-referenced, depending on the "reference" used by whoever is interpreting the outcome. A ***criterion-referenced*** test is so called because the test items themselves (criteria) are used as the ruler with which to measure success. A ***norm-referenced*** test is so called because results shown to be typical (norms) are used as the ruler with which to measure success. Said another way, test-takers whose results are criterion-referenced are competing with the test items, and test-takers whose results are norm-referenced are competing with other test-takers. The population of test-takers whose results are used as norms could be local (even as local as a single classroom), or they could be state, national, or international.

Criterion-referenced testing is associated primarily with school classrooms, and norm-referenced testing is associated primarily with standardized testing. Standardized tests, some of which cover more information than most test-takers can absorb, are designed to discover where individuals fall relative to the population as a whole. As much sense as norm-referenced tests make for standardized tests, an interesting philosophical question is this: do criterion-referenced tests make as much sense for classroom testing as norm-referenced tests make for standardized testing — or might the norm-referenced approach hold some promise for measuring achievement among students in our schools? Teachers who "grade on the curve" apparently believe in the importance of norms, as their approach to interpreting tests is norm-referenced. (In the next chapter you will learn detailed information about "the curve.")

The learning goals that a teacher has for students should dictate the desirability of one type of test interpretation over another. A criterion-referenced testing approach makes sense if students are expected to be engaged in mastery learning, i.e., if all students are expected to learn everything. That makes sense for young children who are expected to learn all of the multiplication tables, or for students in a first-aid course who are being trained to handle all first-aid–level emergencies. But how appropriate is the criterion-referenced approach for broader learning?

By nature, criterion-referenced testing puts a ceiling on expectations. A set body of knowledge is laid out to be learned, and those who learn it score 100% on the test. But is that a formula for narrow teaching? What does the teacher do who wants to open up wide vistas to students and challenge them to extend themselves — the teacher who wants to offer a rich learning experience rather than a ceiling over the heads of students who are capable of much more than answering a list of questions that demand scant thinking? What if that teacher then wants to write an extremely rigorous test that shows differences in levels of understanding among the five or six students who would have scored 100% on a simple mastery test? And what happens to students who then answer a much smaller percentage of that test correctly than they would have under the less-challenging mastery (criterion-referenced) approach?

Under a typical criterion-referenced testing system, students are awarded a grade of A if they answer perhaps 92% to 100% of the items correctly, a grade of B if they answer 85% to 91% correctly, etc. A teacher who wants to challenge students is put into a box. Wanting to (or by public pressure needing to) award a reasonable number of A grades, that teacher is forced to write tests that avoid challenging bright students to a great extent. Criterion-referenced tests must be "dumbed down" to a level that will allow an acceptable number of students to answer 92% of the test correctly.

That limitation of the criterion-referenced approach threatens the morale and motivation of bright students. The answer our schools have found to the danger of boring bright students is to create "gifted" programs to give them some place to exercise their brightness. Another approach might have been to abandon the criterion-referenced approach to testing and embrace the norm-referenced approach. That allows the writing of challenging tests—the stretching of students—without dooming great numbers of students to failure. If a test has 40 items, for example, and the best grade, semester after semester, lies in the mid-30s, let a grade of 75% earn an A. Then the occasional genius can take great satisfaction in scoring the first perfect score in years. The lack of a ceiling on expectation—encouragement to learn beyond a minimum set of criteria—might create a richer learning experience for all.

Keep these two approaches to test interpretation in mind as you read the next few chapters. Think in terms of creating local norms for your tests over time. Think of ways to challenge and excite students rather than have them simply follow a beaten path. An educator some time ago commented that the criterion-referenced approach to testing, because it encourages simple memorization of enough facts to meet the criteria, causes good students and poor students to differ in a much simpler way than one would expect: bad students forget information right away, and good students wait until after the test. Might our approach to testing play an important role in the extent to which students discover their potential and apply it to life after school?

I pose all of these questions to illustrate the extent to which testing touches nerves within various educational philosophies. Educators need to decide not only WHAT to teach and HOW to teach it, but also where they fall philosophically on the relative importance of cushioning the blows for low-performing students and stoking the fires for high-performing students. In the end, your educational philosophy will affect profoundly the kinds of tests you write and the way you interpret results. Your testing, in turn, will affect profoundly the quantity and quality of learning that takes place among your students.

An Overview of Assessment Tools

You will want to assess two dimensions of your students' achievement: what they can do (skills, demonstrated through performance) and what they know (knowledge, demonstrated generally through written responses). Assessing what students know is the basis for most testing as we know it, but assessing what students can do is also important within most disciplines — particularly those having skill development at their core (music, art, physical education, creative writing). A good way to understand assessment tools, then, is to categorize them within two distinct types: performance tests and knowledge tests.

Performance Tests

Tests given by teachers in schools are generally thought of as pencil-and-paper tests designed to measure the extent of information and under-standing students have acquired. Our school experiences have conditioned us to expect success to be indicated by numbers and percentages attached to such traditional testing. A more difficult challenge is to attach quantitative thought to the assessment of a student's display of skill. There is no specific number of correct or incorrect answers associated with a performance test. A percentage score needs to be based on a portion of 100%, and 100% skillful is not as definable as 100% correct from a given number of questions. To think of performance testing in the context of knowledge testing is enough to make a teacher give up, and say "performance is too subjective to measure. I know what's good when I hear it or see it, and that off-the-top-of-my-head judgment will have to be good enough."

But capitulation is not necessary. If you know what you want to teach, you should know what you want to hear or see as an indication of learning. If you can describe what you want to see or hear, you can construct check lists and rating scales that will help you increase the reliability and validity of your judgments. Well-written, wisely used *performance tests*—the subject of Chapter Four—will free you from snap judgments that vary day to day and that leave you with little information on which to base the next round of teaching.

Knowledge Tests

In educational literature, you will see *knowledge tests* labeled as *cognitive tests* to indicate that they test cognition. Because *cognition* is fundamentally a fancy synonym for *knowledge,* I choose to describe these tests with the more immediately understood label *knowledge test.*

No doubt you are familiar with several forms of knowledge tests: short answer, matching, true and false, essay, multiple choice. Tests given in schools vary greatly in both type and quality. Most likely you have taken some very good knowledge tests and some very poor ones. In Chapter Six you will learn to construct high-quality knowledge tests. You will learn also to identify the quality of individual test items and tests as a whole.

Terms Important to This Chapter

instruction (2): a term used in this book to represent a process that encompasses both teaching and learning.

assessment (3): the attaching of a value to something by use of measurement, evaluation, or both.

measurement (3): an objective process that yields specific information, as in the measurement of a room; educational measurement, accomplished through testing, is necessarily less precise than physical measurement because of the unpredictability of human behavior and the imprecision of even well-constructed tests as compared to physical devices such as tape measures.

evaluation (3): a subjective process that yields a judgment, as in deciding what grade to award or who should sit ahead of whom in an ensemble; evaluation gains effectiveness when based on information generated by a reliable, valid measurement tool.

formative evaluation (4): evaluation aimed at guiding the next instructional step, i.e., contributing to the formative process by which one improves musicianship.

summative evaluation (4): evaluation aimed at summarizing a segment of achievement, i.e., generating a grade or some other symbol of what has been accomplished.

music aptitude (5): one's potential to learn music; music aptitude is to music learning as IQ is to academic learning.

music achievement (5): the music learning that one can demonstrate as having been acquired.

reliability (9): the consistency with which something is accomplished; dependability.

validity (9): the extent to which something is accomplished as intended; accuracy.

test-retest reliability (11): process of administering a test twice within a short period of time (2–7 days), and then estimating reliability by calculating the correlation between the two distributions of scores (first and second administration); as applied to performance testing, the process is one of rate–rerate, with the same rater generating two ratings of the same performance and calculating the correlation between the two resulting distributions.

objective validity (12): process for estimating the validity of a test by administering it and a criterion measure (a more comprehensive and trustworthy measure of the same trait the test measures) to the same population, and then calculating the relationship between the test and the criterion measure; used primarily to validate published, standardized tests.

subjective validity (12): process for increasing the validity of a test by making sound judgments about its content and about the process for administering it, thus keeping test-takers free of impediments other than those related to content; involves no statistical value.

content validity (12): a subset of subjective validity; the extent to which the content of a test is congruent with the content taught, and in proportion to the emphasis given to one part of the content over another.

process validity (13): a subset of subjective validity; the extent to which hurdles have been removed from the administration of the test so that students are being tested on content alone rather than on extraneous challenges such as interpreting poorly written items, losing a visual or aural advantage due to placement in the room, suffering distraction due to conditions in or around the testing area, or any other irregularities that might affect the test's outcome beyond knowledge of content.

criterion-referenced (13): a test whose results are interpreted relative to the number of test items answered correctly, without reference to the success of other test-takers.

norm-referenced (13): a test whose results are interpreted relative to the success rate of other test takers, without reference to the number of test items answered correctly.

performance tests (17): tests designed to measure what a person can do (described fully in Chapters Four and Five).

knowledge tests (17): tests designed to measure what a person knows and understands (described fully in Chapter Six).

KEY STATISTICAL TOOLS

Introduction

Statistics! It is here that this book is most likely to strike you as cold, calculating, and at odds with music and the other arts. I understand your discomfort. The arts are rife with nuance and interpretation and stylistic considerations. Art is a form of beauty, and beauty is to an extent (as the ancient Greeks expressed) in the eye or ear of the beholder. When we assess a musical performance, or any artistic endeavor, subjectivity is inescapable.

Still, subjectivity is only part of the picture. Any musical performance entails layers of achievement. Some layers most certainly can be assessed objectively: correct pitches, correct rhythms, characteristic tone quality, basic components of physical execution, and all of the factual information to be learned. Other layers involve judgments on which most musicians agree, e.g., basic considerations of style and interpretation. Still other layers involve highly personal choices, e.g., fine points of style, interpretation, phrasing, and tone.

At that last layer, the personal-choice layer, assessment does tend to become grey. But if you take a quick inventory of what you teach, you will find that most of it can be quantified—particularly for students working at a basic rather than an advanced level. Think back to the WHAT of teaching: if you had no quantitative sense of correct or incorrect, of better or worse, how would you know what to teach—what to tell students to do or avoid doing? Certainly the bulk of what you teach involves quantifiable achievement.

Quantitative assessment requires you to calculate and interpret numerical data. There is no way around that. I think the best way for me to accommodate that need is to present the basic statistical tools of quantitative assessment. That will make this chapter, in effect, a miniature statistics course. I will make it as painless as I know how.

You will use a computer software program for most of your statistical calculations, as described in Chapter Three. Nonetheless, I will present here—along with information about the meanings, uses, and interpretations of the various statistics—formulas for hand calculations. My view may be old fashioned, but I believe that calculating these statistics by hand a few times makes an indelible impression of the logic behind them. That will enhance your subsequent understanding and interpretation of computer printouts. For each statistic introduced, I have presented a sample from which to learn. At the end of the chapter, I have provided exercises to use for practice.

I will mention music only fleetingly, because the content of this chapter bears no direct relationship to the specific task of assessing music learning. Music teachers will need to accept this material (and material in the following chapter) as brief side trips from the primary journey expected here, but readers from other disciplines will be free to associate material from these two chapters with their discipline's content without the distraction of music content.

Learn the material in this chapter thoroughly. In subsequent chapters I will refer freely to statistics and terms presented here. If you have a statistics background you will find this chapter elementary. If not, be assured that I have imposed the bare minimum of information you will need to interpret basic assessment results.

The Standard Normal Distribution

As cold and clinical as the theory of the *standard normal distribution (bell curve)* seems on the surface, it provides a framework by which to manage and interpret quantitative information. The bell curve is not a dreamt-up, ivory-tower theory. It is a virtual picture of how quantities (including quantities of human achievement) are naturally distributed. Because the bell curve is associated with the work of nineteenth-century mathematician Carl Frederick Gauss, sometimes it is called the *Gaussian distribution*.

Whether it's height, weight, shoe size, rate of corn growth, human aptitude, or human achievement, every collection of quantities has a mean (arithmetic average) around which frequencies tend to gather in large numbers, and away from which frequencies tend to diminish with greater distance in either direction. The average distance from the mean (roughly speaking) for all cases of a set of scores is a statistic called the *standard deviation*. Mean and standard deviation will be described in detail in the next section of this chapter.

The theory of the bell curve (based on untold numbers of observations) is that 99 percent of the population, for any variable measured, will fall between three standard deviations above and three standard deviations below the mean, with numbers of cases tailing off dramatically at the extremes. Other predictable percentages of the population will fall symmetrically within sections of the curve related to the standard deviation, as shown in Figure 1.

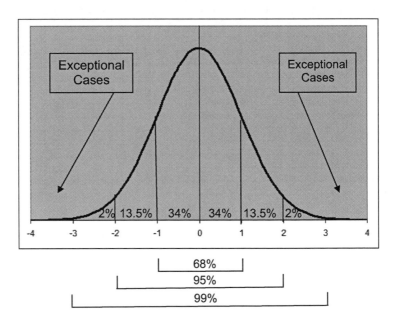

Figure 1. The Standard Normal Distribution (Bell Curve)

Beyond three standard deviation units in each direction lie the exceptional cases. Exceptional cases at the top, for example, would be the height of an NBA center, the IQ of Einstein, or the music aptitude of Mozart.

I learned of the Gaussian distribution late in life, and it helped me understand my capabilities and shortcomings. I wonder what the effect would have been had I known earlier that struggling with difficult tasks did not mean I was dull, but that I simply was not in my element at the time. Now I know from decades of experience, feedback, and testing that my verbal aptitude is in the top tail of the curve, my math aptitude somewhere near the mean, and my mechanical aptitude near the bottom. I wonder if children (beginning probably after primary age) might find peace of mind, insight, and motivation in understanding that (1) weaknesses are a part of the natural order, and (2) each of us has strengths to be identified and used to good advantage.

I think some teachers ignore the candor of the bell curve for fear of lowering children's self-esteem—subscribing to the Lake Woebegone effect: all children are above average. Unfortunately, that leads to teachers pretending that all children are equally capable of each task set before them. Besides frustrating students, that stance leads to an erosion of the teacher's credibility when children's anecdotal evidence eventually tells them otherwise. (Ask a classroom of children who runs fastest, who draws the best pictures, who sings best, who is funniest, etc., and see how quickly they arrive at a consensus.) What if, instead of living in the land of you're-all-wonderful-at-everything, teachers actually pointed out to children the theory of the bell curve? What if we let children know that each of them has challenges that will make them struggle and gifts at which they can excel, and that they are different from one another in these respects? What if we were to excite them about being on the lookout for their strengths and weaknesses?

Children enthused about making the most of strengths and determined to shore up weaknesses might feel that their feet are finally planted on firm personal ground. They might become eager to hear the results of valid assessments. And they might embrace the idea of a teacher/student partnership that puts everyone on an honest, dependable trajectory toward fulfilling potential. They might even tolerate rather than taunt each other's weaknesses, and admire rather than resent each other's strengths. What a boon that would be, to see children strengthen relationships with other at the same time they strengthen themselves!

I should add that I do not envision students "throwing in the towel" where weaknesses are noted. Children by nature love a challenge when they know where they stand. I am betting on the enhancement of all skills, weak and strong, once children are free of flim-flam and uncertainty.

Educators and psychometricians associate the bell curve primarily with innate traits such as IQ and aptitude. But by studying distributions of achievement scores over time, and by comparing them with distributions of aptitude scores and other achievement scores, you can make sense of your students' progress and make the most of your opportunities to advise them wisely and teach them well. Knowing where students stand gives you a good idea of where they should go next. Conversely, ignorance of where students stand—on your part and theirs—can only impede progress. Often heard and variously attributed is the thought that "nothing is so unequal as the equal treatment of unequals." Your obligation as a teacher is to treat children unequally according to what is best for them. High-quality assessment will help you know what is best, and that knowing will lead you to become an ever-more-effective teacher.

Describing Distributions of Scores

The term *distribution* describes any set of scores obtained from measuring any group of subjects by using any measurement tool. A set of scores (each referred to as a *case*) is called a distribution because the individual scores are thought of as distributed from highest to lowest, or distributed around the mean. Figure 2 shows two distributions of fictitious scores that I will carry throughout this chapter and the next to demonstrate various statistics. In reality, most distributions will be larger than these. To keep calculations manageable, I have entered only enough cases to demonstrate the points to be made.

	X	Y
Bert	7	10
Ophelia	6	8
Yonmee	6	5
Ernie	5	4
Rhonda	5	4
Chico	5	3
Obie	4	3
Lois	4	3
Lenyatta	3	2

Figure 2. Two Distributions of Scores for Practice

Another way to list distributions of scores is by use of a *frequency distribution,* a particularly handy device for distributions containing great numbers of scores with many repeated scores. The little nine-case distributions I use here look silly in a frequency distribution, but I have shown the X distribution from Figure 2 as a frequency distribution in Figure 3 so you can see the components. I will make little use of frequency distributions in this book. I am familiarizing you with the technique here only because you are likely to see it in print, and because you may want to use a frequency distribution yourself when circumstances make it practical for you to do so.

X	f	cf	c%
7	1	9	100
6	2	8	89
5	3	6	67
4	2	3	33
3	1	1	11

X	score
f	frequency: number of cases attaining that score
cf	cumulative frequency: number of cases at or below that score
$c\%$	cumulative percentage: percentage of cases at or below that score

Figure 3. Distribution X Shown as a Frequency Distribution

I have labeled this chapter's two sample distributions X and Y just to have a symbol by which to refer to them. Assume that the group of students named took Test X followed by Test Y, and that you want to analyze results of the tests by describing the two distributions as wholes rather than by examining individual results. Three common ways to describe a distribution of scores are by its *shape*, its *central tendency*, and its *variability*.

Shape

A distribution of scores generated by using a perfect assessment tool with a perfectly distributed group of subjects under perfect conditions would be perfectly **symmetrical.** It would, in fact, conform to the **shape** of the standard normal curve (bell curve) shown in Figure 1. A distribution that is not symmetrical (the top half and the bottom half—or as represented by the curve, the right half and the left half—are not mirror images) is described as **asymmetrical**, and the extent of its asymmetry is the extent to which it is said to be **skewed**. A distribution having extreme scores on the high end is said to be **skewed to the right**, or **positively skewed**. A distribution having extreme scores on the low end is said to be **skewed to the left**, or **negatively skewed**. Be careful not to reverse your thinking relative to the type of skew. The high scores that pull the tail of a positively skewed distribution upward raise the mean of the distribution, leaving a larger number of cases below the mean than above it. That bulge of cases at the low end might tempt you to think of the positive skew shown in Figure 4 as negative, and the opposite for the skew having extreme scores at the bottom and a bulge at the top. Remember that the direction of the tail indicates the direction of the skew, because that is the direction in which the extreme scores are pulling the mean. A silly little slogan might help you remember: the tail tells the tale.

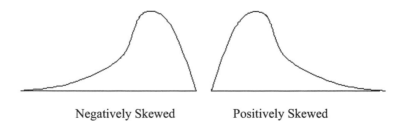

Negatively Skewed   Positively Skewed

Figure 4. A Visual Representation of Skewed (asymmetrical) Distributions

The statistical name used most commonly to describe an ***extreme score*** is ***outlier***. I have seen extreme scores referred to also as ***renegade scores.*** Because scores have no mind of their own ("I'm going to be a renegade today and run out there away from the other scores."), probably they are most appropriately referred to as either extreme scores or outliers.

Note that a distribution with roughly equivalent outliers at each end would not be skewed. The two ends would balance each other, like equal-weight children on the ends of a teeter totter, each exerting about the same influence on the mean. The mean would stay put, so the distribution would not be skewed. Because the extreme scores on both ends would stretch the shape of the distribution, the distribution would not approximate the bell curve despite retaining symmetry. That is, it would become flattened—more horizontal in appearance than the bell curve. The opposite configuration, a distribution whose scores cluster close to the mean, might also retain symmetry without approximating the bell curve. It would become peaked—more vertical in appearance than the bell curve.

That particular property of a distribution is referred to as ***kurtosis***. A distribution whose scores cause it to approximate the shape of the bell curve is described as ***mesokurtic***, a horizontally stretched (flat) distribution is described as ***platykurtic***, and a vertically stretched (peaked) distribution is described as ***leptokurtic***. Those three terms are not among the most important terms for you to know; I offer them because they are used frequently enough to leave you in the dark if you are unfamiliar with them.

One way to create a visual image of the shape of a distribution is to place the scores into a graph known as a ***frequency polygon***, as shown in Figure 5. The lower-case f on the vertical axis of each polygon indicates frequency, i.e., the number of persons who achieved at a particular score. The numbers on the horizontal axis at the bottom of each polygon indicate the scores themselves. If you compare the distributions shown in Figure 2 with the polygons shown in Figure 5, you will see representations, for example, of three persons in the X distribution attaining a score of 5, three in the Y distribution attaining a score of 3, etc. If you were to connect the dots in the polygons, you would see that distribution X is perfectly symmetrical, and distribution Y is positively skewed. By using the frequency polygon technique, you can create a visual representation of the shape of any distribution of scores.

X Frequency Polygon   Y Frequency Polygon

	X Frequency Polygon		Y Frequency Polygon

f 5
      4
      3   .
      2   . .
      1   .   .
      0
        1 2 3 4 5 6 7 8 9 10
              score

f 5
      4
      3   .
      2 .
      1 . .   . .
      0
        1 2 3 4 5 6 7 8 9 10
              score

Figure 5. Distributions X and Y Shown as Frequency Polygons

An absolutely perfect standard normal distribution is known to be an aberration in the world of real-life assessment. Because of the awkwardness of describing a distribution's shape as "approximating the standard normal curve," or even as "approximating the bell curve," persons working with quantitative assessment commonly indulge in the convenience of referring to a distribution of scores that approximates the bell curve as a *normal distribution*—knowing that such a description will be taken to mean an approximation rather than a perfect duplication of normality.

Central Tendency

A distribution's shape describes it only in general terms. To describe a distribution more specifically you must make numerical calculations. Most basic are the numerical calculations that yield measures of a distribution's *central tendency*.

Central tendency statistics yield answers to the question "on the whole, how did they score?" Probably you think immediately of the most obvious way to answer that question: divide the total number of points accumulated by the number of scores in the distribution to arrive at the average score. Because "average" can be thought of in more than one context, another term is needed to represent the strict mathematical average. The term used to indicate the sum of the scores divided by the number of cases is a term described earlier relative to the standard normal curve: the **mean**. Figure 6 shows the simple mathematical formula for the mean score. Learn the meaning of the symbols; you will have extensive use for them beyond this simple formula.

$\overline{X}$	mean
Σ	sum of
X	scores
N	number of cases

$$\overline{X} = \frac{\Sigma X}{N}$$

Figure 6. Formula for Calculating a Mean

You will see that the mean of the X distribution from Figure 2 is 5.00 (45 divided by 9), and the mean of the Y distribution is 4.67 (42 divided by 9). So if you were to compare the means, you might answer the central tendency question "on the average how did they do on these tests?" by saying "on the average they did a bit better on Test X than on Test Y."

Though the mean is the primary statistic of central tendency, some occasions call for another measure to give an accurate picture of how the typical person fared. Imagine a small town in the Middle East with a mean annual income of $247,000. The mean gives the impression of a prosperous community. Now imagine that one person who controls the oil supplies earns tens of millions of dollars each year, a few compatriots live very well, and the 10th most wealthy person in the town earns $2,300 annually. When outliers are so extreme that the mean gives a false impression of the typical score, another measure of central tendency is needed to offer a more representative view. That measure is called the **median,** which is simply the midpoint of the distribution. If you were to rank order the distribution of income for that small town from top to bottom, and count an equal number down from the top and up from the bottom, you might find that the median (midpoint) income is somewhere in the vicinity of $1,200 annually. The disparity between the picture of central tendency given by the median and the mean is astounding.

I should note that there are formulas for the median that take into account repeated scores, and that accommodate a distribution having an even number of cases (the halfway point between the two center scores being the median if repeated scores do not complicate the calculation). Those formulas are not consequential enough to your assessment needs for me to delve into them here. You will do well to think of the median simply as a general midpoint that characterizes the average for a distribution having outrageous outliers. The median cannot be entered into formulas, because each case is not given weight in proportion to its value. In other words, you cannot carry the median forward into formulas used to explore other dimensions of a distribution mathematically. For that you need the mean.

A third measure of central tendency, one that also lacks the mathematical advantages of the mean, is the *mode*. The mode of a distribution is the part of the distribution in which the greatest number of cases is concentrated. You might think of the mode as the most typical score. Just as a mode of dress might be formal or informal, and a mode of business might be aggressive or passive, the mode of a distribution might be low, high, or near the center. Sometimes a single repeated score can be seen clearly as the mode. Sometimes bulges appear in two parts of a distribution, giving two appearances of "mode." A distribution of that kind is commonly described as *bi-modal*.

While the mean, median, and mode are all technically indicators of the central tendency of a distribution, only the mean can be used in formulas to carry out further calculations. For that reason, the mean is the principal statistic associated with central tendency. Think of the median and mode as adjunct expressions of central tendency that amount to "eye-balling" typical occurrences rather than actually arriving at a calculation. Mean, median, and mode will coincide within a given distribution only if that distribution is perfectly symmetrical. Outliers at the top will pull the mean higher than the median, and outliers at the bottom will pull the mean lower than the median. The most volatile of the three measures of central tendency is the mode. It can appear anywhere.

Variability

Now that you are familiar with indicators of central tendency, you might think that two distributions having the same mean, median, and mode would necessarily be similar to each other. That is not necessarily so. Look at the two very small distributions shown in Figure 7, each showing the heights of four men. The mean, median, and mode in each distribution are exactly 6 feet.

X	Y
6' 1"	7' 0"
6' 0"	6' 0"
6' 0"	6' 0"
5' 11"	5' 0"

Figure 7. Two Small Distributions that Demonstrate Variability

If these two groups of men were seen together, those in distribution X would draw no notice at all for their height. Those in distribution Y would. The difference in the two distributions is that one is much more variable than the other. Whereas the central tendency of a distribution answers the question "on the whole, how did they score?" the *variability* of a distribution answers the question "how wide are the differences among the scores?"

One simple measure of variability is the *range* of the distribution, i.e., the number of points between the highest score and the lowest score. The X distribution in Figure 7 has a range of 2 inches, and the Y distribution has a range of 24 inches. The X distribution in Figure 2 has a range of 4 points, and the Y distribution has a range of 8 points.

Range offers a general picture of variability, but it is an extremely volatile characteristic. For example, Bert (the top student shown in Figure 2) could single-handedly change the range of the X distribution from 4 to 7 by scoring a 10. Because extreme scores affect range so dramatically, statisticians sometimes use a statistic called *inter-quartile range* (symbolized by $Q =$). By lopping off the top quarter and the bottom quarter, and stating the range of the inner quarters, they remove the influence of extreme scores. This will not be a particularly useful statistic for you.

Fortunately, you have a statistic available to you that will express the variability of a distribution as effectively as the mean expresses central tendency. That statistic, **standard deviation,** is conceptually similar to an average deviation, but more precise. Calculation of the standard deviation will look complicated at first, but follow the steps patiently. Understanding the standard deviation, including knowing how to calculate it in a way that exposes its logic, will be well worth the learning time it takes.

The columns in Figure 8 show the calculations that underlie the standard deviation. You need to become familiar with two basic symbols and their meanings to make sense of those columns and of the standard deviation formula shown in Figure 9. First $X-\overline{X}$, the symbol for a given score minus the mean of the distribution, is called a subject's **deviation score** (the number of points the score deviates from the mean). Deviation scores will be positive numbers for scores higher than the mean, and they will be negative numbers for scores lower than the mean. The columns headed by the deviation score symbols in Figure 8 ($X-\overline{X}$ and $Y-\overline{Y}$) are lists of the subjects' deviation scores. (Another symbol used to designate deviation score is xd. I will use $X-\overline{X}$.)

Second, $(X-\overline{X})^2$ is the symbol for the squared deviation score, calculated to eliminate negative values. The squared deviation score will always be positive. Knowing these symbols, you will be able to make sense of Figures 8 through 10. Reminder: the mean of the X distribution is 5.00, and the mean of the Y distribution is 4.67.

	X	$X-\overline{X}$	$(X-\overline{X})^2$	Y	$Y-\overline{Y}$	$(Y-\overline{Y})^2$
Bert	7	2	4	10	5.33	28.40
Ophelia	6	1	1	8	3.33	11.10
Yonmee	6	1	1	5	.33	.11
Ernie	5	0	0	4	-.67	.45
Rhonda	5	0	0	4	-.67	.45
Chico	5	0	0	3	-1.67	2.79
Obie	4	-1	1	3	-1.67	2.79
Lois	4	-1	1	3	-1.67	2.79
Lenyatta	3	-2	4	2	-2.67	7.13
			12			56.01

Figure 8. Distributions X and Y, with Preliminary Calculations for Standard Deviation

Having looked at the scores, deviation scores, and squared deviation scores for distribution X and distribution Y in Figure 8, now look at the formula for standard deviation, shown in Figure 9. In narrative form, the formula tells you that the standard deviation is equal to the square root of the value obtained by dividing the sum of the squared deviation scores by one less than the number of cases in the distribution. The squaring of the deviation scores earlier to eliminate negative values causes this formula to produce a value (called the variance) incongruent with original score units until the final operation. That final square root operation then returns the value (standard deviation) to original score units, making it easy to interpret.

SD	standard deviation
$(X-\overline{X})^2$	squared deviation score
N-1	one less than the number of cases.

$$SD = \sqrt{\frac{\sum (X-\overline{X})^2}{N-1}}$$

Figure 9. Formula for Calculating a Standard Deviation

If you put the calculations from Figure 8 into the formula for standard deviation, and then work the formulas to completion, you will have the results shown in Figure 10.

X Distribution

$$SD = \sqrt{\frac{\sum (X-\overline{X})^2}{N-1}} = \sqrt{\frac{12}{8}} = \sqrt{1.50} = 1.22$$

Y Distribution

$$SD = \sqrt{\frac{\sum (Y-\overline{Y})^2}{N-1}} = \sqrt{\frac{56.01}{8}} = \sqrt{7.00} = 2.65$$

Figure 10. Calculation of Standard Deviations for Distributions X and Y

So you now know that the standard deviation (*SD*) for the X distribution is 1.22 and the standard deviation for the Y distribution is 2.65. You also know what steps to follow to arrive at those calculations. What is left is for you to know what those numbers mean.

The standard deviation is easy to interpret, because it is expressed in original score units. In other words, if the scores in distributions X and Y were scores earned by taking two 10-point quizzes, the standard deviations would be interpreted as follows: the average amount that students varied from the mean score of 5 points for quiz X was 1.22 points, or about one and a quarter quiz points; the average amount that students varied from the mean score of 4.67 points for quiz Y was 2.65 points, or a little more than two and one-half quiz points. Therefore, students were somewhat alike in what they knew about the content of the first quiz, but they varied much more in what they knew about the content of the second quiz.

By now you can see that mean and standard deviation are the bread-and-butter statistics of central tendency and variability respectively. You may wonder in absolute terms what a "good mean" or a "good standard deviation" is. For each kind of assessment tool you use, there is a way to calculate what is known as a theoretical mean and a theoretical standard deviation. Those are the means and standard deviations that would be yielded by an ideal test ideally administered after ideal teaching of a perfectly distributed representation of students. You will learn in Chapters Four and Six to calculate those theoretical constructs for individual assessment tools, and to use them as benchmarks against which to compare your test results. Your test results will not match those theoretical benchmarks, as human performance is imperfect and unpredictable, but having the benchmarks will help you stay within reasonable parameters, i.e., help you revise your tests intelligently and monitor relationships between your teaching and your testing.

Describing Individual Scores

Notice that the preceding section's information—about symmetry and skewness, means and medians, ranges and standard deviations—yields information only about distributions as wholes. Scores attained by Bert, Ophelia, and the others have been important to this point only for the weight they contribute to the distribution. To describe individual results you will need to become conversant with a different set of statistics.

You might think of individual scores in one of two ways: absolute value and relative value. With that in mind, read about the following ways to describe individual scores, and about the kind of information each yields.

Raw Scores

A *raw score* offers neither relative nor absolute information. "I scored 27 on yesterday's test," says Pete. If I were curious about the absolute value of Pete's 27, I would ask how many points were possible; 27 of 30 gives a much different impression than 27 of 50. If I were curious about the relative value of Pete's 27, I would ask how others in the class scored. If Pete's 27 was one of the highest scores in the class, my opinion of his score would be elevated (even with a ceiling of 50). If Pete's 27 was one of the lowest scores in the class, my opinion of his score would be lowered (even with a ceiling of 30).

Ranks, Percentages, and Percentile Ranks

A *rank* offers relative information, but no absolute information. "I finished sixth on yesterday's test," says Pete. Information is missing about Pete's success in absolute terms: his sixth-place standing might be either rollicking success or abject failure relative to the test itself. And the size of the population is another piece of important missing information: to finish sixth of 30 is much different than to finish sixth of 10. Further, the distance between sixth place and either fifth or seventh is unknown.

Educators have focused their attention almost solely on the absolute value of individual test results by using *percentage correct* to describe degrees of success. Using that system, we would expect to hear Pete say, for example, "I got a 90 on yesterday's test." We would assume that he answered 90 percent of the items correctly. We would know the level of Pete's success compared to the test itself (absolute value), but we would be in the dark about his relative success. If we knew that the other students had all answered 95 to 100 percent of the items correctly, we would know Pete is lagging behind his peers on that measure. If we knew that the other students had all answered 40 to 70 percent of the items correctly, we would know Pete is performing as a near-genius in comparison to his peers.

Though the absolute measure (percentage correct) is used commonly as a basis for grading student work, national standardized tests require a relative comparison to fulfill their purpose. A statistic used commonly is the percentile rank. **Percentile rank** is expressed **not** as a percentage of the test answered correctly, but as the percentile within which the results fall relative to all other test-takers (norm-referenced). The cumulative percentage (c%) column of a frequency distribution (p. 25) shows percentile ranks, but does so accurately only if the number of cases equals or exceeds 100. To calculate percentile ranks for smaller groups, use the formula shown in Figure 11. It assumes that persons who might be added to expand the distribution to 100 or more would fill in spaces according to the theory of the bell curve. A percentile rank of 90 for Pete would indicate that Pete scored equal to or higher than 90 percent of the other test takers. The percentage of items answered correctly is irrelevant to the percentile rank statistic.

PR	percentile rank
N	total number of cases
N<X	number of cases scoring lower than the case whose PR is being calculated
N at X	number of cases scoring at the value of the case whose PR is being calculated, including the case being calculated.

$$PR = \frac{N{<}X + .5(N\ at\ X)}{N} \times 100$$

Figure 11. Formula for Calculating a Percentile Rank

To make percentile rank calculation clear, I will show calculations of two cases from very small distributions of scores. The distribution at the left margin of Figure 12 is so small as to be ridiculous, but it is valuable for demonstrating the way in which distributions having cases fewer than 100 are filled in by the theory of the bell curve. Common sense tells us that each of the five cases in the distribution represents 20 percent of the 100 cases to which the results need to be generalized. At first thought, then, you might eye-ball the percentile rank of the second case (a score of *4*) as the 80th percentile. That would be in error. Because that case has to represent 20 cases between the 60th and 80th percentile, the best estimate is that it resides at the 70th percentile rank. Notice that the calculations, when the formula is applied, verify that.

$$5$$
$$④$$
$$3$$
$$2$$
$$1$$

$$PR = \frac{N<X + .5(N\ at\ X)}{N} (\text{x } 100) = \frac{3 + .5}{5} = \frac{3.5}{5} = .70\ (\text{x } 100) = 70\%$$

Figure 12. Percentile Rank Calculation

Of course no real-life distributions will be so small or so symmetrically tidy. If I inject one more case into the distribution in Figure 12, the opportunity to eye-ball the percentile rank disappears. The calculations in Figure 13 show the formula applied to a distribution having a repeated score. Note that having a second case at the same score lowers the relative value of that score, and consequently lowers the percentile rank.

$$5$$
$$④$$
$$4$$
$$3$$
$$2$$
$$1$$

$$PR = \frac{N<X + .5(N\ at\ X)}{N} (\text{x } 100) = \frac{3+1}{6} = \frac{4}{6} = .67\ (\text{x } 100) = 67\%$$

Figure 13. Percentile Rank Calculation with a Repeated Score

So percentile rank characterizes each subject's successes relative to others in the population. When a well-constructed standardized test is administered properly to a sample of persons from the population for whom the test has been validated, that relative statistic tells more than any percentage-correct score could. To compare results of individuals to the population as a whole is to compare them to reality; to compare results of individuals to the demands of a test, without regard for the success rate of others, is to compare them to whatever the test-writer judged to be reality.

The distributions first shown in Figure 2 are repeated in Figure 14, with percentile ranks shown. Choose a few cases at random and calculate the percentile ranks to confirm that your use of the percentile rank formula produces the same answers as those shown.

	X	PR	Y	PR
Bert	7	94	10	94
Ophelia	6	78	8	83
Yonmee	6	78	5	72
Ernie	5	50	4	56
Rhonda	5	50	4	56
Chico	5	50	3	28
Obie	4	22	3	28
Lois	4	22	3	28
Lenyatta	3	6	2	6

Figure 14. Two Distributions of Scores for Practice,
with Percentile Ranks Shown

A legitimate question brought to mind by such a ridiculously small distribution is this: if Bert obviously scored higher than all other students on both tests, why does the percentile rank say that "94 percent of others scored at or below Bert's score"? The small number is the key. The formula has to allow for an estimation of where others would score if the test-taking population were large. The theoretical estimate that a number of others would equal or surpass Bert's score depresses his percentile rank within such a small group.

For all its virtues, the percentile rank does have one disadvantage. It lacks a constant relationship to raw score. Raw score and percentile rank would have a constant relationship only if human performance conformed to a rectangular shape around the mean rather than to a bell curve. Because many more cases reside near the mean than away from the mean, a much greater linear distance must be covered in the tails than in the middle of the curve to encompass the same percentage of the population. You can see the disparity at work if in Figure 14 you look at the relationship between Obie's X distribution score (4) and percentile rank (22). If percentile rank had a constant relationship to raw score, you would find that a raw score twice the size of Obie's (8) would equate to a percentile rank twice the size (44), but a cursory check of the other scores and percentile ranks shows that to be absurd.

Standard Scores

The inconstant relationship between percentile rank and raw score gives the percentile rank a disadvantage similar to that of the median and the range: you will recall that their volatility forces us to rely on the mean and standard deviation respectively for statistics that make sense when entered into calculations. Just as we lean on the mean and standard deviation as statistics that describe central tendency and variability relative to the bell curve, we need a statistic that will describe individual scores relative to the bell curve. That statistic is the ***standard score***, expressed in its most basic form as a ***z score***.

Do not let standard scores intimidate you. The z score is a statistic as simple as the mean. To express an individual score in a way that conforms to standard deviation units ($\pm$ 3 from the mean), you need to simply divide the subject's deviation score ($X-\overline{X}$) by the deviation score of the entire distribution (SD). The formula, then, is as shown in Figure 15.

$$z = \frac{X-\overline{X}}{SD}$$

Figure 15. Formula for Calculating a z Score

The result of that calculation will be an expression of individual scores in standard deviation units. That is, a z score of 1.5 signifies that the raw score is one and one-half standard deviation units above the mean, a z score of $-.25$ signifies that the raw score is one-quarter of a standard deviation unit below the mean, etc. Of course all individual scores above the mean will produce a positive z score, and all individual scores below the mean will produce a negative z score. Like standard deviation units, z scores range, for all practical purposes, from -3 to $+3$, with cases beyond -2 or $+2$ being rare. Note that the z

symbol used is lower case. That is important, as an upper case Z signifies another statistic, one not pertinent to this textbook.

The distributions first shown in Figure 2 are repeated in Figure 16, with z scores shown. Choose a few cases at random and calculate the z scores to confirm that your use of the z score formula produces the same answers. To arrive first at a deviation score for a given case, you need to subtract the mean of 5.00 from any score in the X distribution, or you need to subtract the mean of 4.67 from any score in the Y distribution. Then to arrive at a z score for a given case, you need to divide the deviation score by the standard deviation, which for the X distribution is 1.22, and for the Y distribution is 2.65.

	X	z	Y	z
Bert	7	1.64	10	2.01
Ophelia	6	.82	8	1.26
Yonmee	6	.82	5	.12
Ernie	5	.00	4	– .25
Rhonda	5	.00	4	– .25
Chico	5	.00	3	– .63
Obie	4	– .82	3	– .63
Lois	4	– .82	3	– .63
Lenyatta	3	–1.64	2	–1.00

Figure 16. Two Distributions of Scores for Practice, with z Scores Shown

Test results reported as standard scores quite often are not reported as z scores. That is an odd sounding statement now that you have learned that standard scores are called z scores, but let me explain.

Because z scores relate directly to standard deviation units, z scores have a mean of 0 and a standard deviation of 1. That means that a person's score reported as a z score might be, for example –.20. That is cumbersome, so z scores sometimes are transformed into more reader-friendly figures. The process is similar to translating a language. I can take something written in German or Spanish and make it readable to more Americans by translating it into English. Similarly, I can create a more readable statistic by transforming z scores. The formula for a ***transformed z score*** is this: $z' = z (SD) + \overline{X}$. The symbol z' is read "z prime," and it is simply a generic symbol for whatever new standard score you create. The new mean and standard deviation can be anything the transformer wants them to be.

One common z score transformation is the ***McCall T***. McCall (about 90 years ago) used a mean of 50 and a standard deviation of 10. The formula for a McCall T, then, is $T = z(10) + 50$. A z score of $-.20$ then becomes a T score of 48, a z score of 1.00 becomes a T score of 60, etc. In some standardized test manuals you will see norm tables with figures that are predominantly in the 30s, 40s, 50s, and 60s. When you see that, you will know you are looking at standard scores expressed as McCall T scores (with a mean of 50 and a standard deviation of 10), a language that has become widely accepted.

The transformed standard score most familiar to you is one that you probably have never understood as a standard score: the SAT score. The SAT has a mean of 500 and a standard deviation of 100 (as do some other tests) because it is a transformed standard score: $SAT = z(100) + 500$. The mean of 500, plus three standard deviations, takes you to the top score of 800. The mean of 500 minus three standard deviations takes you to the bottom score of 200—a score known as "chance score," because chance would have you answer that many items correctly if you answered randomly without knowing anything.

You can see that the standard normal curve, a.k.a. the *bell curve*, does indeed underlie much of our lives. Educational institutions, testing services, pollsters, and others depend heavily on the bell curve to make sense of their assessments. That is why I asserted earlier that we should make children conscious of the curve, its use, and its implications for them. To keep them blind to a system by which they are being judged from all quarters seems at least negligent, if not deceitful.

Describing Relationships Between Distributions of Scores

In the first major section of this chapter I showed ways to describe distributions of scores (shape, central tendency, variability), and in the second I showed ways to describe individual scores (rank, percentage correct, percentile rank, standard score). A third and final type of statistical task that you will find important to many quantitative assessment processes is to describe relationships between two distributions of scores. You will use only one statistic to calculate relationships: ***correlation***.

I want to begin by orienting you to what correlation is and how it is interpreted. Then, when I show you the calculations, you will appreciate where you are going, why you are going there, and what you will have after you have arrived.

An important term that you need to become comfortable with is ***variable***. A variable is anything that can be measured and is subject to change from one group of subjects to another or from one time to another. That encompasses about everything that can be expressed numerically. For easy identification, variables are commonly labeled with letters: X and Y, A and B. Sometimes variables are labeled in a way that makes the nature of the information apparent. For example, a researcher might label an experimental group E and a control group C, or two experimental treatment groups E1 and E2. When I show you how to calculate correlation, I will use the two distributions we have been using since they appeared in Figure 2. You will remember that I have already labeled those distributions of test scores as X and Y.

The three basic possibilities for a relationship between two variables is that they have a positive relationship (X and Y tend to vary in the same direction), a negative relationship (X and Y tend to vary in opposing directions), or no relationship (X and Y function unpredictably relative to each other). Of course there are many gradations along the way. The relationship between X and Y (positive or negative) could be weak, moderate, strong, very strong, or perfect. You are highly unlikely to find a perfect correlation (positive or negative) between two variables in human behavior, i.e., between two distributions of scores. Perfect correlations are usually physical relationships, like the perfect positive correlation between how far upward you move your finger on a violin string and how high the pitch sounds, or the perfect negative correlation between the speed an object travels and the time required to cover a given distance.

Think of a few pairs of variables for which you would predict an imperfect but positive relationship: height and shoe size, music aptitude and music achievement, SAT scores and college GPA. Think of a few pairs of variables for which you would predict an imperfect but negative relationship: age of adults and reaction time, weight of a truck's load and average speed through the mountains, number of students in a classroom and teacher time given to individuals.

A key word from the previous paragraph is ***predict***. The stronger the correlation between two variables, the more confidently you can predict what Y will do if you know X. For example, if the correlation between height and shoe size is strong, and if you are given a list of names and shoe sizes, you can guess relative heights with something approximating accuracy. You will have made a prediction based on your knowledge of the correlation between the two variables. You can make predictions based on any strong correlation, even one that is negative. If you were told that an elementary school teacher had a class size of 18 this year, as compared to last year's class size of 27, and if you knew of a high negative correlation between class size and individual attention, you would predict that this year's students receive more individual attention.

So if X and Y are strongly correlated, you can predict one from the other. Might you also infer that one causes the other? For example, given a high correlation between the number of dollars spent per student by a school system and the number of graduates those systems send to college, could you infer that the lack of money explains the lower incidence of college enrollment? Though people try to make causative arguments from correlation, they are on shaky ground doing so. To illustrate the fallacy vividly, let us assume a high correlation between ice cream sales and number of persons who drown in Atlantic City. If correlation is linked to causation, we would shut down the ice cream stores to reduce the number of persons drowning. But a third factor—warm weather—affects each of the variables independently. Keep that in mind, and be very cautious about implying causation from correlation. Common sense sometimes leads us to believe in a strong causative relationship. Certainly we believe that the smaller class size for the elementary teacher causes that teacher's increased individual attention on students—and to an extent we may be right. Still, the possibility that an untold number of other factors impinges on the result should dictate caution.

The time has come to learn to calculate the correlation statistic, symbolized with a lower case "*r*" for relationship. The formula for correlation looks complicated at first sight, but all of the symbols it contains are now familiar to you, except for the numerator. You will see an interpretation of the numerator in the box next to the formula shown in Figure 17.

$$r = \frac{[\ \sum(X-\bar{X})\,(Y-\bar{Y})\ ]}{\sqrt{\sum(X-\bar{X})^2\ *\ \sum(Y-\bar{Y})^2}}$$

> The symbol in the numerator represents the sum of the deviation score products. Each person's X and Y deviation scores are multiplied by each other, and that column of products is added to create the numerator.

Figure 17. Formula for Calculating a Correlation Coefficient

You will understand what a key the numerator of this formula is if you realize that no other calculations we have carried out thus far have shared information between the two distributions. Common sense dictates that data from the separate distributions must be interlocked to arrive at a statistic that reveals a relationship between them. That interlocking is done by multiplying the X deviation score for Bert by the Y deviation score for Bert, entering the product in its own column as shown in Figure 18 (to the far right), and then doing the same for each case. The sum of those products then becomes the binding agent when it is put into the formula as the numerator. Figure 18 consists of all the columns of data involved in the calculation: raw scores for each distribution (X or Y); deviation scores for each distribution ($X-\bar{X}$ or $Y-\bar{Y}$); squared deviation scores for each distribution ($X-\bar{X}^2$ or $Y-\bar{Y}^2$); the sum of the squared deviation scores for each distribution ($\sum X-\bar{X}^2 = 12;\ \sum Y-\bar{Y}^2 = 56.01$); deviation score products ($X-\bar{X})(Y-\bar{Y}$); and the sum of those deviation score products (23).

The *r* statistic that this calculation yields is called a **correlation coefficient**. Correlation coefficients range each direction from zero, to a perfect positive correlation at one pole (1.00) and a perfect negative correlation at the other (−1.00).

	X	X–$\overline{X}$	(X–$\overline{X}$)²	Y	Y–$\overline{Y}$	(Y–$\overline{Y}$)²	(X–$\overline{X}$)(Y–$\overline{Y}$)
Bert	7	2	4	10	5.33	28.40	10.66
Ophelia	6	1	1	8	3.33	11.10	3.33
Yonmee	6	1	1	5	.33	.11	33
Ernie	5	0	0	4	– .67	.45	.00
Rhonda	5	0	0	4	– .67	.45	.00
Chico	5	0	0	3	– 1.67	2.79	.00
Obie	4	–1	1	3	– 1.67	2.79	1.67
Lois	4	–1	1	3	– 1.67	2.79	1.67
Lenyatta	3	–2	4	2	– 2.67	7.13	5.34
			12			56.01	23.00

Figure 18. Distributions X and Y, with Preliminary Calculations
for Correlation

In Figure 19 you will see the steps taken to calculate the correlation coefficient by entering the data from Figure 18 into the correlation formula.

$$r = \frac{[\sum (X-\overline{X})(Y-\overline{Y})]}{\sqrt{\sum (X-\overline{X})^2 * \sum (Y-\overline{Y})^2}} = \frac{23}{\sqrt{12 * 56.01}}$$

$$= \frac{23}{\sqrt{672.12}} = \frac{23}{25.95} = .89$$

Figure 19. Calculation of the Correlation Between Distributions X and Y

To be sure you are clear about the entire process, I will list the steps taken in estimating the relationship between two distributions of scores by the calculation of a correlation coefficient.

<u>For each of the two distributions</u>

1. Subtract the mean from each score to create the distribution of deviation scores.

$$X-\bar{X}$$

2. Multiply each deviation score by itself to create the distribution of squared deviation scores.

$$(X-\bar{X})^2$$

3. Add the columns of squared deviation scores.

$$\Sigma(X-\bar{X})^2$$

<u>To interlock the two distributions</u>

4. Multiply each person's X deviation score by that person's Y deviation score to create the distribution of deviation score products.

$$(X-\bar{X})(Y-\bar{Y})$$

5. Add the column of deviation score products.

$$[\,\Sigma(X-\bar{X})(Y-\bar{Y})\,]$$

<u>To calculate *r* by use of the information generated in steps 1–5</u>

6. Place the two values obtained in step 3 and the value obtained in step 5 into the correlation formula.

In Figure 20 you will see a graphic portrayal of the range of correlation coefficients. Imagine the placement of coefficients at various points along that continuum, and think about what their placement means to their strength, and consequently to the confidence they engender in prediction of one variable from knowledge of the other.

Negative Correlation   Positive Correlation

−1.00-----------------------------------0---------------------------------- +1.00
Stronger   Weaker   Weaker   Stronger

Figure 20. A Graphic Portrayal of the Range of Correlation Coefficients

Important to your interpretation of correlation coefficients is recognition that weak relationships gather around the center point, which signifies no relationship at all. Strength of relationship increases with movement toward the ends, toward a perfect positive or a perfect negative relationship. Think of the sign of a coefficient (+ or −) as indicative of the direction of the relationship, but unrelated to its strength. Think of the absolute value (the numerical value of the coefficient without regard to sign) as indicative of the strength of the relationship, regardless of direction. A correlation of −.86, for example, indicates a stronger relationship than does a correlation of .74, even though the relationship between the two variables in the first case is a matter of the extent to which they are in opposition.

In Figures 21 and 22 you will see examples of a technique for representing a relationship between two variables visually. The pictures shown are called *scattergrams* or *scatterplots*. In Figure 21, the X and Y distributions we have been working with are represented on a vertical and horizontal axis. Placing a point on the scattergram to indicate the X/Y intersection for each case creates a picture of the direction and strength of the relationship.

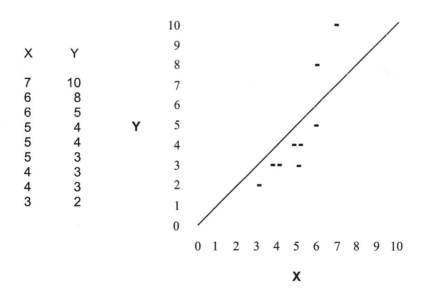

Figure 21. A Scattergram Depiction of the Relationship Between
Distributions X and Y

The line cutting upward at 45 degrees through the center of the scattergram shows where a perfect positive relationship would fall. That is, if the relationship were 1.00, all the points would fall exactly on that line. The closer a collection of points comes to describing that line, the closer the relationship is to 1.00. As you can see, the .89 correlation that we calculated for this X and Y distribution is reflected in the clustering of the points around that line. A perfect negative correlation, by contrast, would have the points placed on a line running 45 degrees from top left to bottom right. As an illustration of the interpretation of scattergrams, I have drawn a set of four hypothetical scatterplots in Figure 22 (without values attached, they cannot be referred to as scattergrams), and I have given them labels that indicate roughly how they would be interpreted.

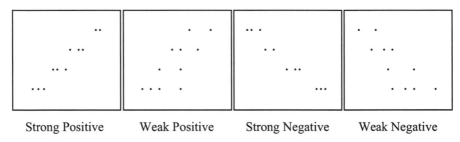

    Strong Positive   Weak Positive   Strong Negative   Weak Negative

Figure 22. An Array of Hypothetical Scatterplots Interpreted

Finally, you should know that the world of statistics involves several kinds of correlation. Some of them you will need only if you become involved in research. I have described only the most basic type of correlation. It is called the ***Pearson product moment correlation,*** a long and awkward name that you will not need to remember. The simple term *correlation* is generally taken to mean this particular type of correlation. Sometimes it is nicknamed the ***Pearson correlation*** or the ***Pearson r.*** It is limited to the task of comparing distributions of scores, and it is limited to variables that function in a ***linear relationship*** (conforming to a straight line). For example, you could not use a Pearson *r* to calculate the relationship between age and bone strength. Why? Because bone strength does not change linearly with age. A young child's bones are weak, they become strong up through the adult prime, and then they become weaker again. Statisticians would say that bone strength and age have a *curvilinear relationship* (conforming to a curved line). Therefore, the Pearson correlation could not be used to calculate the relationship between those two variables (unless a particular age bracket were specified during which the relationship is linear, e.g., age 10 to 20 or age 60 to 70).

Note that a correlation coefficient does not represent the percentage of common ground between two variables. That is, if two variables have a correlation of .80, they do not overlap at a rate of 80%. To find the percentage of common ground, you need to square the correlation coefficient. So in the example of a correlation of .80, the common ground would amount to 64% (.80 x .80). Because your purpose in calculating r^2 is to determine the percentage of common ground, r^2 is sometimes referred to as the *coefficient of determination*.

Parting Thoughts

You may have found this chapter exhausting. For a person unfamiliar with statistics, it certainly contains a great amount of new information. Think of all that information as a collection of tools to be put into your assessment tool box and used along the way. Your having these tools will benefit both of us. I will be able to move freely through many processes that rely on them, and you will be well positioned to familiarize yourself with various approaches to assessment without having to stop and learn a new statistic every few pages.

For practice, calculate the statistics called for on pages 54–57 of this chapter. Notice that each page after the first has two functions: it reveals the answers to calculations asked for on the previous page, and it becomes the basis for the next set of calculations to be worked. If you encounter difficulty, re-read the corresponding portion of the chapter. If statistical calculations are new to you, you may find that you need to spend more time with this chapter than with any other.

Terms Important to This Chapter

standard normal distribution (bell curve) (21): a model that shows the way in which variables of all kinds—animate and inanimate, human and non-human, physical and behavioral—tend to be distributed from one extreme to another, with a gathering of greatest frequencies around the center point.

Gaussian distribution (21): a synonym for "standard normal distribution," so named because of its association with nineteenth-century mathematician Carl Frederick Gauss.

distribution (24): a term used to describe an array of scores obtained from testing a group of persons, the logic being that an array of scores can be thought of as being "distributed" from highest to lowest, or "distributed" around a central point (mean).

case (24): any particular score within a distribution of scores.

frequency distribution (25): a method of displaying a distribution of scores compactly by showing the number of times each repeated score appears rather than listing every individual case regardless of repetitions.

shape (26): one of the three principal ways to describe a distribution of scores (the others being central tendency and variability); the symmetrical, bell-shaped standard normal distribution is the standard against which other shapes are compared.

symmetrical (26): the shape of a distribution whose mean, median, and mode coincide, and whose upper half (distribution of scores above the mean) is a mirror image of its lower half (distribution of scores below the mean).

asymmetrical (26): a general term to describe any distribution whose shape is not symmetrical.

skewed (26): pulled out of shape; the property of a distribution that is asymmetrical.

skewed to the right, or *positively skewed (26):* the specific description of a distribution whose asymmetrical shape is caused by extreme scores at the high end of the distribution pulling the mean (arithmetic average) above the median (mid-point) of the distribution.

skewed to the left, or *negatively skewed (26):* the specific description of a distribution whose asymmetrical shape is caused by extreme scores at the low end of the distribution pulling the mean (arithmetic average) below the median (mid-point) of the distribution.

extreme score (27): a score so unusually high or unusually low as compared with the body of scores that it skews the distribution in its direction.

outlier (27): a term used commonly as a synonym for *extreme score.*

renegade score (27): a term used less commonly as a synonym for *extreme score.*

kurtosis (27): a measure of the relative peakedness or flatness of the curve described by a distribution of scores; a function of variability.

mesokurtic (27): label given the shape of a distribution whose kurtosis has it approximate the kurtosis of the standard normal distribution.

platykurtic (27): label given the shape of a distribution whose kurtosis has it stretched horizontally, producing a flat shape as compared to that of the standard normal distribution (greater-than-normal variability).

leptokurtic (27): label given the shape of a distribution whose kurtosis has it stretched vertically, producing a peaked shape as compared to that of the standard normal distribution (less-than-normal variability).

frequency polygon (27): a graph created by placing frequencies on the vertical axis and scores on the horizontal axis, and then placing a point at each intersection of score with frequency to create a graph that shows the shape of the distribution.

normal distribution (28): a nickname used commonly to describe a distribution that approximates the standard normal distribution, a.k.a. bell curve.

central tendency (28): one of the three principal ways to describe a distribution of scores (the others being shape and variability); central tendency, which answers the question "on the whole, how did they score?" describes the distribution's typicality mathematically by use of the mean (arithmetic average), or relatively by use of the median (central score) or the mode (most frequently occurring score). The mean, as the staple of central tendency, is entered into further calculations.

mean (29): the arithmetic average of a distribution of scores, which theoretically coincides with the crown of the bell curve; the point around which frequencies tend to gather in large numbers, and away from which frequencies tend to diminish with greater distance in either direction.

median (29): the mid-point of a distribution of scores, without regard for arithmetic value; the median thus eludes the influence of extreme scores.

mode (30): the most frequently occurring score in a distribution.

bi-modal (30): a term that describes the shape of a distribution as having dual points at which the frequency of scores tends to peak.

variability (31): one of the three principal ways to describe a distribution of scores (the others being shape and central tendency); variability, which answers the question "how wide are the differences among the scores?" is described by the range (top score minus bottom score), the inter-quartile range (not practical for you as a teacher), or the standard deviation (roughly, the average number of score points away from the mean). The standard deviation, as the staple of variability, is entered into further calculations. (Another expression of variability, the variance—standard deviation squared—is also impractical for you as a teacher.)

range (31): the span of scores in a distribution from highest to lowest.

inter-quartile range (31): an infrequently used statistic showing the range of the two middle quartiles of a distribution, designed specifically to blunt the effect of extreme scores that can make the range of a distribution a volatile statistic.

standard deviation (32): the average distance (roughly speaking, though not precisely so mathematically) that cases within a distribution of scores vary from the mean; a key benchmark within the theory of the standard normal distribution.

deviation score (32): a given score minus the mean of the distribution within which it lies, causing the deviation score for each person who scores above the mean to be a positive number and the deviation score for each person who scores below the mean to be a negative number.

raw score (35): simply the number of items from a measurement tool that a given person answered correctly.

rank (35): placement of a given person's score relative to the scores of others in a particular group measured by the same measurement tool, e.g., first, second, etc.

percentage correct (35): the percentage of the measurement tool's items that a given person answered correctly, e.g., 90 percent, 86 percent.

percentile rank (36): the percentage of the larger population of scores (perhaps national norms) that are equal to or lesser than a given person's score, e.g., "her score is at the 74th percentile rank."

standard score (39): an expression of an individual score relative to the standard normal curve.

z score (39): the most basic of standard scores, corresponding directly to the standard deviation units of the standard normal curve, with a mean of 0 and a standard deviation of 1.

transformed z score (40): a standard score transformed from the *z* value to a more readable form whose values are all positive. The transformation is made by inserting the standard deviation and mean of choice into this transformation formula: $z' = z (SD) + \bar{X}$.

McCall T (41): the transformed standard score most widely used, particularly in norms tables of standardized tests; based on a mean of 50 and a standard deviation of 10.

correlation (42): the type (positive or negative) and degree of relationship between two variables.

variable (42): anything that can be measured and is subject to change from one group of subjects to another or from one time to another; the opposite of a constant.

predict (43): this very common word is included here for an opportunity to emphasize the power of a strong correlation; the stronger the relationship (correlation) between two variables, the greater is the power to predict one from knowing the other.

correlation coefficient (44): the number that identifies numerically the correlation (relationship) between two variables, expressed as a coefficient that varies from −1.00 (a perfect negative relationship) to 1.00 (a perfect positive relationship), with a mid-point of 0 (no relationship).

scattergram, scatterplot (47): a graphic illustration of the relationship between two variables, generally shown with values from one variable displayed on the vertical axis and values from the other variable displayed on the horizontal axis. If values are omitted, showing only a visual representation of the relationship, the term *scatterplot* is more precise than the term *scattergram.*

Pearson product moment correlation, Pearson correlation, Pearson r (48): several labels for the most common among several types of correlation statistics. The Pearson *r*, used to estimate the relationship between two distribution of scores, is one of two correlation calculations used commonly in the interpretation of test results; the other (point biserial correlation) will be explained in Chapter Six.

linear relationship (48): a relationship that conforms to (moves in, describes) a straight line, e.g., the relationship between speed and distance of a moving body.

curvilinear relationship (49): a relationship that conforms to (moves in, describes) a curved line, e.g., the relationship between time and physical development for living things, which evolve from weak to strong to weak.

coefficient of determination (49): a value equal to the correlation coefficient squared (r^2), and representing the percentage of common ground between the correlated variables. Another perspective on r^2 is to think of it as the percentage of one variable that can be explained by the presence of the other.

TWO DISTRIBUTIONS OF SCORES FOR PRACTICE CALCULATIONS

Assignment: Calculate the mean, median, mode, range, and standard deviation for each of these distributions of scores. Notice that the scores in the Y distribution are not in descending order. Do not rearrange them. They are as they should be.

Case	X	$X-\bar{X}$	$(X-\bar{X})^2$	Y	$Y-\bar{Y}$	$(Y-\bar{Y})^2$
1.	26			22		
2.	25			27		
3.	21			25		
4.	18			12		
5.	11			6		
6.	9			6		
7.	6			12		
8.	5			18		
9.	5			6		
10.	3			6		
11.	2			16		

> The solutions to this assignment are shown on the next page.
> To be sure you are facile with these calculations as you move
> ahead from this chapter, diligently avoid looking ahead until
> you have made the most you can of this assignment.

TWO DISTRIBUTIONS OF SCORES FOR PRACTICE CALCULATIONS

Assignment: Calculate percentile rank and z scores for all cases. Calculate McCall T scores for cases 1, 4, and 9. When calculating percentile ranks for cases in the Y distribution, note that you will be counting numbers of scores lower in value than the score whose percentile rank you are calculating, not necessarily scores located lower on the page.

Case	X	$X-\bar{X}$	$(X-\bar{X})^2$	PR	z	Y	$Y-\bar{Y}$	$(Y-\bar{Y})^2$	PR	z
1.	26	14.1	198.81			22	7.8	60.84		
2.	25	13.1	171.61			27	12.8	163.84		
3.	21	9.1	82.81			25	10.8	116.64		
4.	18	6.1	37.21			12	− 2.2	4.84		
5.	11	− .9	.81			6	− 8.2	67.24		
6.	9	− 2.9	8.41			6	− 8.2	67.24		
7.	6	− 5.9	34.81			12	− 2.2	4.84		
8.	5	− 6.9	47.61			18	3.8	14.44		
9.	5	− 6.9	47.61			6	− 8.2	67.24		
10.	3	− 8.9	79.21			6	− 8.2	67.24		
11.	2	− 9.9	98.01			16	1.8	3.24		
	131		806.91			156		637.64		

$\bar{X} = 131/11 = 11.9$ $\bar{Y} = 156/11 = 14.2$

$SD_X = \sqrt{806.91/10} = 8.98$ $SD_Y = \sqrt{637.64/10} = 7.98$

Median	9	Median	12
Mode	5	Mode	6
Range	24	Range	21

The solutions to this assignment are shown on the next page. To be sure you are facile with these calculations as you move ahead from this chapter, diligently avoid looking ahead until you have made the most you can of this assignment.

TWO DISTRIBUTIONS OF SCORES FOR PRACTICE CALCULATIONS

Assignment: Calculate a correlation coefficient between the two distributions. Note that multiplying like signs yields a positive value and multiplying unlike signs yields a negative value.

Case	X	$X-\bar{X}$	$(X-\bar{X})^2$	PR	z	Y	$Y-\bar{Y}$	$(Y-\bar{Y})^2$	PR	z	$(X-\bar{X})*(Y-\bar{Y})$
1.	26	14.1	198.81	95	1.57	22	7.8	60.84	77	1.02	
2.	25	13.1	171.61	86	1.57	27	12.8	163.84	95	1.68	
3.	21	9.1	82.81	77	1.01	25	10.8	16.64	86	1.42	
4.	18	6.1	37.21	68	.68	12	− 2.2	4.84	45	− .29	
5.	11	− .9	.81	59	− .10	6	− 8.2	67.24	18	−1.08	
6.	9	− 2.9	8.41	50	− .32	6	− 8.2	67.24	18	−1.08	
7.	6	− 5.9	34.81	41	− .66	12	− 2.2	4.84	45	− .29	
8.	5	− 6.9	47.61	27	− .77	18	3.8	14.44	68	.50	
9.	5	− 6.9	47.61	27	− .77	6	− 8.2	67.24	18	−1.08	
10.	3	− 8.9	79.21	14	− .99	6	− 8.2	67.24	18	−1.08	
11.	2	− 9.9	98.01	5	−1.10	16	1.8	3.24	59	.23	
	131		806.91			156		637.64			

$\bar{X} = 131/11 = 11.9$ $\bar{Y} = 156/11 = 14.2$

$SD = \sqrt{806.91/10} = 8.98$ $SD = \sqrt{637.64/10} = 7.98$

Case #1   Case #1

$T = 1.57 \times 10 + 50 = 65.7$ $T = .98 \times 10 + 50 = 58.9$

Case #4   Case #4

$T = .68 \times 10 + 50 = 56.8$ $T = −.28 \times 10 + 50 = 47.2$

Case #9   Case #9

$T = −.77 \times 10 + 50 = 42.3$ $T = −1.03 \times 10 + 50 = 39.7$

The solutions to this assignment are shown on the next page.
To be sure you are facile with these calculations as you move
ahead from this chapter, diligently avoid looking ahead until
you have made the most you can of this assignment.

TWO DISTRIBUTIONS OF SCORES FOR PRACTICE CALCULATIONS

Case	X	$X-\overline{X}$	$(X-\overline{X})^2$	PR	z	Y	$Y-\overline{Y}$	$(Y-\overline{Y})^2$	PR	z	$(X-\overline{X})*(Y-\overline{Y})$
1.	26	14.1	198.81	95	1.57	22	7.8	60.84	77	1.02	109.98
2.	25	13.1	171.61	86	1.57	27	12.8	163.84	95	1.68	167.68
3.	21	9.1	82.81	77	1.01	25	10.8	16.64	86	1.42	98.28
4.	18	6.1	37.21	68	.68	12	-2.2	4.84	45	-.29	-13.42
5.	11	-.9	.81	59	-.10	6	-8.2	67.24	18	-1.08	7.38
6.	9	-2.9	8.41	50	-.32	6	-8.2	67.24	18	-1.08	23.78
7.	6	-5.9	34.81	41	-.66	12	-2.2	4.84	45	-.29	12.98
8.	5	-6.9	47.61	27	-.77	18	3.8	14.44	68	.50	-26.22
9.	5	-6.9	47.61	27	-.77	6	-8.2	67.24	18	-1.08	56.58
10.	3	-8.9	79.21	14	-.99	6	-8.2	67.24	18	-1.08	72.98
11.	2	-9.9	98.01	5	-1.10	16	1.8	3.24	59	.23	-17.78
	131		806.91			156		637.64			492.18

$\overline{X} = 131/11 = 11.9$ $\overline{Y} = 156/11 = 14.2$

$SD = \sqrt{806.91/10} = 8.98$ $SD = \sqrt{637.64/10} = 7.98$

Case #1

$T = 1.57 \times 10 + 50 = 65.7$

Case #4

$T = .68 \times 10 + 50 = 56.8$

Case #9

$T = -.77 \times 10 + 50 = 42.3$

Case #1

$T = .98 \times 10 + 50 = 58.9$

Case #4

$T = -.28 \times 10 + 50 = 47.2$

Case #9

$T = -1.03 \times 10 + 50 = 39.7$

$$r = \frac{[\sum (X-\overline{X})(Y-\overline{Y})]}{\sqrt{\sum (X-\overline{X})^2 * \sum(Y-\overline{Y})^2}} = 492 / \sqrt{806.91 \times 637.64} = 492 / \sqrt{514{,}518} = .69$$

Chapter Three

ANALYZING STATISTICS BY USING MICROSOFT® EXCEL

This may be the shortest, most simple (least comprehensive) software guide ever written. My purpose in this chapter is to acquaint you with the basic operations of a software program that you will find helpful when you need to calculate the statistics described in Chapter Two. Microsoft® Excel has capabilities far beyond what I describe here, but in the interest of brevity and simplicity I will let you discover other operations as you find use for them.

To calculate basic statistics using the Excel program itself, follow the procedures below. The sample data used are the X and Y distributions introduced in Chapter Two.

Entering Data

- Open an Excel Document. Save it with an appropriate name for future retrieval.

- Label the A Column "Test X" in Cell A1. Enter practice data X beginning in Cell A2.

- Label the C Column "Test Y" in Cell C1. Enter practice data Y beginning in Cell C2.

(Leave the B and D columns empty for figures yet to come.)

When you have finished, your screen should look like the screen shown in Figure 1 if you are using a PC. The Mac screen is configured a bit differently, but the same components are present. I will show PC screens only.

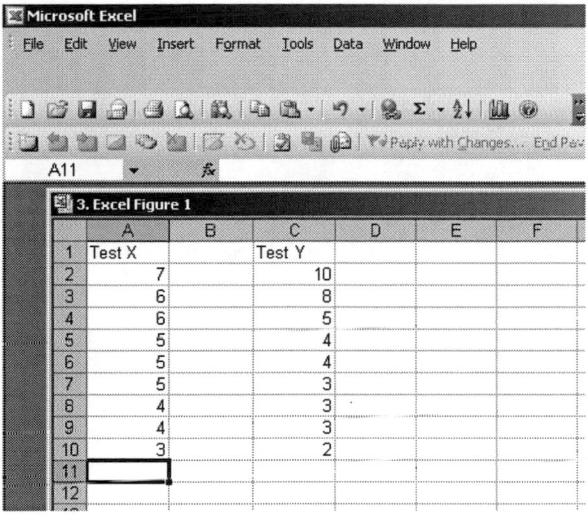

Figure 1. Excel Screen After Entering Data From Distributions X and Y

The selected cell (black outline) shown in Figure 1 just happens to be the cell on which I clicked after finishing the function described. Each time I complete a function I will park the cursor on some neutral cell.

Calculating the Mean

First you will sum the two distributions of scores. To alleviate any later confusion about what the values on your spread sheet mean, insert labels above all new categories of data. So in cells A11 and C11, type the word "Sum." Then, to sum the X distribution,

• select (highlight) the column of values from A2 through A10.

• click on the Σ sign shown on the toolbar.

Do the same for the Y distribution. When you have finished, your screen should look like the screen shown in Figure 2.

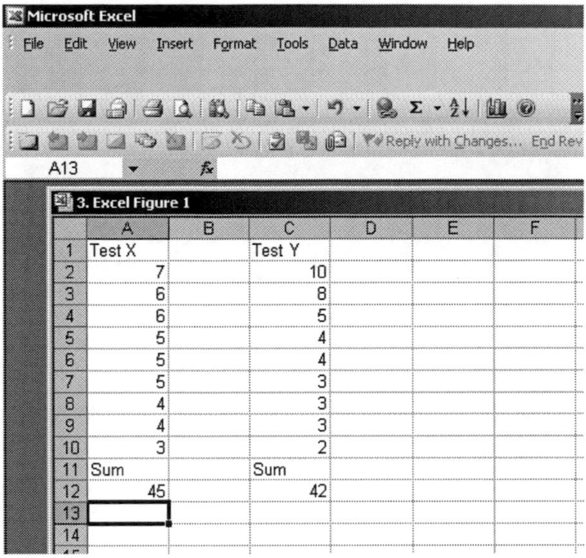

Figure 2. Excel Screen After Calculating the Sums of Distributions X and Y

In cells A13 and C13, type the word "Mean." To calculate the mean for the X distribution,

• select the original column of values again.

• open the drop-down menu to the right of the $\sum$ symbol (▾), and click "average."

Do the same for the Y distribution. When you have finished, your screen should look like the screen shown in Figure 3.

Calculating the Standard Deviation

In cells A15 and C15, type "SD" for "standard deviation." You may calculate the standard deviation by one of two methods. Choose the method you find most comfortable. The dominant task for the first method is typing; the dominant task for the second method is opening windows and responding to menus. I will show each method.

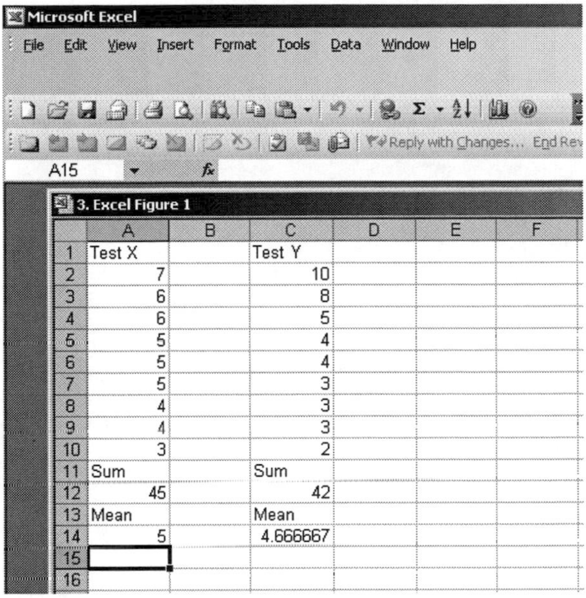

Figure 3. Excel Screen After Calculating Means for Distributions X and Y

Typing Method

- Select cell A16 as the cell in which you want the standard deviation to appear.

- Type the following formula into that cell: =stdev(A2:A10)

- Push ENTER. The standard deviation will appear in cell A16.

- Repeat the steps for distribution Y, using cell C16 and cells C2 through C10.

When you have finished, your screen should look like the screen shown in Figure 4.

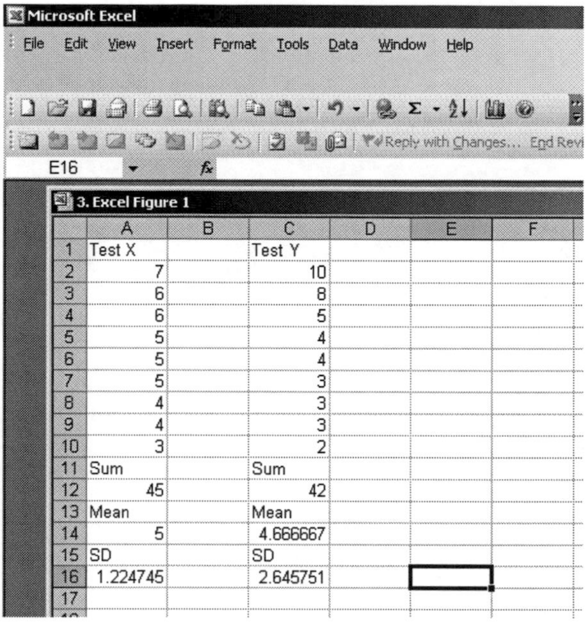

Figure 4. Excel Screen After Calculating the Standard Deviations
for Distributions X and Y

You can achieve the same results as shown in Figure 4 without typing the formula into the cell. If you want to compare the two methods, select and delete the standard deviations shown in cells A16 and C16, and then recalculate them by using the menu method. Follow the steps below.

Menu Method

 • Select cell A16 as the cell in which you want the standard deviation to appear.

 • Open the drop-down menu next to the ∑ symbol, and click "More Functions." (An = sign will appear in the selected cell.)

 • For category, select "Statistical."

 • For function, select "STDEV."

At this point, your window should look like the one shown in Figure 5.

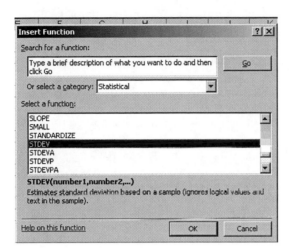

Figure 5. Window Selections Needed for Standard Deviation Calculation

Click "OK." The window will change. Select the cells for which you want the standard deviation calculated—in this case, cells A2 through A10. Click "OK" in the new window. The standard deviation will appear in cell A16. Repeat the steps for Column Y, placing the standard deviation in cell C16. When you have finished, your screen should look like the screen you achieved when you used the typing method. That screen is shown in Figure 4.

Calculating Correlation

To be consistent, and to keep yourself oriented to which statistics are located in which cells, type "r" for "correlation coefficient" in cell E15, immediately above the cell that will receive the coefficient. As with calculation of the standard deviation, you may calculate correlation either by a typing method or by a menu method. Because this calculation interlocks the two distributions, there will be no separate operations for the X distribution and the Y distribution.

Typing Method

- Select cell E16 as the cell in which you want the correlation coefficient to appear.

- Type the following formula into that cell: =correl(A2:A10,C2:C10).

- Push ENTER. The correlation coefficient will appear in cell E16.

When you finish, your window should look like the window shown in Figure 6.

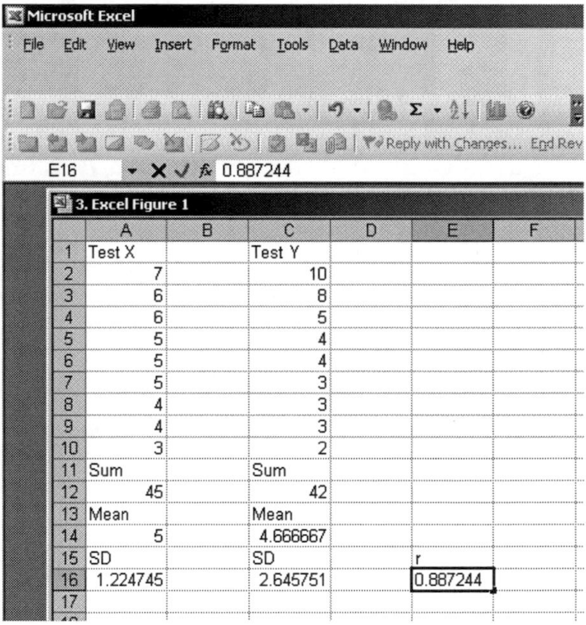

Figure 6. Excel Screen After Calculating the Correlation Between Distributions X and Y

You can achieve the same result as shown in Figure 6 without typing the formula into the cell. To learn the menu method for calculating correlation coefficients, delete the contents of cell E16 and follow the steps below.

Menu Method

- Select cell E16 as the cell in which you want the correlation coefficient to appear.

- Open the drop-down menu next to the $\sum$ symbol, and click "More Functions." (An = sign will appear in the selected cell.)

- For category, select "Statistical."

- For function, select "CORREL."

- Click "OK." The window will change.

- With the cursor in Array 1, select cells A2 through A10.

- With the cursor in Array 2, select cells C2 through C10.

At this point, your window should look like the window shown in Figure 7.

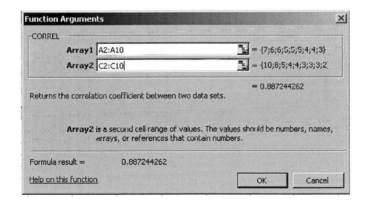

Figure 7. Window Selections Needed for Correlation

Click "OK." The correlation coefficient will appear in cell E16. When you finish, your screen should look like the screen you achieved when you used the typing method. That screen is shown in Figure 6.

Calculating Standard Scores

In cells B1 and D1, enter "z" for "standard score." I will show you the method for calculating standard scores for the X distribution as an example. Select cell B2. You will calculate a z score for that first case by typing in a formula, and then I will show you how to apply that formula to all cases in the distribution to avoid your having to calculate each z score individually.

The following formula, which you will now build in cell B2, will make sense to you if you remember that the formula for z score is the score minus the mean, divided by the standard deviation. Enter this formula into cell B2 by use of a combination of typing and clicking:

- Type =(

- Click on the cell containing the first value (cell A2)

- Now the formula in cell B2 will read =(A2

- Type a minus sign from your number pad, click cell A14, and then type)

- Now the formula in cell B2 will read =(A2-A14)

- Type a divide sign from your number pad, and then click cell A16

- Now the formula in cell B2 will read =(A2-A14)/A16

This next operation may be foreign to you. Because you will want to apply the mean and the standard deviation as a constant to each value in the distribution, you need to command them to remain as constants. To do that you will insert a dollar sign on either side of their column designations. Using cursor and keyboard, type in dollar signs so the formula becomes this: =(A2-A14)/A16.

Locate the cursor in the lower right corner of the cell until you see a bold plus sign at the intersection of B2, B3, C2, and C3, then depress and hold down the left mouse button. A *z* score will appear in the cell. The window should look like the window shown in Figure 8.

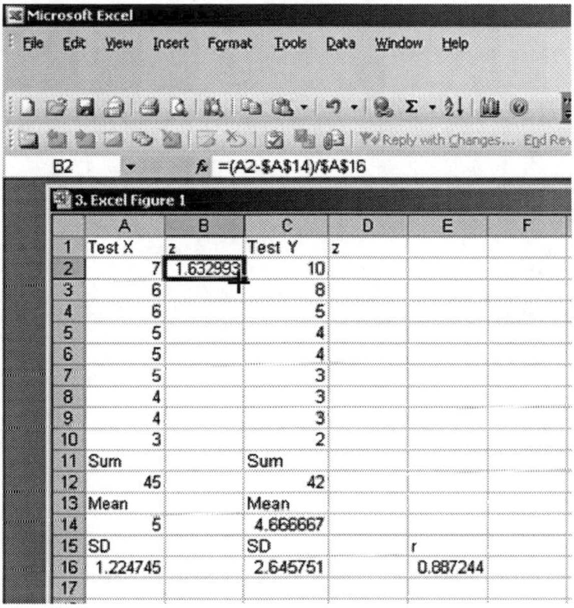

Figure 8. Placement of the Cursor in Preparation to
Drag in the Column of *z* Scores

Holding the left mouse button down, drag the mouse straight down to the bottom of cell 10. Release the mouse button. The full array of z scores will appear in the B column.

Repeat the entire process to calculate the *z* scores in the Y distribution. Of course you will use all the values of the Y distribution from their corresponding cells. Specifically, you will enter the formula into cell D2, you will take the mean from cell C14, and you will take the standard deviation from cell C16. You will surround the C on C14 and the C on C16 with dollar signs, the command that causes that mean and that standard deviation to function as constants. Then you will drag the D column as you did the B column. After you have calculated all *z* scores, your window should look like the window shown in Figure 9.

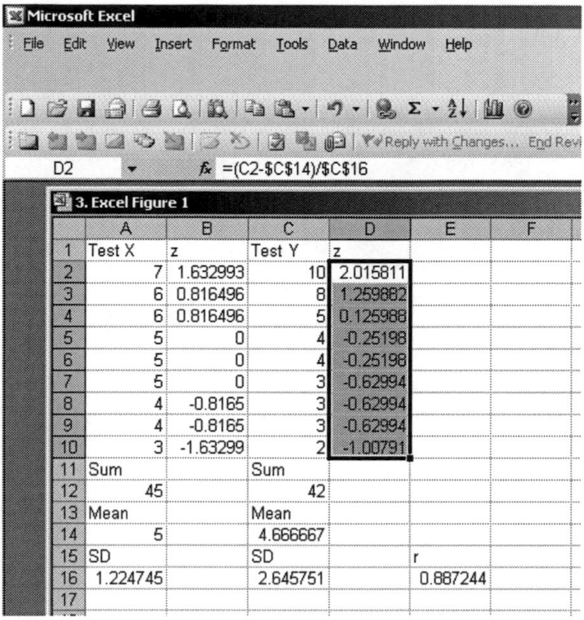

	A	B	C	D	E	F
1	Test X	z	Test Y	z		
2	7	1.632993	10	2.015811		
3	6	0.816496	8	1.259882		
4	6	0.816496	5	0.125988		
5	5	0	4	-0.25198		
6	5	0	4	-0.25198		
7	5	0	3	-0.62994		
8	4	-0.8165	3	-0.62994		
9	4	-0.8165	3	-0.62994		
10	3	-1.63299	2	-1.00791		
11	Sum		Sum			
12	45		42			
13	Mean		Mean			
14	5		4.666667			
15	SD		SD		r	
16	1.224745		2.645751		0.887244	
17						

Figure 9. Excel Screen After Calculating *z* Scores for Cases in Distributions X and Y

To show you the appearance of a column after dragging the formula through it, I left the cursor at its resting place for this last screen rather than park it in an empty cell.

If you want to transform *z* scores, you can do that easily enough without using a computer calculation. For the McCall *T* ($T = z\ (10) + 50$), simply move the decimal point one place to the right and add 50. For example, the first case in the X distribution would be assigned a *T* score of 66 (16 + 50), and the second-to-last case in the Y distribution would be assigned a *T* score of 44 (–6 + 50). For a standard score equivalent to an SAT score, you would move the decimal point of the *z* score two places to the right (x 100) and add 500.

Excel, in essence, is a large calculator by which you can organize data, enter it into innumerable calculations, locate results at specific places on the page, graph information, store it, print it, and send it by e-mail. Various statistics software packages will allow you to use more advanced operations easily, but I think Excel offers you what you need for purposes of this book. Other statistics software may be helpful to you if you conduct research, but even then I recommend storing your data in Excel. You can easily import an Excel spread sheet into another software's document for analysis—and meanwhile, you have your data stored in a convenient format. Just as other software applications assign identifying extenders to stored files (.doc or .docx for Word and .ppt or .pptx for PowerPoint), stored Excel files take on the identifying extender .xls or .xlsx.

PERFORMANCE TESTING FOR
INSTRUCTIONAL IMPROVEMENT

Introduction

For teachers of music—or any skill-based endeavor—information about performance testing is primary. Whether your purpose is to learn what you should teach next, record information for students and parents, or decide about an award (grade, ensemble placement, scholarship), you will need to create a system by which your assessment of student performance is reliable. That is, you will need assurance that you are consistent—from student to student and time to time—in the assessments you make. Validity is a concern as well, but throughout my presentation of performance-testing tools I will focus my attention first on reliability. As you will remember, reliability is a prerequisite for validity. Near the end of the chapter I will advise you directly about safeguarding the validity of your performance tests.

Some processes described in this chapter may seem rigorous, perhaps impractically so—particularly where I write about using and evaluating rating scales. Still, those processes are invaluable to *systematic assessment*. Much later in the chapter I will show you some usable *shortcut assessments*, but to use shortcuts exclusively is to impair the quality of your assessments.

Levels of Performance Assessment

Off-the-cuff general judgments might be considered a crude form of performance assessment: "I don't like that," or "she can do better than that." A person having some details in mind might add a bit of specificity to the judgment: "That tone isn't very good," or "the rhythm is all over the place." Still, such crude evaluations are notoriously unreliable for lack of *criteria* by which to judge the performance.

One way to organize performance assessment relative to criteria is to decide what characteristics are desirable to observe, and then write a *checklist*. You must write the criteria for a checklist clearly to accommodate a "yes" or "no" answer. Then when you evaluate a performance you put a check on the line corresponding to each *criterion* met by the performer, and leave blank the lines corresponding to criteria yet to be met. Some judgment will always be required, but you can reduce the room left for interpretation by using language well. Look at the checklist for a beginning instrumentalist's basic competence, shown in Figure 1.

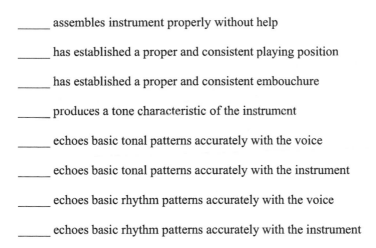

Figure 1. Checklist for a Beginning Instrumentalist's Basic Competence

You might use a group checklist to record individual progress within a group if the criteria serve as motivation, not as embarrassment. Be sensitive to individual feelings. Only you, as the teacher, know the students and the criteria well enough to decide when a public posting is appropriate. The sample checklist shown in Figure 2 has criteria at the top (represented arbitrarily by letters) and student names down the side. The opposite arrangement may work best, depending on class size, number of criteria, and the shape of the posting area.

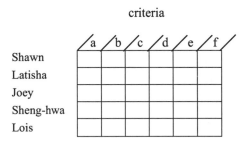

Figure 2. Sample Group Checklist

Checklists are useful tools for performance assessment as far as they go, but they limit you as the teacher to answering the question "is that criterion present?" For more complex performance assessments you will want to answer the question "to what extent is the criterion present?" One tool for measuring extent is a ***Likert scale***, an example of which is shown in Figure 3. The Likert scale is used most commonly in survey research to solicit levels of agreement. It is likely to be useful to you as a teacher of music more for soliciting opinions (student responses) than for measuring achievement (your responses).

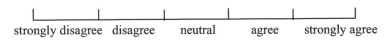

Figure 3. Example of a Likert Scale

Teachers sometimes record the extent of student achievement by use of a five-point scale similar to the one shown in Figure 4.

5 = outstanding
4 = good
3 = average
2 = below average
1 = unsatisfactory

Figure 4. An Achievement Scale Used by Some Teachers

One advantage of the scale in Figure 4 is that it allows you as the teacher to record degrees of achievement rather than simply stating presence or absence. Still, this scale is not as useful as it might be to your achieving the primary purpose of assessment: to improve instruction. By using this scale you will record no specific shortcomings that account for a student's having been rated "average" rather than "good" or "outstanding." That will leave you with no information from which to choose specific content or devise specific teaching strategies aimed at elevating the student's skills. If the purpose of your assessment is purely summative, the scale in Figure 4 may help you award grades, but you will glean little formative information from such general terms as "average" or "good." To say "she's a good singer" or "he's a good musician" is not to say "good in every respect." Human performance stems from multiple dimensions of skill.

To create a profile of achievement, you will need to isolate those various dimensions of your students' skills, and then observe each dimension relative to a list of specific, informative criteria. (Note: I will use *observe* and *observation* in reference to scrutiny by any means, recognizing that musical *observation* is accomplished primarily by hearing.) The multi-dimensional profile that you create will enable you and your students to understand what has been achieved and what direction is needed for the next round of instruction. An effective tool by which to achieve such a profile is a ***rating scale***.

Constructing Rating Scales

Dimensions and Criteria

How good is her tone quality? How accurate are his rhythms? How expressively does she play? These questions are inquiries about various *dimensions* of a person's musical performance. No doubt you have encountered someone whose sense of pitch is faulty but who plays rhythms well—or perhaps the reverse. Nearly everyone's strength and ease of performance varies from one dimension to another. Because that is so, you will need to isolate dimensions of each student's performance in a way that will enable you to identify strengths and weaknesses. Then you can share that information with the student, and the two of you can form a partnership to make the most of strengths and shore up weaknesses that would—if left unchecked—cripple the student's efforts to advance as a musician.

In specific terms, you will be using *systematic observation* to measure the condition of the student's tone quality, rhythm accuracy, expression, or any of a number of other dimensions of performance. *Measure* is a key term in that last statement. You will remember from Chapter One that measurement is an objective process, but that objectivity is relative. Measurement of human behaviors will never be accomplished as objectively as measurement of physical properties. The goal in writing a rating scale aimed at a particular dimension of performance is to make the process as objective as it can be for the purpose of measuring learning. **The closest we can come to acquiring a tape measure for performance is to construct a good rating scale.**

To make systematic, intelligent observations relative to each dimension, you will need to establish specific criteria for each. How many criteria should a given dimension encompass? Too few will restrict the range of judgment, leaving you torn between one criterion that overstates the performance level and another that understates it. That lowers reliability (consistency of judgment) by creating errors on the high side one time and on the low side another. Too many criteria will blur your judgment, frequently leaving you torn between two criteria so similar that either could be justified. That lowers reliability through indecision and vacillation.

Researchers over the years have found that five criteria generally yield the highest reliability. I theorize that five-point rating scales yield optimal results for the same reason that a five-line staff yields optimal results for music notation: the eye and mind can perceive and make quick, accurate judgments where one central choice is flanked on either side by two others. Imagine the visual confusion if a music staff were to have six or seven lines. Whatever the explanation, a rating scale having five criteria—referred to commonly as a five-point rating scale—is a standard worthy of acceptance.

Further clarification of terminology is in order here. I will refer to a series of five criteria as a "rating scale." When it stands alone, it is in fact a *one-dimensional rating scale.* For a given performance assessment you may construct criteria for two or three such dimensions. In that case, the whole also would be referred to as a rating scale: a "two-dimensional rating scale" or a "three-dimensional rating scale." But even then, each dimension, when referred to in isolation from the other dimensions, is called a "rating scale."

While studying and practicing the use of rating scales in the pages immediately ahead, you will be laying a foundation for writing and using an assessment tool ubiquitous among today's educators: a rubric. As an offshoot of the well-established, long-respected rating scale, the so-called "rubric" reminds us that knowledge of and facility with rating scales is foundational to all approaches to performance assessment.

The Continuous Five-Point Rating Scale

The most powerful form of rating scale is called a *continuous rating scale,* because its five criteria constitute a continuum. That is, they function like a rising thermometer: the performer will pass "1" to get to "2," then "2" to get to "3," etc. A good continuous rating scale can be difficult to write, but the rewards of doing so are substantial. The better conceived and better written a scale is, the higher its reliability and the more useful its results to teaching. A good scale is worth hours of working, piloting, and reworking for the long-term advantages it gives once it becomes a part of your teaching repertoire.

In Figure 5 you will see a continuous rating scale that I used for a research project. I needed to measure the ability of children in grades K through 3 to synchronize movement with music at a variety of tempos. I prepared a recording containing 14 brief musical items that ranged in tempo from mm 57 to mm 130, arranged in random order. As each item was played, a wood block showed the tempo for a few bars. Subjects were asked to pat their laps (bilateral parallel motion) along with the wood block sound, and then keep patting with the beat of the music after the wood block sound stopped. My aim in constructing the rating scale was to write five criteria that operated continuously and allowed me to score the extent to which each subject was able to synchronize movement to the music of a given item.

| Dimension Label | → | Synchronization Ability |

Ratings	Criteria
5	synchronous; in addition, acknowledging such musical considerations as emphasis and phrase endings
4	synchronous; locked into the tempo throughout
3	nearly synchronous, but not "locked in"
2	unsynchronous, but exhibiting some sense of the task
1	erratic; as if not hearing the music

Figure 5. An Example of a Five-Point Continuous Rating Scale that Works Well

The best way for me to orient you to the creation of a continuous rating scale like the one shown in Figure 5 may be to re-trace the steps I took. I wrote a scale that looked effective, then used it (pilot tested it) with children who would not be participating in the study. I learned from that *pilot study,* and then made adjustments to the scale. Had the scale been made for classroom use, I would have simply used it with a few classes, adjusted it, used it again, and adjusted it again until I arrived at the optimal scale.

One fault I found in the scale at the time I pilot tested it surprised me greatly. Criterion 5 in the first draft of the scale eventually became Criterion 4 in the revised scale shown in Figure 5. When I wrote the original scale, logic told me that a child who locked into synchronization throughout a piece would have scored at the top. Then a few pilot subjects surprised me with moves that indicated sensitivity to phrasing. I needed a way to rate that ultimate sign of synchronization ability, so I rewrote the scale.

The number of exceptionally musical children in my sample—those who indicated phrasing—was small. Why did I feel compelled to accommodate them with a revised fifth criterion? A continuous scale should accommodate all the dimension-related skills that might be displayed by those being measured. The very small number of students scoring 5 was not a concern. Because performance skill ratings tend to conform in frequency to the shape of the bell curve, ratings of 1 and 5 will be rare for a well-conceived rating scale. The most-used rating **across a large number of subjects** should be 3 (crown of the bell), with a large number of 2s and 4s representing the sides of the bell, and a small number of 1s and 5s representing the tails. Ratings that conform to the shape of the bell curve in this way show that your writing of the scale and your use of it fit the population for whom you designed it, i.e., discriminate among performances roughly in proportion to the expected rate of occurrences within a population.

Any time you try to write and make use of a continuous rating scale, be sure the criteria actually function continuously. If you write criteria in such a way that a student might accomplish criterion 3 or 4 but fail criterion 2, you could find yourself torn. For a student who fails criterion 2 but accomplishes criterion 3, for example, you would have to either award a score of 1 to acknowledge that the student did not negotiate the bridge between criterion 1 and criterion 3, or award a score of 3 as you turn a blind eye to the student's failure to satisfy criterion 2. Figure 6 shows such a dysfunctional scale.

A surface problem with the scale shown in Figure 6 is that it conforms only to a piece whose tonal patterns are limited to those listed. That means this type of scale, even if it did function well, would be applicable only to very elementary performances. Assuming that it was designed specifically for just such a performance, the content of the scale would be fine. A problem that cannot be solved situationally, though, is the undependability of the implied continuum. True, pitch errors are more likely to occur in the high-numbered criteria than in the low-numbered criteria, but a few students are likely to succeed at a criterion higher than one at which they failed. At that point the premise of the scale as continuous crumbles.

Pitch Accuracy

Ratings	Criteria: The student plays correctly all
5	dominant skipping patterns
4	tonic skipping patterns
3	subdominant stepwise patterns
2	dominant stepwise patterns
1	tonic stepwise patterns

Figure 6. An Example of a Dysfunctional Five-Point Continuous Rating Scale

In addition to being sure that your continuous scale operates continuously, be sure the criteria match the content you taught and the skills you expect from a particular group of students at a particular level of development. The continuous rating scale shown in Figure 7 might be appropriate for elementary instrumentalists, but at the high school or college level Criterion 1 would be unused and Criterion 5 would be insufficient.

Tone Quality

Ratings	Criteria
5	clear and resonant enough for a secondary school ensemble
4	unusually well developed, but lacking full clarity and resonance
3	typical of a developing elementary student
2	recognizable, but dramatically deficient
1	unrecognizable as the instrument

Figure 7. A Five-Point Continuous Rating Scale Appropriate for Elementary Instrumentalists

The Additive Five-Point Rating Scale

Probably you sense that a continuous rating scale is difficult to write, and that much of what you will want to measure inherently fails to function on a continuum. To assess dimensions of performance that will not conform to a continuous approach, you may want to revert to the checklist: a list of criteria that you can identify as present or absent. If you limit your check lists to five criteria, you will benefit in two ways. First, five is a comfortable number of criteria: it imposes neither the frustration of too few criteria nor the rigor of too many. Second, to accommodate multiple dimensions within the same assessment task, you are likely to use some checklists and some continuous rating scales. Having the same number of criteria in each dimension of the assessment tool helps you interpret results in ways that soon will become apparent.

When you construct a multi-dimensional assessment tool that mixes checklists and continuous rating scales, you might want to think of the five-point checklist as a non-continuous five-point rating scale. Because the score on a five-point checklist amounts to an adding of the check marks earned rather than the achievement of a particular number on a continuum, such a checklist is sometimes called an ***additive rating scale***. Notice in Figure 8 that an additive rating scale is written with lines to check rather than with numbers from which to choose.

General Performance

Ratings	Criteria
_____	accurate rhythms
_____	accurate pitches
_____	acceptable tone quality
_____	good intonation
_____	expressive performance

Figure 8. A Five-Point Additive Rating Scale for Assessing General Performance

The very nature of the criteria in the scale shown in Figure 8 creates wide swaths within which to make judgments. In preparation to use such a general scale you will have to decide ahead of time the extent of accuracy needed, the level of intonation needed, etc. for students to receive a check mark.

An additive scale, though not as inherently powerful or reliable as a good continuous scale, can be constructed to assess skills more specifically than shown in Figure 8. One way to move from general to specific is to take a criterion from a general additive scale like the one shown in Figure 8, make it the dimension for a more specific additive scale (or for that matter, for a continuous scale), and then create specific criteria within the new dimension. In Figure 9 you will see a more specific additive scale created by using the last criterion in the Figure 8 scale as the new dimension.

Expressive Performance

Ratings   Criteria

_____   musically phrased

_____   dynamically controlled

_____   rhythmically flexible

_____   stylistically appropriate

_____   uniquely rendered

Figure 9. A Five-Point Additive Rating Scale for Assessing Specific Performanc

Guidelines for Writing a Rating Scale

When you write rating-scale criteria, use language that is concise, specific, and parallel. Concision is important to your being able to attend to the performance rather than to lengthy descriptions. Specificity is important to your making quick decisions rather than pondering over vague descriptions with multiple meanings. Parallel language is important to your being able to think through the criteria in the scale and compare them easily. To appreciate that last point fully, read the non-parallel language in Figure 10 and compare it to the parallel language in Figure 9.

Expressive Performance

Ratings	Criteria
_____	musically phrased
_____	good control of dynamics
_____	the rhythm is not stiff and mechanical
_____	plays in the appropriate style
_____	personalized with rubato, etc.

Figure 10. A Five-Point Additive Rating Scale with Non-Parallel Language

The order in which you place criteria within an additive rating scale is never as crucial as for a continuous scale. The very reason you need the additive format is that the criteria do not lead logically from one to another. Still, if you see an order that looks less than random, use it. It will make your assessments easier. In Figure 8, for example, I chose to group the most basic accuracy issues together at the top (accurate rhythms; accurate pitches), and I put the criterion most distinct from the others at the bottom (expressive performance). The order in which you arrange the criteria of an additive scale is just a matter of organizing your thinking for maximum efficiency while you are listening to a performance.

Other assorted pieces of advice for writing rating-scale criteria follow. Some seem obvious, but these suggestions stem from flawed scales written by students making their first attempt. That seems to suggest that they represent legitimate dangers worth reading and thinking about.

- Limit criteria to a single dimension.

   If you write "the rhythm and melody were accurately reproduced," you will allow yourself to approve neither skill until both are demonstrated. That will lower the diagnostic power of your scale.

- Use positive language.

   Write "rhythmically accurate" rather than "the rhythms were not accurate." Write "played through without stopping" rather than "did not stop before reaching the end." You can assess the presence of a condition more efficiently and more reliably than you can assess its absence.

- Use consistent language.

   If you use the term "correct pitches" in one criterion, continue that wording wherever the issue arises in other criteria. "Correct pitches" in one criterion, "pitches OK" in another, and "hit pitches" in still another imposes a translation job that detracts from the job of assessment.

- Use descriptive language.

   If you write simply "attacks," the question becomes "what about them?" By contrast, "clean, correct articulation" describes the trait sought.

- Use precise language.

   "Musically phrased" is superior to "Phrasing in logical places," because music is a matter of artistic expression, not logic.

- Be realistic.

   Tailor all criteria to conform to skills that you can realistically expect to hear at some point from members of the population you are assessing. To write "perfect intonation" for an elementary rating scale is to overshoot the top of the spectrum, and to write "no resonance, pitch center, and control" is to overshoot the bottom.

- Write only criteria that are measurable (observable).

   If you are making an assessment from an audio tape, do not write criteria that involve posture, embouchure, and other factors that need to be assessed visually. Whether you are assessing performances live or by tape, do not write criteria such as "good effort," or "correct counting system" unless your assessment entails an interview or a counting exercise. In short, refrain from writing criteria involving factors that can only be inferred. Every criterion must be directly observable to be measured.

I need to elaborate on that last point. Think of your performance assessment as a two-stage process. The first stage is the *what* stage (measurement): what do I observe in this performance? You will complete that stage by using rating scales, and that is why every criterion you write must be tied to a directly observable (visual or aural) act. The second stage is the *why* stage (evaluation): why did the act occur as observed? You will complete that stage by investigating probable causes and by exercising judgment as a teacher. For example, a flabby-sounding tone on a wind instrument may stem from a poor airstream, a poor embouchure, or some other cause. To write a criterion with language about the airstream or the embouchure rather than about the sound of the tone is to ask yourself to rate the performance on the basis of an inference about the cause rather than on the basis of your direct observation.

Using Rating Scales

Performance testing differs fundamentally from knowledge testing in an important way: you as the teacher (assessor) intervene between the test item and the written response. When you measure students' knowledge by using a multiple choice test, for example, they react to written items by writing their responses directly onto a piece of paper without your intervening. When you measure students' performance skills by using rating scales, they react to the performance tasks by performing, and you then use your judgment to decide upon a notation that you believe represents their performance response. The "chain of custody," to use a medical laboratory term, passes through you. You are in a position to contaminate the results. Because you want an accurate (valid) measurement, you need to not only write a scale that has the potential to work well, as described in the previous section, but you need to use it competently and responsibly. That makes the information in this section extremely important.

Measurement/Evaluation Perspective

When I wrote about measurement and evaluation in Chapter One, urging you to think of those terms as distinct entities having an objective nature (measurement) and a subjective nature (evaluation), I tempered my remarks by saying that "the two sometimes bend in each other's direction" (p.5). This is the point at which elaboration on that point is appropriate.

The first condition to acknowledge is that a rating scale, because it is designed to measure human behavior, will never be as objective a measurement tool as a tape measure. When you compare a point on a tape measure with a mark on a wall, it either reads 10 feet or does not. There is no judgment to be made. By contrast, when you compare a criterion on a rating scale with what you hear from a student performance, the number you record is affected by an element of judgment (subjectivity).

This introduction of judgment creates an interesting irony: while those five criteria are designed to function collectively as an objective measurement tool, individually they call for you to make evaluations—which by nature are subjective. It is this reliance on evaluation within the use of a measurement tool that separates the rating scale from the tape measure. So what is it about a rating scale that justifies our classifying it as an objective tool of measurement?

My answer to that question is that we write criteria within tight parameters to create a system we can use with consistency. We close as many loopholes as possible by writing criteria in specific, concise, parallel language, effectively reducing subjectivity by narrowing the choices within which the judgments are made. We organize those criteria into a well-designed scale based on the responses that our experience tells us are possible for the population being measured. And through practice, elaborated upon in the next section, we become mindful of specific standards that allow or do not allow the awarding of a given number. In doing all this, we create an opportunity for consistent (reliable) results as compared to conjuring up new criteria on the spot each time we have an assessment to make. Rating scales, then, constitute a systematic process that comes as close as we can expect to measuring human performance. That is why rating scales are said to be "objective" in a relative sense. Even though the measurement process has a modicum of evaluation working within it, our care in designing, writing, and using rating scales enables the whole to function as an effective instrument of measurement—at least to the extent that the measurement of human behavior is possible. The rating scale is our best substitute for a tape measure. Therefore, we feel confident when we use rating scale measurements of what we hear, perhaps incorrect pitches, to guide broader evaluations about the needs of the student, perhaps greater awareness of tonal functions.

Practice

Just as you cannot expect to write ideal criteria the first time you put words on paper, you cannot expect to make ideal judgments the first time you put a scale into use. In the last section I suggested pilot testing as a way to check the quality of a scale, and I said you can expect to make revisions after pilot testing the scale (as I did with the synchronization scale). Similarly, you will need to pilot test your use of the scale. You will do that to some extent simultaneous to your pilot testing the scale itself, but you will want to solidify your rating process further by practicing with the scale after you have settled on a final version. You will need to anchor in your mind a firm concept of what you will and will not give credit for in response to the scales call for "clean, clear articulations," or "proper style," or whatever criteria you have written. In short, you will remove as much subjectivity as possible so as to move the process closer to the objectivity needed in a tool of measurement.

To groom a scale for use in your teaching, begin by recording (audio or video) a sample of student performances. Choose students who collectively represent the widest possible cross-section of skill levels within the perform-ance task you are measuring. Then listen to the performances in private while looking at the scale. The easiest performances to rate will be those few conforming to criteria at the scale's extremes. To make judgments for less clear-cut performances, listen repeatedly until you have created a mind-set that lets you discriminate dependably between, for example, a rating of 3 and a rating of 4 on a continuous scale. By having the freedom to listen to the performances any number of times, and in the absence of students, you will be able to devise a studied, systematic approach to using the scale. You may find that even though you constructed the scale carefully and decided on a final draft, some small final adjustments to the scale are merited. That is, the process of preparing the scale and the process of preparing yourself to use the scale interact in unpredictable ways. At some point you will feel confident with both. To prepare the scale for wider use, you might even record "anchor" performances that demonstrate ratings of 1, 2, 3, 4, and 5 for each dimension.

You might be thinking "this seems like a lot of work." It is, but the product will be well worth it. Once you have created a series of rating scales and become comfortable with their use, you will have a treasury of assessment tools to use year after year. And as your experiences as a teacher grow, you will tinker with them and fine-tune them now and then.

Guarding Against Bias

In a struggle between logic and feelings, logic will not necessarily prevail. Logically, you know that your purpose in assessing student skills is to know your students' abilities and needs so you can do a better job of teaching them. Logically, you know that students lose as much in the long run by being rated spuriously high as they do by being rated spuriously low. Logically, you know that nothing will help you help your students so much as an assessment that describes, or at least approximates, the truth. But that is all logic, and logic goes out the window when feelings creep into play. No matter how much you believe in the efficacy of valid measurement, you will naturally feel that you are doing something *for* a student when you give a high rating, and doing something *to* a student when you give a low rating. Further, you will naturally be more sympathetic to hard-working, cooperative students than to slothful trouble makers. You will try to be impartial, but you will tend to give a break here and there to some students.

To counteract tendencies toward personal biases, rate performances without knowing the identities of the students. Set up a room with a recording device and have students record performances individually while you work with the rest of the class. You could have a responsible older student, an aide, a student teacher, or a parent-volunteer supervise the recordings and write students' names on a numbered list. Or you could instruct students to sign on numbered lines on a clipboard prior to recording their performances. Then you would rate the performances by number, and check the identities on the list only after you have finished the ratings.

This system is far from foolproof, because some students will have tone qualities or other characteristics that are unmistakable. Still, this system will increase the objectivity of your ratings enough to be worth the effort for high-stakes assessment. Also, having performances recorded enables you to listen multiple times. If you have written three dimensions to be rated for a particular performance, you can listen three times—each time isolating in your mind only the dimension you are rating. Rating only one dimension at a particular listening is extremely important to the quality of your results (as you will see in specific terms when you read soon about the halo effect). Further, you may decide to listen to particular students' performances multiple times for the rating of a single dimension when you encounter difficult judgments. Virtue lies not in listening to each person an equal number of times, but in making each rating as close as possible to a true representation of the performance. If that will be accomplished best by an unequal number of listenings, so be it.

Bias can creep in even when you have done your best to hide student identities. Suppose that you hear the performance of the first player on a recording, and you rate that player *4* for dimension one. If you have that score in view as you listen again to rate dimension two, and if you ponder briefly about whether to award a rating of *3* or *2*, the previous rating of *4* will influence you toward the *3*. Human nature has us look for clues when we have a judgment to make, and past performance, e.g., reputation, is a powerful clue.

Researchers refer to this tendency for previous scores to influence current judgment as the ***halo effect***—expectations of good results from one who has shown good results previously. You can avoid the halo effect. Any time you will be rating the same group of performers multiple times for any reason, keep the record of all previous ratings out of sight as you rate anew. Do not tell yourself "all that trouble is unnecessary; I have a strong enough will to overcome a small tendency toward bias." The effect is not a matter of will; it is a matter of undeniable human nature, proven over and over again.

Recording and Calculating Results

I recommend that you create a master *tally sheet* on which to record your ratings of each dimension of a performance for a given group of performers. Figure 11 shows a tally sheet for a three-dimensional performance assessment. I will describe the use of each feature shown on the tally sheet. (Just as the earlier sample distributions involved fewer cases than you are likely to see, this tally sheet—for efficiency's sake—accommodates a distribution of only nine performers. You will design tally sheets that fit the reality of your classroom.)

The heading shown on the tally sheet is arbitrary. If you are the only person rating students, you will not need a line for "rater." Design the heading to carry whatever information you need.

Dimensions 1 through 3 could be whatever you want them to be. You might, for example, have a melodic dimension, a rhythmic dimension, and a tone quality dimension. Then you would label them as such at the tops of the columns rather than labeling them simply "Dimension 1," etc. You may use more than three dimensions, or fewer.

"Composite" is simply a place to record the sums of all the ratings across dimensions to yield an overall performance score. For example, a person who scored a 3 on Dimension 1, a 4 on Dimension 2, and a 3 on Dimension 3 would have a composite score of 10.

Notice that I have provided two columns for each dimension, labeled "first rating" and "second rating." **You will not use double columns on your tally sheets once you have established your rating scales and have confidence in them.** The tally sheet in Figure 11 is designed to accommodate a form of test-retest reliability similar to that described in Chapter One. For performance testing, a more accurate term would be *rate-rerate reliability*: the purpose is not to measure the consistency of student responses across two performances, as with knowledge testing, but rather to measure your consistency as a rater across two listenings of the same performance. Nonetheless, *test-retest* is the term used most commonly, even in reference to rating scales. To estimate test-retest reliability, you will need to use recorded performances. Generally an audio recording will suffice, as you will be rating aural dimensions. If you want to rate visual dimensions as well (posture, hand position, etc.), you will need to use video recordings.

Rating Scale Tally Sheet

Class _____ Rater_____

Piece Performed_____ Date_____

	Dimension 1		Dimension 2		Dimension 3		Composite	
Case	first rating	second rating	first rating	second rating	first rating	second rating	first rating	second rating
1.								
2.								
3.								
4.								
5.								
6.								
7.								
8.								
9.								
Σ								
$\overline{X}$								
SD								

$r =$ _____ $r =$ _____ $r =$ _____ $r =$ _____

Inter-correlations:

$1,2 =$ _____ $1,3 =$ _____ $2,3 =$ _____ $1,C =$ _____ $2,C =$ _____ $3,C =$ _____

Figure 11. A Sample Tally Sheet for Recording Ratings of a Distribution of Performances Across Three Dimensions

This is how the test-retest (rate-rerate) process works. You will listen to the performances with the rating scale for Dimension 1 in front of you, and mark a rating of 1, 2, 3, 4, or 5 in the "first rating" column for each performer. Then to avoid the halo effect, you will put the tally sheet out of sight and listen to the performances again, recording Dimension 2 ratings (first rating) for each performer on a sheet of scrap paper. You will repeat that process for Dimension 3 on another piece of scrap paper, with your ratings for Dimensions 1 and 2 out of sight. After you have finished rating each dimension, you will transfer the Dimension 2 and 3 scores from the scrap paper onto the tally sheet, then add across the rows to calculate the first-rating composite scores for all cases. At this point you will calculate the sum, mean, and standard deviation for each of the four first-rating distributions (three dimensions and the composite) and enter those numbers in the appropriate cells. Now you have all columns labeled "first rating" filled from top to bottom, and all columns labeled "second rating" empty.

To estimate the reliability of your rating process—for this rating scale applied to this particular performance with this group of students—wait long enough to clear your mind of recall, perhaps two or three days (not more than a week). Then, using pieces of scrap paper to record your ratings for each dimension in isolation from each other, repeat the entire rating process. When you have finished, enter all the figures from the scrap papers onto the tally sheet in the "second rating" columns. You will have no reason to calculate sums, means, and standard deviations for the second ratings (though you may), because their role is simply to make a calculation of test-retest reliability possible.

Can you see what you have before you at this point? The extent to which your first ratings and your second ratings are in agreement is the extent to which you are using the rating scale consistently, i.e., the extent to which your rating process has reliability. The $r =$ showing below each pair of columns is intended to hold a test-retest reliability coefficient. You will calculate that coefficient by considering the first rating for each dimension the X distribution and the second rating for each dimension the Y distribution. Calculate the correlation coefficient as you learned in Chapter Two, or by use of Microsoft®

Excel as you learned in Chapter Three. Calculate a coefficient for the composite column just as if it were a separate dimension that you had rated.

You still have some blanks on the rating sheet under the heading *Intercorrelations*. Intercorrelations are correlations between dimensions of the rating scale rather than between multiple ratings of a single dimension. Whereas you will expect a high coefficient between your first and second ratings, because you are rating the same dimension of the same performance by use of the same scale, you will expect a much lower coefficient when you calculate intercorrelation. Why? Because you have designed your dimensions to measure separate aspects of each person's performance, and each person has strengths and weaknesses that will cause higher scores for one dimension of performance than for another. If intercorrelation coefficients approach the strength of the reliability coefficients, probably your scale is doing a less-than-adequate job of measuring discrete dimensions of the performances. (Use first ratings to calculate intercorrelations. The second ratings are there for one purpose only: calculation of test-retest reliability.)

Should you expect positive coefficients for your intercorrelations? Yes, because rarely is a performer so strong in one dimension and so weak in another that the two dimensions relate negatively. But neither should the relationship normally be anywhere near as strong as the relationship between your own two ratings of the same performance, i.e., your test-retest reliability. A rule of thumb described later in some detail is that your intercorrelation coefficients should fall approximately halfway between your reliability coefficients and 0.

Giving It a Try

To practice writing and using rating scales, you will need a body of content with which to work. You may have, or be able to create, a collection of performances to use for that purposes. If not, you will find some help on the disc that accompanies this book. One of the items on that disc is a set of nine instrumental performances of *When the Saints Go Marching In,* performed by students in grade five. The notation of the song is shown in Figure 12.

Figure 12. Notation of the Performance Piece on the Compact Disc

Listen a few times to the performances you will use for this exercise, and decide on three dimensions to rate. Then write three rating scales—one continuous scale and two additive, or one additive and two continuous (to give yourself practice with both). Read over your scales, think about what you have written relative to the advice given earlier about writing rating scales, and revise the scales to what you consider a final form. Photocopy the tally sheet shown in Figure 11, and then systematically rate the performances on the disc according to the procedures just described. Remember that the score for a dimension whose scale is continuous will be the number that the performer reached, whereas the score for a dimension whose scale is additive will be the number of checkmarks achieved, i.e., the number of criteria that you found present. When you have the tally sheet filled out, including all the calculations for test-retest reliability and intercorrelation (a task measured in days, not hours), read the next section for insight into the implications of your results.

Interpreting Results With the Help of Theoretical Constructs

So now you have a tally sheet filled with means, standard deviations, and correlation coefficients, generated from your multi-dimensional ratings of a series of student performances. It may look similar to the tally sheet shown in Figure 13, which consists of purely hypothetical data provided here so you have something with which to compare your tally sheet for general appearance.

Rating Scale Tally Sheet

Class _____ Rater_____

Piece Performed_____ Date_____

	Dimension 1		Dimension 2		Dimension 3		Composite	
Case	first rating	second rating	first rating	second rating	first rating	second rating	first rating	second rating
1.	3	3	5	4	4	4	12	11
2.	3	2	2	2	3	3	8	7
3.	2	2	2	2	3	3	7	7
4.	4	3	3	2	3	3	10	8
5.	1	1	3	3	2	3	6	7
6.	4	4	3	3	3	3	10	10
7.	3	2	4	4	5	4	12	10
8.	2	2	2	2	3	3	7	7
9.	3	3	2	2	3	3	8	8
Σ	25		26		29		80	
$\overline{X}$	2.78		2.89		3.22		8.89	
SD	.97		1.05		.83		2.20	

r = .86   r = .91   r = .87   r = .91

Inter-correlations:

1,2 = .21   1,3 = .67   2,3 = .38   1,C = .69   2,C = .80   3,C = .83

Figure 13. A Sample to Show the Kinds of Figures Likely to
Fill Your Tally Sheet (Hypothetical)

If you choose to calculate the statistics by using Microsoft® Excel, which I recommend, your Excel spreadsheet will look similar to the one shown in Figure 14 (same hypothetical data). Note that I have, as I recommended in Chapter Three, provided labels in cells immediately above calculations on the Excel sheet to make specific results easy to locate.

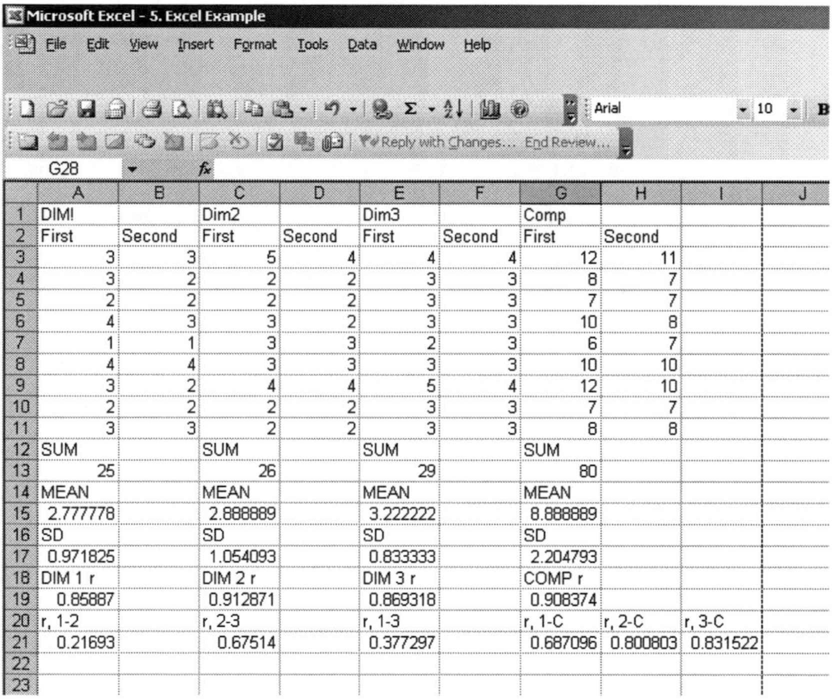

	A	B	C	D	E	F	G	H	I	J
1	DIM!		Dim2		Dim3		Comp			
2	First	Second	First	Second	First	Second	First	Second		
3	3	3	5	4	4	4	12	11		
4	3	2	2	2	3	3	8	7		
5	2	2	2	2	3	3	7	7		
6	4	3	3	2	3	3	10	8		
7	1	1	3	3	2	3	6	7		
8	4	4	3	3	3	3	10	10		
9	3	2	4	4	5	4	12	10		
10	2	2	2	2	3	3	7	7		
11	3	3	2	2	3	3	8	8		
12	SUM		SUM		SUM		SUM			
13	25		26		29		80			
14	MEAN		MEAN		MEAN		MEAN			
15	2.777778		2.888889		3.222222		8.888889			
16	SD		SD		SD		SD			
17	0.971825		1.054093		0.833333		2.204793			
18	DIM 1 r		DIM 2 r		DIM 3 r		COMP r			
19	0.85887		0.912871		0.869318		0.908374			
20	r, 1-2		r, 2-3		r, 1-3		r, 1-C	r, 2-C	r, 3-C	
21	0.21693		0.67514		0.377297		0.687096	0.800803	0.831522	
22										
23										

Figure 14. Data as Recorded and Calculated by Using Microsoft® Excel

The next questions are these: What do all these figures mean? What should you consider good? What do these figures imply about your scales, and about your use of them?

You need some benchmarks against which to compare your results. Those benchmarks are the ***theoretical constructs*** (***theoretical mean*** and ***theoretical standard deviation***) of a five-point rating scale, derived from the theory of the standard normal curve. First, think about the theoretical mean.

You would expect the theoretical mean to be 3, because that is the mid-point (median) and the mean of the five-point scale. The wrinkle in that logic is that a rating of 0 is always a possibility: theoretically, a student could fail to reach the first level of a continuous scale or fail to satisfy any of the criteria of an additive scale. The possibility of a 0 boosts the number of potential ratings to six, and that lowers the theoretical mean to 2.5, as shown by the formula in Figure 15.

$$\overline{X}_{THEO} = \frac{\sum \text{Potential Ratings}}{N \text{ Potential Ratings}} = \frac{15}{6} = 2.5$$

Figure 15. Formula for the Theoretical Mean of a Five-Point Rating Scale

Because a rating of 0 will be rare, you might want to think of the theoretical mean as floating somewhere between 2.5 and 3. Still, for calculations you will use 2.5.

The theoretical mean allows you to see if your obtained means are somewhere "in the ballpark." Means for well-written, well-used rating scales will vary from perhaps 2 to a little less than 4. If you obtain means near or above 4, you should check to be sure you have not written a scale that demands too little relative to the students' abilities. Another possibility is that you fell into the I'm-a-nice-person trap, handing out ratings as if they were prizes rather than objective judgments. If you obtain means below 2, you should check to be sure you have not written a scale that demands too much relative to the students' abilities. Another possibility is that you fell into the I-can-be-a-taskmaster trap, and rated students as if you were determined to maintain a high standard. An important mind-set for you to adopt when you are measuring performances is one of complete neutrality, coupled with a fierce determination to identify the scale number that comes closest to representing the truth as you hear it. When you rate in that way, using a well-written scale appropriate to the circumstances (students; teaching objectives), your obtained mean is likely to approximate the theoretical mean.

The first place to look for an explanation of an extreme mean is at the scale and your use of it. If you conclude then that you have a good scale, and that you have used it well, the explanation may be simply that you have an exceptionally gifted class, or the reverse, as compared to the larger population for whom you designed the scale. Every group of students you work with will not conform to the shape of the bell curve. You will find results much easier to interpret after you have had a few years experience using rating scales. The larger body of students over the years, taken as a collective distribution, will tend to conform to the bell curve. The more you see that happening, the more confident you can be that your process is sound, and that small groups that deviate wildly are simply aberrations.

You will understand the theoretical standard deviation of a five-point rating scale best if you think in terms of the three standard deviations that lie between the mean and either tail of the standard normal curve. Considering that the top of your rating scale is 5, and the theoretical mean is 2.5, the span of points between the theoretical mean and the top is 2.5. That same span traverses three standard deviation units. Therefore, to calculate the theoretical standard deviation you will divide that span of points (2.5) by 3, as shown in Figure 16.

$$SD_{\text{THEO}} = \frac{\text{Top Score} - \bar{X}_{\text{THEO}}}{3} = \frac{5 - 2.5}{3} = \frac{2.5}{3} = .83$$

Figure 16. Formula for the Theoretical Standard Deviation
of a Five-Point Rating Scale

The theoretical standard deviation allows you to see if your obtained standard deviation is reasonable. A standard deviation radically higher than .83, e.g., approaching 1.5, might indicate a set of criteria with a hollow center—one that pushes you toward either high scores or low scores. If the high scores and low scores in a hollow-centered distribution cancel each other out mathematically (the teeter-totter effect), your mean might well be in the expected range even though you award few scores near the center. That should prompt you to re-examine your scale.

A standard deviation radically lower than .83, e.g., approaching 0, might indicate that you are failing to discriminate among differences that are truly there. You might do that either in the mid-range (nearly everyone scores 3), the upper range (few score lower than 4), or the lower range (few score higher than 2).

The first place to look for an explanation of extreme standard deviations is at the scale and your use of it. If you conclude then that you have a good scale and used it well, the explanation may be simply that you have a wildly divergent or oddly homogeneous class. Every group of students you work with will not conform to the shape of the bell curve. As I mentioned relative to the mean, some groups of students are true exceptions to the norm. If the large body of students over time shows a reasonable degree of variability, you should give yourself some latitude to assume that wildly deviating small groups are aberrations. Legitimately large standard deviations for isolated groups can, in fact, help explain why some groups are more difficult to teach than others: for some groups of students, you will find yourself boring the highest-performing students while struggling to maintain the lowest-performing students. That is the kind of group that will yield large standard deviations when rated by use of a well-written, well-administered rating scale.

I should make a final point about the theoretical constructs of a rating scale so you are clear about how they relate to the composite score. The theoretical mean and standard deviation for the composite score will be a simple multiple of the number of dimensions combined to create the composite. Because the theoretical mean for one dimension is 2.5, the theoretical mean for the composite score of a two-dimensional rating scale will be 5.0 (2.5 x 2), for a three-dimensional scale 7.5 (2.5 x 3), etc. Similarly, because the theoretical standard deviation for one dimension is .83, the theoretical standard deviation for the composite score of a two-dimensional rating scale will be 1.66 (.83 x 2), for a three-dimensional scale 2.5 (.83 x 3), etc.

You still need to interpret the correlation coefficients—those used to estimate reliability and those used to estimate intercorrelation between the dimensions. Neither can be interpreted in an absolute way. Generally, a reliability coefficient that exceeds .80 for a single dimension is considered a strong indicator that the consistency of the rating process warrants acceptance and re-use. You might consider reliability coefficients between .70 and .80 acceptable but borderline. If your reliability coefficient is lower than .70, probably you should try to improve the scale, your use of the scale, or both.

Expect reliability coefficients for composite scores to be higher than those for individual dimensions. In Figure 13, the equal reliability coefficients for Dimension 2 and the Composite (.91) are unusual, and the lower coefficients for the other dimensions as compared to the Composite are typical. Reliability increases with the number of scores involved because each inconsistency is a smaller percentage of the body of scores, and the composite for a three-dimensional rating scale encompasses three times as many scores as does any one dimension alone.

You will need to interpret intercorrelation coefficients through an entirely different lens. Because your intention in constructing the multi-dimensional scale was to measure distinct dimensions of a performance, and because results between the dimensions are not expected to coincide if the scale has done the job of making those distinctions, you will expect a much lower coefficient for intercorrelations than for reliability estimates. A rule of thumb is that intercorrelations coefficients generally fall about halfway between the corresponding reliability coefficients and 0. Intercorrelation coefficients for dimensions whose reliability falls in the mid .80s, then, should be expected to fall somewhere in the neighborhood of the .40s. This is only a broad rule of thumb. An intercorrelation of .57, for example, would not be at all alarming, but an intercorrelation of .78 should cause you to question the degree of independence between your dimensions. Where the line of acceptability falls between those examples (.57 and .78) is highly subjective.

Expect intercorrelations between individual dimensions and the Composite to be higher than those between individual dimensions, because each dimension is itself a part of the Composite. As a dimension is being correlated with the Composite, then, it is simultaneously being correlated, in part, with itself. You can see that tendency at work in the intercorrelation coefficients shown in Figure 13.

Pursuing Validity

You are highly unlikely to achieve any measure of objective validity for your rating scales. Probably the closest you will come will be to have a colleague conduct a second rating and calculate the consistency between the two of you. That is called *inter-rater reliability* (or *inter-judge reliability*, a term used commonly in research studies). A high level of consistency between two persons indicates some likelihood that a scale is measuring what it is intended to measure. For that reason, inter-rater reliability is sometimes referred to as *quasi-validity*. A high level of agreement between two competent raters is a strong endorsement of the quality of the rating scale.

If you check inter-rater reliability, be sure to first spend time with your colleague explaining exactly how you think of the criteria and how you use the scale. A little joint practice is also a good idea, and will not mask deficiencies in any way. If the scale is poorly constructed, reliability will break down no matter how much preparation you put into the process. Preparation and practice will only raise reliability (and by extension, validity).

If you can achieve a high level of consistency between persons, you will have achieved a measure of quasi-validity for your scale. More important in practical terms, you will have a scale that multiple persons can use, perhaps within a department, and have confidence that comparisons between students, between classes, and even between schools can be relied upon. A staff consisting of teachers all knowledgeable about performance assessment and committed to using it well could, over time, create an invaluable battery of system-wide measurement instruments for performance assessment. I would not, on the other hand, recommend that you search for commercially written scales. The content of a good rating scale is dependent on the circumstances of the students, teacher, materials, and teaching objectives. For that reason, generic scales tend to be inferior to teacher-made scales.

Subjective validity is more easily accounted for than is objective validity. For content validity, simply be sure that the dimensions you write measure what you have been teaching, and that the criteria match realistic, specific teaching objectives. For process validity, be sure students are in a comfortable, safe environment, that you have become confident in the scale as written, that you have become comfortable and decisive in your use of the scale, and that you have used the bias-fighting processes described above. All those factors boost the subjective validity of your results.

Rubrics

Description

Dictionaries define *rubric* as a title emphasized by printing it in red (*ruber*), or secondarily as "any established procedure." At some point, the term came to be adopted by educators to describe a tool for *measuring degrees of performance quality*. That last phrase probably sounds familiar to you now, because rubrics are a variation of the rating scale approach to measuring performance. Everything you have learned about rating scales will help you understand, write, and use the tool that has come to be known as a "rubric."

The most comprehensive rubrics are akin to multi-dimensional continuous rating scales. Specifically, each dimension of the rubric shows levels of potential achievement arranged in a continuum. Rubrics are designed and used to measure either a performance or a non-performance product. For reading efficiency here, I will use the term *performance* in the broadest sense—to represent any skill displayed in any form, including those that might be described more technically as a *product*.

Though rubrics sometimes are used exactly as multi-dimensional rating scales are used, commonly they are used to measure whole performances in a single observation rather than making multiple observations dimension by dimension. Risks to reliability and validity, particularly due to the halo effect, are accepted as reasonable exchanges for accomplishing more measurements of more performances in less time. School schedules and class sizes make that trade-off tempting more often than not.

Rubric terminology is not congruent with rating scale terminology, nor is it consistent within itself. In rubric language, what would be called a *dimension* in a rating scale is likely to be called a *criterion*, but not exclusively so. What would be called *criteria* in a rating scale are likely to be called *levels*, but not exclusively so. Further, the number of levels is not necessarily five, and in fact is commonly four—sometimes fewer. For the rubric shown in Figure 17, for example, the terms in the left column would most likely be known as *criteria*. The four descriptions in the other columns would most likely be known as *levels*. If a five-dimensional, five-point rating scale were constructed to measure the same performance, each of the rubric criteria (melody, rhythm, etc.) would be considered a *dimension* of the performance. Beneath each dimension would be five (not four) descriptions of what the rubric terminology calls *levels*—known in rating scale terminology as *criteria*. (Pages 74–75 will refresh your knowledge of rating scale construction.)

Rubric for the Singing of a Song			
	4	3	2	1
Melody	Correct pitches throughout	Melody is less than perfectly accurate	Much of the melody is flawed	Very little of the melody is as it should be
Rhythm	Correct rhythms throughout	Rhythm is less than perfectly accurate	Much of the rhythm is flawed	Very little of the rhythm is as it should be
Voice Quality	Pure and lovely	Enjoyable	OK, but not particularly attractive	Seriously deficient
Musicality	Beautifully expressive	Moderately expressive	Some sense of phrasing	Devoid of musicality
Lyrics	Correct throughout	Nearly correct throughout	Hit and miss	Troublesome throughout

Figure 17. Example of a Rubric (sometimes called an "analytic" rubric)

Guidelines for writing the levels of a rubric are the same as guidelines for writing the criteria of a rating scale. First, focus yourself on a target for the assessment by deciding precisely what you want to hear or see before you begin to write. Then write descriptions that are (1) brief, specific, and mutually exclusive, (2) arranged to constitute a continuum of achievement from the lowest level to the highest, and (3) expressed in parallel language. Those attributes are even more critical in writing rubric levels than in writing rating scale criteria, because rubric users are likely to attend to a great number of levels and criteria simultaneously. The last thing you need is to have the waters muddied by confusing or bloated language.

To do a comprehensive job of measuring performance over the course of a full school year, you might want to use both rubrics and rating scales. You should select the most appropriate tool for each circumstance. Once or twice each school year you might want to invest in the rigor of a comprehensive assessment with optimal reliability and validity. For those occasions you would use rating scales as previously described. To accommodate more frequent performance assessments in the face of limited time and large numbers of students, you might want to use rubrics (or, thought of in another way, apply multi-dimensional rating scales to single observations).

The rating scale tenet that each dimension should be rated in isolation from the others is only one compromise that rubric users accept in exchange for efficiency. An even more fundamental rating scale tenet is that multiple dimensions of the performance should be kept separated from each other within a given criterion. The reason is that assessors otherwise face a quandary when part of the criterion has been satisfied and part has not. Sometimes even that tenet is sacrificed in favor of efficiency. In Figure 18 you will see a version of the Figure 17 rubric with all the levels collapsed in a way that calls for a single value to be ascribed to the overall performance. This compromise is commonly called a *holistic rubric*, leaving the standard rubric in Figure 17 to be called, by comparison, an *analytic rubric*.

What the holistic rubric amounts to is a quick, surface judgment of the quality of a performance. Few performers who earn, for example, a rating of 3 will have satisfied every factor within the corresponding description. And some may have exceeded a factor or two. That is because nature will not have performers achieve at the same level for every dimension (melody, rhythm, etc.) of a task. Therefore, assessors using a holistic rubric have to cast a blind eye to some of the detail and choose the number whose description most closely represents the performance. As great a compromise as that is over an analytic rubric, and especially over a rating scale, the descriptions still have more value than numbers alone, or than such vague labels as "good" or "fair." The descriptions keep the assessor listening or watching for the achievement of specific objectives, and it is by the comparison of a performance to those objectives that assessments contribute to their primary function: improve instruction.

Rubric for the Singing of a Song	
4	Melody and rhythm are accurate, voice quality is lovely, expression is beautiful, and lyrics are correct throughout.
3	Melody and rhythms are nearly accurate, voice quality is enjoyable, musicality is moderately expressive, and lyrics are nearly correct throughout.
2	Much of the melody and rhythm are flawed, voice quality is OK, some sense of musical expression is apparent, and lyrics are hit and miss.
1	Little is correct about the melody and rhythm, voice quality is difficult to listen to, musicality is absent, and lyrics are troublesome.

Figure 18. Example of a "Holistic" Rubric

You can see that each time-saving retrenchment—from rating scale to analytic rubric to holistic rubric—leads backward toward the simple numeric scale that has no descriptive criteria at all. Continued retrenchment, theoretically, would lead to a simple "I like it" or "I don't like it." For each performance assessment you undertake, you will need to decide where on the performance measurement hierarchy you should function. Your decision will depend on interplay among several considerations: the importance of reliability and validity to that particular assessment, the number of performances you have to assess, and the amount of time available. Regardless of compromises, any systematic, objective-driven measurement tool will lead to more valid assessments than will off-the-cuff judgments. Valid assessments not only improve instruction, but they offer rationale to students, parents, and administrators for the decisions you make (including grades).

Of course the ultimate in assessment flexibility is to take the tack of creating whatever tool works for you. It may be something quite unlike the tools others are using. Terminology, rules, and assessment formats you see in print were all born of someone having done exactly that. It does pay to study what has become widely used by others, because those models (1) give you benefit of the thinking others have invested, and (2) enable you to talk easily about assessment tools with others and work cooperatively with them beyond your own classroom. Still, if you find something that works well for you outside the formats you see, use it. You may create a new format that others decide to adopt.

Student Involvement

A value of rubrics beyond helping you make assessments as the teacher is that students can use them to get a taste of assessment and a perspective on your expectations for achievement. By contrast, most students' patience and attention spans would be stretched to the breaking point by the more rigorous dimension-by-dimension rating scale approach. Some teachers have students make self-assessments by use of rubrics. Some also have them make peer assessments. True, the task of assessing performance is demanding beyond the average student's ability to produce consistently valid results. But then, teachers encourage students to exercise any number of skills that will be accomplished well only after considerable practice, e.g., pitching a baseball or playing a violin. So expect your students to be immature novices as assessors. Also, expect them to need minimally complex rubrics—rubrics that contain fewer criteria than you might use. That means only that your assessment must constitute the final judgment.

Despite these limitations, teachers who teach students to use rubrics to assess their own work and the work of their peers find that the practice generates several worthwhile results:

1. By becoming familiar with the rubric, students become familiar with your expectations.

2. Struggling to use a rubric well gives students insight into the chore of assessment, and perhaps some appreciation for your responsibility as teacher.

3. Students will make some assessment judgments that are insightful to themselves, their peers, and you.

4. The value students see in the information that rubrics yield elevates their appreciation for assessment and their willingness to submit to it.

5. Assessing their work and the work of peers gives students a perspective on their standing relative to the work of others, and to your expectations as the teacher.

6. Student assessments of themselves and peers might give you insight that helps you make subsequent assessments more efficiently.

7. Knowing how students see their own work and the work of their peers will help you teach more empathetically and efficiently.

8. Each student becomes aware, in specific terms, of improvement needed. That puts you and the student in a good position to plan and prepare for selective re-assessments.

For some assessments, you might want to involve students in the creation of the rubric. That encourages them to think about what they should be accomplishing. It also encourages them to invest in the assessment process more heavily than if you imposed everything on them. I hasten to add that you need to maintain the role of expert and authority at all times. Student-written rubrics and student assessments should never become so prevalent as to overshadow your own thoughtful and comprehensive assessments.

Further Compromises

I am not using the term *compromise* derogatorily. Most circumstances call for some level of compromise. The longer you teach, and the more assessment tools you create and use, the more you become a candidate for effective compromises. If you learn comprehensive assessment processes well, beginning with rating scales, and you work diligently at learning how to create and use them, you acquire along the way assessment instincts that allow you to effectively mix many compromises into your repertoire of assessment tools.

Look, for example, at the checklist for a trumpet hand position shown in Figure 19 (not a 5-point scale). It looks like a checklist that would work well and cover the important points of the objective. The question is this: how practical would this checklist be? As a beginning teacher, you might find such a checklist useful. In a very short time, however (if not right away), you would find that you can see and correct these elements of the trumpet hand position so efficiently during the course of a lesson that you would waste time keeping a record of the problems in such detail. (Incidentally, such a list might be valuable to student self-assessment. It would give students a means of checking themselves and making corrections in preparation for your assessment.)

Trumpet Hand Position

Left Hand

_____ Thumb around 1st valve casing

_____ First two fingers around 3rd valve casing

_____ Third finger in ring on 3rd valve slide

_____ Small finger on top of third valve slide

_____ Wrist straight; trumpet slightly angled

_____ Arm relaxed and away from side

Right Hand

_____ Thumb concave; under lead pipe between valves 1 and 2

_____ Palm concave, a few inches from valve casing

_____ First three fingers concave, with pads on buttons

_____ Small finger concave, resting atop hook

_____ Arm relaxed and away from side

_____ Not holding the weight of the trumpet

Figure 19. Checklist for Trumpet Hand Position

So for such perfunctory elements of instruction as instrument position, you are likely to make on-the-spot assessments that you act on immediately—simple instinctive reactions to teachable moments. On-the-spot assessments amount to teaching techniques, and as such are the province of a different kind of textbook. The purpose of this text is to familiarize you with the more systematic assessments that give you precise records periodically, provide you with valid information for your planning of subsequent teaching, offer rationale to others for your decisions, and contribute subliminally to the quality of your on-the-spot assessments.

As you gain experience, you will find that you can make ever more assessments quickly, in a way that a casual observer might consider rash. By then you will have used enough check lists, rating scales, and rubrics over enough years that your mind will make many valid judgments by almost instantaneous use of its stored information, much as a computer does. You will find yourself blurring the line between measurement and evaluation all the more. I want to finish by emphasizing three important thoughts relative to such shortcuts.

1. You will make hundreds of instant assessments moment by moment as you teach. That is the nature of good teaching. The kind of systematic assessment processes described in this chapter are a means organizing your thinking, taking inventories to assure comprehensive treatment, and recording results so as to guide future teaching plans. These processes also create a consistency that allows you to operate at the same level year after year rather than re-inventing your approach repeatedly and suffering inconsistent results.

2. If you decline to think extensively about the assessment process—and if you fail to write measurement tools, use those measurement tools, and evaluate and revise those measurement tools—you are likely to be deceiving yourself about the efficacy of your shortcut assessments. In the absence of periodic assessment that is rigorous and systematic, your mind will become like a computer asked to do a job without the necessary software having been installed.

3. Regardless of your experience and competence with shortcut assessments, you should not rely on them exclusively. At particular points throughout a school year you will need to assess student progress systematically. There is no substitute for becoming familiar with good assessment processes and putting them to use when their thoroughness is called for.

Terms Important to This Chapter

systematic assessment (70): assessment by using a planned, practiced, systematic approach that produces a written record and is high in subjective validity (content and process) and reliability.

shortcut assessment (70): assessment by a process lacking the thoroughness of systematic assessment, but justifiable in many circumstances; quality is heavily dependent on the assessor's teaching experience and previous experience with systematic assessment.

criteria (71): standards against which something being judged is compared.

checklist (71): a list of criteria for performance that can be answered by "yes" or "no; during assessment, the criteria met are checked and the criteria unmet are left blank.

criterion (71): singular form of the term *criteria.*

Likert scale (72): a response scale used commonly in survey research to solicit levels of agreement or disagreement.

rating scale (73): a scale consisting of a list of criteria that describe in a concise, specific way the levels of achievement a teacher might identify in a performance.

dimension (74): a category of achievement measured by use of a list of criteria; a dimension might be rhythm accuracy, pitch accuracy, tone quality, intonation, expressiveness, etc.

systematic observation (74): a key tool of systematic assessment.

one-dimensional rating scale (75): a rating scale designed to measure only one dimension of achievement, as compared to a multi-dimensional rating scale designed to measure two, three, or more dimensions of achievement.

continuous rating scale (75): a specific type of rating scale designed as a continuum of achievement that requires students to pass through lower levels on their way to achieving higher levels, with the level achieved constituting the score.

pilot study (76): use of a measurement tool such as a rating scale with a test group to identify strengths and weaknesses of the tool, revise it as needed, and establish guidelines for its use.

additive rating scale (79): a five-point check list used to measure a dimension of performance not suited to a continuous rating scale; the score is expressed simply as the number of criteria satisfied by the performance.

halo effect (87): the effect that knowledge of a person's previous achievement has in biasing one's assessment of current achievement.

tally sheet (88): a form designed to hold results of an assessment and its subsequent statistics for convenient referral.

rate-rerate reliability (88): a term that describes more accurately (as compared to *test-retest*) the process of estimating reliability for a rating scale, because the two measurements correlated are not of separate events, but rather two independent ratings of the same event by the same person.

intercorrelations (91): correlations between the dimensions of a multi-dimensional rating scale used to assess performance skills of a given set of students.

theoretical constructs (94): theoretical benchmarks of a measurement tool based on the theory of the standard normal curve, benchmarks that can be compared to obtained statistics to judge the typicality of those obtained statistics.

theoretical mean (94): a benchmark mean, which will be approximated by administering a well-designed, well-administered measurement tool to a normally distributed sample.

theoretical standard deviation (94): a benchmark standard deviation, which will be approximated by administering a well-designed, well-administered measurement tool to a normally-distributed sample.

inter-rater reliability (99): an estimate of the reliability of a measurement instrument made by calculating the correlation between the ratings of two persons who used the same rating scale independently to rate the same set of performances.

quasi-validity (99): a term sometimes applied to inter-rater reliability, because agreement between two persons increases the chance that the scale is measuring what it was intended to measure.

rubric (100): a term adopted by educators to describe an assessment tool based on rating scale principles and used to measure degrees of performance quality.

analytic rubric (102): a rating scale-based tool used to measure separate dimensions of a performance, but not necessarily through separate observations—as with the traditional rating scale approach.

holistic rubric (102): a rubric in which levels are collapsed, allowing the assessor to ignore the assessment of separate dimensions in favor of quickly producing a single value that represents the quality of the overall performance.

Chapter Five

PERFORMANCE TESTING FOR AUDITIONS
AND OTHER COMPARISON TASKS

Introduction

This will be a short chapter, but it does deserve a place of its own because of the uniqueness of the tools involved. Any music teacher who works with ensembles has occasional cause to assess performance for the sole purpose of deciding whether one person or ensemble deserves to be rated more highly than does another person or ensemble. That kind of performance assessment, because it is aimed at comparisons rather than at diagnosis and improved instruction, calls for a unique approach. The three circumstances for which I will give advice here are ensemble auditions, individual challenges, and ensemble competitions. I will reflect back on performance testing practices described in Chapter Four, because some of those practices are worth borrowing and because your understanding of them will improve your use of comparison techniques.

Ensemble Auditions

For illustration, assume you have 10 student musicians vying for a place in a six-person section. You need to decide whom to admit. If you use a performance-based seating arrangement—and to accommodate all the possibil-ities, I will assume here that you do—you will also need to decide in what order they should sit. If formative assessment were your aim, you would be interested in each student's strengths and weaknesses, and in what specific learning each needs most. In contrast, for this audition you need to focus on one objective only: what is the rank order of their musicianship skills relative to the needs of the ensemble.

Probably you conduct such auditions only once each year. Your decisions, then, will affect the character of the ensemble, the quality of your rehearsals and performances, and the lives of the individual students for an entire school year. With an effect that far-reaching you will want to commit yourself to a thorough job of assessment.

I have participated in auditions in which everyone auditioning was in the room together. As they took turns playing, the auditioner rearranged them in order of performance quality—with some asked to play several times until the auditioner felt comfortable with the judgments. I believe that experience, sheer terror for the faint of heart, is unconscionable. Variability in fearfulness and stamina from one player to another, along with lack of uniformity in what the auditioner hears while poking here and there for comparative information, causes me to recommend strongly against that approach.

One important tenet is this: unless differences between two performers are profound, a single listening is unlikely to be sufficient to make accurate judgments about differences in their skill and musicianship (one argument for rejecting a strict performance-based seating system). Chances are good that you will need multiple listenings to many of the performances to make confident judgments. That suggests the use of recorded auditions as an alternative to the terroristic personal group auditions described above.

The wrinkle is that a live hearing—and interaction between you and those you are auditioning—seems important. You feel a need to be present to be sure the process is uniform for everyone, to answer questions, to calm nerves, and maybe to allow a restart if you have reason to believe you are not hearing a representative performance. And you want to talk to each person at the time of the audition to learn more about attitudes and aspirations and determination—intangible aspects of each performer's makeup.

To cover all the bases, you may want to audition students in a way that captures every advantage. The best approach may be to have each student meet with you at an appointed time to talk with you and play the audition. Explain that you are recording the audition at the same time so you can replay segments as needed, because you want to be sure to make the best possible judgments. Probably an audio tape recording will be sufficient, but you can use video tape if you think you will want to compare students on the basis of visual factors — and if clearance to video tape is not a problem.

In keeping with the rest of this book, I will not recommend particular content for an audition. That is a matter of pedagogy, not assessment. Generally the audition will involve some prepared piece and some sight-reading. Those decisions are yours.

At the time you hear each performer in person, make a general judgment — one to be confirmed and solidified a short time later by use of the tape. You will need to make notes to help remember details about person number 4 or 5 at the time you are listening to person number 9 or 10. To organize those notes, you might want to use a general additive scale (check list) similar to the one shown in Chapter Four, Figure 8, but modified in some way — maybe as shown here in Figure 1, or maybe in some other fashion.

Because your focus is on comparison, you might not want to treat the criteria as solely additive, but rather rate the level of each criterion with a number from 1 to 5, and then make brief comments following each criterion. The rank (top right) of the first person you hear will be 1, and after you have heard a second person that rank will either remain 1 or become 2, etc.

Because this is a grand compromise as compared to the separate-dimension measurements shown in Chapter Four, you will be bothered by uncertainty. The numbers and comments are intended to help you resolve some of that uncertainty, but you will have to carry a great amount of recall in your head from one performance to the next. That reliance on short-term memory makes it very important for you to hear everyone from one section consecutively during the same period of time.

Proceed as if you intend to complete the audition then and there, having heard each person only one time. When you finish, you will have a ranking — but you are not bound to it. Unless all judgments were absolutely clear cut, you should consider the ranking tentative. Having the recordings will give you the security of knowing you can listen as frequently as needed until you have

Name _____ Inst._____ Date_____

Prepared Piece   Rank ☐

Rating   Comments

_____   accurate rhythms   _____

_____   accurate pitches   _____

_____   acceptable tone quality   _____

_____   good intonation   _____

_____   expressive performance _____

Sight Reading

Rating   Comments

_____   accurate rhythms   _____

_____   accurate pitches   _____

_____   acceptable tone quality   _____

_____   good intonation   _____

_____   expressive performance _____

Figure 1. One Option for a Personal Template to Use
at the Live Hearing of an Audition

cemented all of your judgments with certainty. Do exactly that, and do it as soon as possible to make maximum use of recall before it dissipates. Where you are sure of placements, no further listening is needed. Where perform-ances are close to each other in quality, listen as many times as necessary to be sure of your judgment. If you cannot decide between two persons, use guidelines for the challenge, described in the next section, to bring the two together and achieve resolution.

I realize that your auditions may involve elements not shown in the Figure 1 audition sheet: scales, vocal exercises, improvisation, selected solo, orchestral excerpts, etude, or any of a number of other elements. The purpose of the form shown in Figure 1 is to show, in a compact way, one approach to audition record-keeping. You need to devise a form that is comfortable for you, and one that encompasses all the factors you want to consider for a specific audition.

Individual Challenges

Whether you use a performance-based seating system for an ensemble, and therefore need a challenge system, is a matter of philosophy. In any case, a challenge system would be used only at the secondary level or higher.

Some directors believe that a system of rotating responsibilities without internal competition is healthier and more humanizing. That becomes difficult to accommodate where widely varying abilities and technical demands put some performance responsibilities out of reach for many players. The natural solution then becomes a hierarchical assignment of responsibilities. Under those conditions, many directors see a range of values in a challenge system. They believe that it (1) provides motivation for lower-placed players who might otherwise feel "stuck" or "typecast," (2) keeps higher-placed players from becoming complacent, and (3) leads to increased practice of ensemble music in all quarters. My experience, as a student and teacher, has been that such a system can spur self-improvement, healthy competition, and respect for the ensemble itself. In retrospect, I sense that the music ensemble system I lived with as a student oriented me subtly to an important democratic life-lesson: work hard, earn your way, be the best you can be, and you can continue to rise with no ceilings over your head other than those you impose.

All this comes with an important qualifier. Such a challenge system must be managed responsibly. Any amount of arbitrariness or unfairness can instantly convert a healthy motivational tool into a corrosive, destructive force antithetical to the ensembles' intended value to students.

An assumption is that members of the ensemble see status in their position within the section, and are motivated by opportunities to challenge another person for an improvement of status. A challenge is similar to a two-person audition, but having only two persons to compare allows for a more direct comparison—one you can conduct easily and fairly by a method slightly different from that used for auditions, and without the use of a recording.

Giving a set of printed challenge rules to everyone will bring order and organization to the challenge process and reduce the time you spend responding to questions and complaints. The sample set of rules shown in Figure 2 is accompanied by a corresponding column showing the rationale for each rule. You might post such a set of rules in the rehearsal room (senza rationale), or have copies available to students by request. Another option is to print the rules on the reverse side of the challenge application form, so all challenge-related information is available to students on a single sheet of paper.

An example of a challenge form is shown in Figure 3. You might keep a supply of forms in a convenient place for students to pick up, and might even use a ballot-box style depository for completed forms.

The reason I emphasized earlier the importance of good management is that a challenge system is a tool that can do either a great amount of good or a great amount of harm, depending on how it is handled. If it is handled poorly, the competition and emotion it ignites can become disruptive and distracting. But if it is handled well, it can excite students in a healthy way about improve-ing their playing and advancing their status as musicians. To avoid the first effect and engender the second, you must apply all rules even-handedly. Students will accept results and thrive if they are convinced that the system is absolutely fair.

Besides laying down and abiding by an effective set of rules, you must administer the challenges themselves in an even-handed way. A good method is to place the two parties together in a room and then seat yourself outside the open door, out of sight, with pencil and paper for note-taking. Have the challenging parties flip a coin to decide who will be performer number 1. Then

Challenge Rule	Rationale for the Rule
1. You may challenge only the person immediately ahead of you in the section.	This avoids having anyone lose position to another with whom he or she has not competed, an unfair and demoralizing practice.
2. To initiate a challenge, you must fill out your portion of the challenge form and give it to the person you are challenging. That person has two school days to fill out the remainder of the form (except the bottom line) and return it to you.	Without the two-day provision, the person challenged could stall unreasonably.
3. You are to submit the challenge form to the director, who will schedule the challenge and return a copy of the completed form to each party.	Note: the director should be timely about scheduling challenges.
4. The music chosen must be from the current folder. If the challenge involves a change of parts, the part to be used is the part played in the ensemble by the person being challenged. You may designate either the whole piece or segments of the piece, e.g., from Letter B to Letter C.	The ensemble music is common ground, and the parts used for the challenge need to be the parts for which the winner of the challenge will be responsible.
5. The director reserves the right to add a piece of sight-reading, and is likely to do so in case of a close judgment.	The director should always have an option to assess independent musicianship, and sight-reading is a perfect way to do that.
6. If you lose a challenge that you have initiated, you may not give a new challenge form to the same person sooner than one week after the loss.	There is no reason to believe circum-stances will change in just a few days. A flurry of challenges between the same two persons harasses both the person challenged and the director.
7. You may challenge the same person no more than two consecutive times per semester.	This will discourage shot-in-the dark challenges, two of which would seal the challenger into place for the semester.
8. If someone hands a challenge form to you, and if you fail to fill out your portion and return it to the challenger within two school days, you risk losing your chair by default.	The director needs the discretion to decide whether a warning or a loss of position is appropriate to the circumstances of the tardiness.
9. No challenges will be scheduled during the two weeks preceding a major performance.	During these times the director needs to be free to put maximum attention on other matters, and needs stability of part assign-ments within the ensemble.

Figure 2. A Sample Set of Rules for an Ensemble Challenge System,
With Rational Given for Each Rule

CHALLENGE FORM

A person wanting to challenge the person sitting in the next seat ahead will complete the first three lines of this form, then give it to the person being challenged (challengee). The challengee will be obligated to complete the next two lines and return it to the challenger within two school days, for example, 2:00 p.m. Monday to 2:00 p.m. Wednesday. The challenger will give it to the director, who will schedule the challenge and give a copy to each party. If the challengee fails to return the signed form within two school days, the challenger may report that to the director.

, _____ , want to challenge _____

_____

Challenger's choice of music

_____   _____
Challenger's signature   Date/Time given to challengee

_____
Challengee's choice of music

_____   _____
Challengee's signature   Date/Time returned to challenger

_____   _____
Director's choice of music   Date/Time of challenge

Figure 3. A Sample Challenge Form

instruct performer 1 to play a particular passage, followed by performer 2 playing the same passage. That allows you to make comparative notes while all the sounds are fresh in mind. Do the same for a second passage, this time having player 2 play first. Continue that system, alternating which person performs first (essential when sight reading), until you have heard everything. Consult your notes and announce the winner as either performer 1 or performer 2. You may know characteristics of the students as musicians that will reveal the identities despite this blind system, but the system gives you a chance of anonymity and lets students know that you are doing everything you can to be impartial in your judgment. Those efforts on your part, along with a kind and respectful demeanor, go a long way toward boosting the morale of your student musicians and motivating them to strive for improvement.

Ensemble Competitions

Competition among music ensembles has become an industry unto itself. My bias is that teachers hired by schools are obligated first to teach students, and to help them develop independent musicianship skills that will serve them well for life. Competition that enhances that aim, or at least refrains from impeding it, is desirable. Competition that detracts from that aim is unjustifiable as part of a school program.

The judging of ensemble competitions amounts to a form of performance assessment. Because judgments are being made relative to full ensembles rather than individuals—and because restrictions are imposed by the time available, the number of judges, and the background of judges—this particular kind of performance assessment necessarily succumbs to a great many compromises. All that can be done is to examine the compromises being made, and then examine the extent to which good performance assessment practices might be adapted to competitions to blunt damage done by those compromises.

Ensemble adjudication forms typically consist of many dimensions, sometimes 10 or more. In many cases the number of points given for each dimension varies, generally to assure a sum of 100 points. The first thing that might be done is to free our minds of that artificial 100 point barrier, and think instead in terms of rating scales that work well without regard for point totals.

To listen to and judge more than one dimension of performance simultaneously is difficult. As the number of dimensions grows, the danger of meshing them together (halo effect) and impairing reliability increases. When I have judged ensemble competitions calling for assessment of a great number of dimensions simultaneously, I have seen the following steps generally practiced by judges as a way to survive the chaos:

1. Do not allow your sheets to be collected and recorded until after you have heard a number of ensembles, probably at least three.

2. Sketch ratings for those first few ensembles in light pencil.

3. Compare the numbers on those first few sheets with your overall impression of their rankings as first, second, and third best.

4. Change numbers as needed to make them conform to the outcome you feel is most justifiable (the tail wagging the dog).

5. Turn the sheets in, and try your best to maintain consistency throughout the day, with those first few ensembles functioning as the baseline.

Anyone who has judged such a competition knows the impossibility of remembering the 9:00 a.m. interpretation of criteria across all dimensions while listening to a performance by the 2:00 p.m. ensemble. In terms of good assessment practices, these conditions present a nightmare of unreliability. What might be done?

Assuming the availability of three judges, the assessment could be built on six dimensions of performance. Each dimension could have five criteria built into it, using either a continuous or additive design, depending on which is more appropriate for the dimension. Then two dimensions could be assigned to each judge, who would block out all other considerations while listening for and assessing those two dimensions alone. Instead of each of the three judges trying to wrestle the same ungainly monster in hopes of duplicating each others' result (or nearly so), each would be responsible for one-third of the whole. The work of the three judges then would be additive rather than repetitive, and reliability would be increased by limiting each judge's attention to two dimensions (still a compromise). The combined assessments of the three judges would then determine the overall ratings of the ensembles. Concentrating each judge's assessment on two dimensions would also allow each to write more detailed comments on the sheet to be returned to the director—comments that would be unlikely to duplicate other judges' comments, and would be helpful to the ultimate goal of the entire process: education.

A more radical reform would be to eliminate ratings altogether. The system as described above could be used to provide judges with a record of what they have heard, and to generate helpful comments to be forwarded to the director. But instead of awarding ratings at the end of the day, judges would convene to make a judgment of a different sort—a judgment tied to the real-world rewards of outstanding musical performance. What reward is enjoyed by an outstanding musical ensemble in the real world of music? The common reward is that many other persons want to hear the ensemble perform, so the ensemble makes a recording. The recording is disseminated, and with it their reputation spreads. Could our school ensembles be given a similar award in lieu of a rating? Imagine having state recordings made each year, one recording for each genre: concert band, string orchestra, full orchestra, jazz band, concert choir, etc. Rather than award ratings, the judges could convene to decide which performances of which pieces should be put on the state recording. The goal of each ensemble would be to receive helpful comments and to have a piece chosen for the state recording. The recording would be bought by students all over the state, and profits could be used to hire the best judges available.

Think of the educational benefits of a state recording. Schools could collect a library of recordings over time, and have students listen to them individually and as a group. Shining moments would take on a life of their own: "you have to hear the XXX school's 2010 recording of YYY." Indirectly, directors would be sharing interpretations of pieces. Students would become more thoughtful about the effects of playing something X way as compared with Y way. Years after graduation, students could play recordings for reminiscence, or for comparison with current performances. In short, all the thoughts and actions generally associated with musicianship would be encouraged. The educational value of ratings and trophies pales by comparison.

Chapter Six

Note: terms in **_bold italics_** are defined at chapter's end
(in order of appearance), and in a glossary (alphabetically).

KNOWLEDGE TESTING

Introduction

Probably music history, music theory, and other kinds of "academic" learning come to mind first when you think of knowledge testing, but the need is broader than that. If you are comprehensive in your teaching of general music or music performance, you will need to measure what students know as well as what they can do. Only if you work solely with performance, perhaps as a high-level conductor or a one-to-one studio teacher, might you limit your assessment of student achievement to performance testing.

The best way for you to assess what your students know is to send them into the real world for a few years to see what they accomplish with the knowledge you helped them acquire. Of course that is impractical, so you need to create shortcut methods of discovering what they know and understand. That is what a test is: a **_shortcut_**. An important part of your job as a teacher is to create good tests—good shortcuts—that come as close as possible to yielding valid information. Only you, as the teacher, can do that. No commercial test writers know your content, teaching objectives, or students well enough to accommodate subjective validity (content and process).

You are familiar with knowledge tests. You have taken hundreds during your years as a student. At first you might think an acceptable approach to testing is to write tests similar to the tests you have taken, and then calculate a percentage correct (because most of your teachers did that), give grades based on those percentages, and move to the next unit of learning. You can do better than that. You would never base your daily teaching on what you pick up through casual observation. For students, tests are an important challenge, and test results affect them profoundly. It is only right, then, that you put as much thought, study, and effort into preparing tests as you expect students to put into taking them. The information in this chapter will help you do that.

Types of Knowledge Tests

This list of tools for testing knowledge will look familiar: short answer, matching, true/false, essay, multiple choice. As with any undertaking, choose the tool best suited to accomplish the specific task you have in front of you.

Short answer, matching, and true/false formats are effective for elementary and middle school students, and for quizzes that prepare older students for more comprehensive tests. The essay format is a specialty item: if your purpose is to plumb the depths of a narrow topic, survey opinion, or probe student thinking, essay tests work well. The multiple choice format—despite much criticism—still offers the greatest potential for testing a broad range of information, knowledge, and understanding. All test formats have strengths and limitations. I will point them out, along with other characteristics, in the next three major sections.

Short Answer, Matching, and True/False Formats

When you use a short answer, matching, or true/false testing format you ask students for brief, factual answers. Your tests are quick to write and quick to grade as compared to the more complex essay tests and multiple choice tests—tools used widely for comprehensive testing of knowledge.

Short answer, matching, and true/false formats serve a variety of assessment needs:

1. Measure knowledge among students for whom more complex formats present unreasonable challenges, either because of age or circumstance.

2. Assess key knowledge among students in settings that do not lend themselves to more complex testing, e.g., music ensembles.

3. Give frequent, smaller-scale assessments (quizzes) to students whose major examinations will be written in an essay or multiple choice format. Frequent assessments spur students to stay current with their studying and keep them aware of what they do and do not know (quintessential formative evaluation). Considering the lower reliability of such short tests, you may want to grade them liberally and sometimes offer retakes, thinking of them more as alarm bells than as measurement tools.

4. Give students a variety of ways to express what they know, thereby reducing frustration among students who fare better with one format than with another.

Short Answer

For each item of a test written in the ***short answer format***, you ask students to supply a word or a few words to fill in a blank or respond to a statement or question. The short answer format is ideal for testing knowledge of a narrow body of facts (In which symphony does Beethoven use vocal soloists?) or terminology (The string technique of plucking rather than bowing is called _____.). (Answers: Beethoven's Ninth, and pizzicato.) An advantage of the short answer format is that you demand some rigor of students by forcing them to supply the answer. A disadvantage is that you restrict substantially the extent of knowledge you can cover and the extent to which you can prompt students to think with that knowledge (make inferences). That disadvantage becomes even more pronounced if you supply a word bank from which students can choose the correct response.

The following guidelines will help you write effective short answer items.

1. Design your short answer test items to elicit responses that are not only short, but specific. Write the second item below, not the first.

Bach wrote music in the _____.

The era in which Bach wrote music goes by the name _____.

You may write the first example above expecting students to answer *Baroque era*, but the wording opens other possibilities: Bach wrote music in the *church*, or in the *music room*, or in the *evening*. The second example requires *Baroque* as an answer. Make the wording of each item airtight, leaving students no place to go for an answer other than to the answer you are trying to elicit. If you fail to do that, and if a student provides a poor answer that is tenable because of your imprecise construction, you will be in an awkward position. To give credit for the spurious response is to damage the test's validity, and to not give credit is to damage your credibility. Because your credibility is more precious over the long haul than is the validity of one test, you will have to (begrudgingly) give credit for the poor response.

2. For completion items, avoid mid-sentence blanks if you can do so gracefully. A consistent pattern of blanks will help test-takers concentrate on content, and therefore answer items more in keeping with what they know (raising reliability and validity). Also, if all statements end with a blank—intended either for a completion of the statement or a response to it—you can organize the page visually to have all the blanks run down the right margin. That will help students read items efficiently to double-check their responses before handing their tests to you, and it will help you scan the pages more efficiently when you grade the tests.

3. Make all blanks equal length to avoid giving clues to the expected length of the answer. If you need to use an extra page to avoid a crowded presentation, do so: protecting a test's process validity is worth the cost of a few sheets of paper.

4. If the blank after an item calls for an answer to be given in a specific unit, help test-takers think in those units by adding, for example, $ for dollars, % for percent, *mm* for metronome marking, etc.

Matching

For a test written in the ***matching format***, you ask students to pair items that have some logical basis for association. You will arrange two sets of items in side-by-side columns, and have students associate the pairs across columns either by drawing a line that connects the pairs or by entering the number or letter of a right-column item into a blank that precedes the corresponding left-column item. The number/letter approach is easier to grade, and probably no more difficult to take. Upper case letters create less ambiguity than do lower case. For example, a carelessly written *d* or *a* could be mistaken for each other if the length of the stem on the right side were questionable.

Advantages of the matching format are that it is compact and easy to construct (though finding enough homogenous material can be a challenge), and it requires minimal reading and writing by students. A disadvantage that it shares with the short answer format is that you restrict substantially the extent of knowledge you can cover and the extent to which you can prompt students to think with that knowledge (make inferences).

A sample item from a matching test is shown in Figure 1. Following the figure is a list of guidelines for writing such an item. The figure and the list together should give you a good feel for writing matching items.

Match names of composers in the right column with descriptions in the left column by placing the correct letter in each blank. Names may be used once, more than once, or not at all.

____ Known as a great composer of symphonies,   A. Bach
       he wrote nine, and in the ninth he used singers.
                                             B. Mozart

____ He was a church organist and choirmaster.
                                             C. Beethoven

____ He wrote many hundreds of art songs, called
       lieder.   D. Schubert

____ He wrote many operas, symphonies,
       concertos for various instruments, and other   E. Brahms
       works—all in a relatively short time.
                                           F. Ravel

____ He didn't compose his first symphony until   (Note: answers are
       he was in his forties, but it was a great success.   C, A, D, B, E)

Figure 1. A Sample Test Item Written in the Matching Format

These guidelines, all of which apply to the sample item shown in Figure 1, will help you write effective matching items.

1. Use only homogenous material. For example, do not mix composers with music theory terms.

2. Have the two columns differ in number so the final answer cannot be arrived at by default, and point out to students that some items may not be used or may be used multiple times.

3. Make the list long enough to reduce guessing (4 or more) but short enough to keep the task manageable (7 or fewer). Older students can handle a longer list than can younger students.

4. Place the shorter items in the right column.

5. If a logical order is apparent, use it unless it gives clues to the answers. In the case of Figure 1, listing composers in chronological order does not give a clue to any of the answers, and it might reinforce some learning. Never miss an opportunity to have a test help you teach.

6. Give clear directions for the matching task.

7. Place all items for a given matching task on one page.

True/False

For a test written in a pure ***true/false format***, you ask students simply to identify statements as true or false. Precede each statement with a T and F and instruct test takers to circle the correct choice, or precede each statement with a blank and ask test takers to enter *true* or *false* (better for clarity than *T* vs. *F*) to indicate the correct choice. Make blanks long enough to accommodate the words *true* and *false* comfortably. Those two approaches to presenting items in a pure true/false format are shown in Figure 2.

If a statement is true, circle T. If it is false, circle F.

T   F   1. The English Horn is a member of the brass family of instruments.

T   F   2. The clarinet and saxophone are single reed instruments.

If a statement is true, print *true* in the blank. If it is false, print *false* in the blank.

_____   1. Impressionistic music was written beginning in the late 1800s.

_____   2. One of Mozart's most famous compositions is The William Tell Overture.

(Note: Answers are F, because the English horn is a double reed woodwind instrument; T; *true*; and *false*, because Rossini wrote the William Tell Overture.)

Figure 2. Two Ways to Present Items in a Pure True/False Format

I recommend the first of the two approaches shown in Figure 2, for two reasons. First, looking at the T and F preceding each entry, as compared to looking at blanks, prompts students to focus their thinking more constantly on the task of identifying statements as either *true* or *false*. Second, identifying the location of a circle is easier for you than reading student handwriting.

True/False Alternative Response

True/false tests prompt students to (1) identify facts, definitions, and principles, (2) make judgments about cause and effect, and (3) evaluate logic. By making alterations to the pure true/false format, you can ask students for an *alternative response* that enhances the power of the true/false format to accomplish some of those objectives. Two ***true/false alternative response*** approaches are shown in Figure 3.

In each of the following statements, the first parts are true and the second parts may be. If the second part **does** explain why the first part is true, circle YES. If the second part **does not** explain why the first part is true, circle NO.

YES NO 1. The clarinet, oboe, and saxophone are called woodwinds *because* all three are made of wood.

YES NO 2. Percussion instruments were given that name *because* the term *percuss* means to strike or hit, and when a percussion instrument is played, something is struck or hit.

If a statement is true, circle T. If it is false, circle F and then replace the underlined word with a new word that makes the statement true. Write your new word in the blank.

T F _____ 1. A conductor's preparatory beat should indicate the desired dynamic level and <u>meter</u>.

T F _____ 2. A conductor stands on a box called the <u>podium</u>.

(Note: Answers are NO, because the saxophone is not made of wood; YES; F, tempo; and T)

Figure 3. Two Approaches to an Alternative Response
True/False Format

An advantage of the true/false format, both in the pure approach and the alternate response approach, is that it lets you encompass a body of factual knowledge quickly and efficiently. Another advantage is that true/false tests are easy to construct and even easier to grade. One disadvantage of the true/false format, tempered somewhat by an alternative response approach, is that luck plays too great a role. Guessing damages test reliability, particularly when items give the person who does not know the answer a 50% chance of answering correctly. Another disadvantage is emphasis on purely knowing information as compared to thinking with information (drawing inferences).

The examples in Figures 2 and 3 will help you write true/false items. Other suggestions that will increase the quality of your items are as follows:

1. Make statements so specific as to be airtight. For example, after teaching students about bows and how they are made, you may think of this statement as true: "Musicians play stringed instruments by drawing the hair of a bow across the strings." Even though drawing bow hair across strings is the standard technique, students who know about pizzicato playing and other exceptions may answer *false*.

2. Make statements as short, simple, and direct as you can without compromising your objective of assessing a particular piece of knowledge.

3. Write statements of somewhat equal length to allow test-takers to get into a rhythm and avoid distraction.

4. Put only one idea into each statement to avoid your having to interpret a student's mind-set.

5. Write a somewhat comparable number of true items and false items, and place them in a way that avoids a detectable pattern.

The Essay Test

The essay test is indispensable. Sometimes no other format will do. Still, its limitations keep me from seeing it as the format of choice for broad-based knowledge testing. Below you will read about the strengths, uses, and drawbacks of the essay test format, along with advice for administering essay tests, scoring them, and interpreting results.

Strengths and Uses of the Essay Test

One benefit of the essay format, according to some claims, is that it teaches writing skills. To that claim, I can only answer "I doubt it." If the essay format were used specifically to judge writing skills, and students were given ample time to make several revisions, the claim would be true. In fact, only by use of an essay test could such a test of writing be accomplished. But writing extensive essay answers aimed at course content within tight time restrictions is as likely to blunt one's writing skills as to advance them. When content alone is the aim, the teacher may abandon all consideration for writing by allowing test takers to respond with a variation (outlines, lists) on the *pure essay format*. That kind of flexibility of response is sometimes termed a *constructed response format*.

Whether you ask students to respond in a pure essay format or a constructed response format, you have two perspectives from which you can formulate essay items. An *extended response item* is aimed at a broad survey of thought. For example, you might ask students to "Tell what you would do to promote world-wide music learning," or "Choose a time period (one century or less) and speculate about how daily life might have influenced musical style." An extended response item requires you as the teacher to read and assess responses from a perspective broader than course content. The way you interpret and use responses to such items is highly personal.

A *restricted response item*, by contrast, is aimed at testing knowledge of specific course content. For that purpose, the multiple choice format is generally more effective. I would use an essay test only if I could restrict items tightly enough to put clear parameters around potential responses. Such items might be "Write about how J.S. Bach's personal relationship with Carl Philipp Emanuel appears to have differed from his relationship with Wilhelm Friedemann," or "Compare the first and second themes of the excerpt below in melodic and harmonic terms." Items with such specificity as these will yield responses that can be scored with some objectivity (though scoring is one of the great challenges of the essay format).

Drawbacks of the Essay Test

Students learn minimally while taking the test. Your principal product as a teacher is student learning. It follows, then, that the ideal test would be one that prompts students to learn even while they are taking the test. To some extent, you can write an essay item to prompt more thinking rather than less. For example, rather than "Describe the periods in which Beethoven's compositions can be categorized," you might ask "Listen to this excerpt, identify the period to which it belongs, and list the traits that gave clues to your answer." Still, as compared to the multiple choice format, the essay format restricts teachers' opportunities to control content and channel students into specific lines of thought.

For a realistic perspective on how students will approach your essay items, think about the approach you have taken as a student. You know that students will study by cramming as much information as possible into their minds as close in time to the test as possible. Then if an item coincides exactly with material they memorized, they will respond as if taking dictation from a mental tape recorder. If the item does not coincide exactly with material they memorized, they will write a transition paragraph to align the question with what they know—then write as if taking dictation from a mental tape recorder. Thinking and learning are at the margins of that kind of testing experience.

Items are not easily reusable. The number of items answerable in an essay test is small, because each takes a large portion of the testing time. That small number of items lets students carry the test out with them in their heads (or on paper if they are industrious and furtive). That precludes your reusing items within a short period of time, as those items are likely to be in circulation. When you teach multiple sections of the same subject, afternoon test-takers can even shake down morning test-takers for the questions.

Scoring tends to be laborious and unreliable. Even if you write essay items with great care (and you should do that to put parameters around responses), you will write them in very little time as compared to writing multiple-choice items. Scoring is the arduous aspect of an essay test for you, the teacher—both for the time needed and for the stress of uncertainty. Students become experts at writing "good sounding stuff" that forces you to decide what is worth credit. Though subjectivity in scoring makes essay test results less reliable than multiple choice test results, you can reduce uncertainty and boost reliability by using an effective scoring system. Helpful details follow.

Administering and Scoring the Essay Test

The scoring system described here applies only to essay tests driven by course content, e.g., restricted response items rather than extended response items. The purposes of this system are to reduce bias, increase reliability, and remove some of the uncertainty that makes the grading of essay tests generally difficult and demanding. To make the descriptions easier to follow, I will present each component as a numbered step.

Step One: Prepare a Template. Write the test items, then write what you consider to be an ideal, comprehensive response to each. You might write in a list format to save time, but do get onto paper the elements you expect to see in the best answer you could expect to receive. That gives you a template for comparison with student answers. You might, in the course of writing a response to one of your questions, see ways to improve the question with a slight alteration—probably an alteration that helps put parameters around the response.

Step Two: Prepare the Students. The last time you meet students before administering the test, give them written information about content parameters, format, procedures, scoring system—whatever will help them know what to expect. That will reduce distractions and give them more time for the test itself. The Figure 4 example is a pretest handout from a college course I taught involving non-music content. It amounts to the cover sheet for the exam itself, a sheet that students will receive anew when they take the exam. The format of this particular exam was not purely essay, because the task was to revise writing rather to write. Still, the instructions illustrate a principle of preparing students for what they will find on test day.

It is interesting to see exam preparation sheets grow over time. Many of the directives given in Figure 4 were born of student missteps from previous testing. Over time you will develop air-tight instructions.

Academic Writing Skills: Mid-term Exam Instructions

Revise each of the following 12 entries: cross out words, insert words, circle material and relocate it with an arrow. **Revise only as extensively as necessary to repair the flaws you see. DO NOT RE-WRITE WHOLE PASSAGES.** Feel free to eliminate words, but be sure you retain the original message; that is, limit changes to enhancements such as specificity, grammatical correctness, parallel form, etc. **If you reduce the quality of the original in any way, including changing the meaning, you will have points subtracted from your total.**

You will be wise to skip items where flaws are not apparent to you, then return to those items when you have finished the others. If you are short of time, or if you see a problem clearly but cannot see a solution, circle the area in question and note the nature of the problem (passive voice, pretentious word choice, misused colon). I will award partial credit for your seeing and understanding a problem that you do not have time to repair. (Note: A circle alone will mean nothing; you must at least describe the nature of the problem. You need not describe problems that you repair; a repair is a higher-order response than a description.) **Print legibly throughout.** Assessment for this type of exam is time-intensive. I will **ignore** illegible writing, which means I will consider the item unanswered. You will be prudent to use a pencil and have a good eraser with you.

The exam consists of twelve items, each having multiple flaws written into it. When I read your revisions to see how successfully you have identified and removed those flaws, I will use this point system:

You repaired a flaw written intentionally by the instructor:	+2
You identified (but did not repair) a flaw written intentionally by the instructor:	+1
You repaired a flaw not written intentionally by the instructor (clear improvement):	+1 or +2
You revised without repairing a flaw (maybe a style change), but did no damage:	0
You revised in a way that created a flaw or changed the meaning:	−1 or −2

Figure 4. Student Preparation Sheet for a Writing Skills Revision Test

Step Three: Prepare the Environment. Think about testing conditions ahead of time in case you need to alter your classroom. You may want to re-arrange seating, or even use a different room if yours is inadequate in some way (crowded, noisy, etc.). You might give essay tests in a computer labora-tory so students can type their responses and either print them or e-mail them to you. The legibility alone is worth the trouble.

Step Four: Guard Against Bias. Find a way to hide student identities. A code number would work, but so does a sticky note over the top of the name (double-thickness to be sure nothing shows through). Place a line or box for the name on the cover sheet (instruction sheet) so all names are in a comparable location, have students cover the name with a sticky note, and then have them staple that cover sheet over the answers. Two advantages of this are that you will not be distracted by knowing whose paper you are reading (unless content reveals the identity), and students will have faith that you graded the papers as objectively as possible. Simple as it is, Figure 5 shows information from the top of one of my exam sheets. The more explicit information you give students in writing, the less you have to disrupt them with annoying verbal directions—and the more quickly they can set to work.

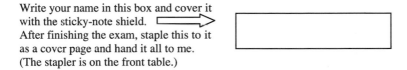

Write your name in this box and cover it
with the sticky-note shield.
After finishing the exam, staple this to it
as a cover page and hand it all to me.
(The stapler is on the front table.)

Figure 5. A Way to Prepare the Top of a Test for Anonymity

Step Five: Use Your Template With a Numerical System. You can make your scoring of essay test items more reliable by using some kind of numerical system. I have had good results using the system shown in Figure 6 (similar to the system I used for the editing exam shown in Figure 4). You may find it usable for your exams, or you may create a system of your own.

+1   each piece of information that matches something from the template

−1   each piece of information that is faulty

0   each piece of information that is irrelevant or of little importance

+1 or +2   each piece of good information not in the template

Figure 6. A System for Scoring Items in an Essay Test

The logic of the system shown in Figure 6 is this: students deserve credit for information you have entered into your template, but they should not be able to take a shotgun approach—write anything they can think of and hope something hits the mark. You guard against that by subtracting credit for inaccuracies, and by ignoring the padding that looks like something of note but is not. Finally, the student who gives good information beyond your template deserves credit, perhaps even more so than for the answers you did have in your template.

For some tests you may need to create a variation on this point system. For example, I have administered essay tests designed to measure the quality of student writing. I give students 2.5 hours to produce about 300 words— plenty of time to revise multiple drafts and finish with a piece that feels pristine. I cannot write a template for that exam. Instead, I have created a six-dimensional five-point rating scale. I read each exam multiple times, each time attending to one or two specific dimensions. I use the rating scale as if I were rating a performance. (I give the rating scale dimensions and criteria to students a week before the exam.) You may find other scoring variations useful for specialty exams. The important principle is that your system allows you to be consistent, which gives you reliability (a prerequisite for validity).

Step Six: Guard Your Concentration. Do not score one student's test in its entirety before moving to the next. If you have three essay items on the test, that approach will pull your concentration from Item 1 to Item 2 to Item 3, and then back to Item 1. Instead, read and score Item 1 from each person's test. That will allow you to keep your template and your criteria for awarding points for that particular item firmly in mind throughout the entire stack of tests, thus improving your reliability. Then repeat that process for each of the other items. Between items you might shuffle the order of the papers as an additional precaution against the halo effect.

Step Seven: Create Your Distribution and Reveal Identities. Write the score total for each exam on the sticky note covering the name. Put the tests in distribution order from top to bottom. Remove each sticky note to reveal the identity of the student, and record the distribution of scores by name.

Optional Step Eight: Estimate Reliability. If you think you will want to estimate your test-retest reliability, you can photocopy all the exams before scoring them. Then, after scoring the whole set as described above, wait a few days. Using the photocopies, repeat the entire process. Then list all the students' names, followed by the score you awarded the first time (X distribution) and the score you awarded the second time (Y distribution). Calculate a correlation coefficient between the two distributions. That is an arduous process that you will want to perform very infrequently. However, even one such exercise will give you empirical evidence of the reliability of your approach. Assuming that your approach will either stay consistent or improve with time, a strong coefficient (greater than .70, and preferably .80) should assure you that you are scoring essay tests with a reasonable level of reliability.

Interpreting Scores from Essay Tests

You may be wondering about how to control the point totals of an essay test. Commonly, teachers who write three essay items give two items a value of 30 points each and the other a value of 35 (or some variation thereof) to reach the traditional total of 100. I recommend that you abandon that kind of restrictive thinking.

There is nothing magical about having a 100-point total for a test. If you write your own ideal answers to the items into a template, as I recommended in Step One of the preceding section, the number of points possible will be wholly unpredictable. To write the best possible items, and to craft the best possible responses, you need to be free of the 100-point handcuffs. Let the content dictate the point total. One essay exam may total 83 points, another may total 112, and another may total 127. Point totals are irrelevant to your ability to interpret results.

If you need a percentage-correct score, you can calculate it easily: just divide the number of points a student accumulates by the number of points possible (the number of points in your template). Having said that, I must add that I am pessimistic about the value of calculating such a percentage. Your extensive responses to rich essay items will have so much depth to them that the best students are highly unlikely to score a high percentage of the total shown in your template. If you are accustomed to your best students scoring 95%, or 98%, or 100%, the percentages you obtain in this way will shock you.

At this stage I am going to point out a departure you might take from common practice. To equate high grades with high percentages would cause great numbers of students to fail the kind of rich essay test I have described. One solution to that problem is to write essay items shallow enough to allow the expected success rate. That solution is common, but is it desirable? You need to ask yourself if you are willing to remove rich, thought-provoking experiences from bright students in exchange for a criterion-referenced grading system that "comes out right" in terms of percentage correct. Assuming that you want to retain the rich, thought-provoking experiences, you might want to consider an alternate solution. If the best students score in the 60s on a test having, for example, 87 points possible (percent correct in the 70s), then students who score in the 60s deserve a grade of A. Sometimes that is referred to as *grading on the curve*, meaning the theory of the bell curve is used. That is, students are compared with each other rather than with the potential of the test. Another term for that approach, as you learned earlier, is norm-referenced.

Where exactly do the A, B, and C grades fall when you use a norm-referenced system? That is a matter of judgment. A raw score is a measurement (arrived at through a process as objective as you can make it), and the grade attached to that score is an evaluation (a judgment you make, admittedly subjective). Only you—the person who taught the material, who has gotten to know the students, and who read their answers—can make that judgment with some degree of wisdom. The newer your experience with the students and the newer the test, the more cautious you will be about awarding low grades. Then, after you become familiar with test results across a large number of students, and you begin to see the bell curve form, you will have more information on which to base your grading judgments.

One way to improve your view of the distribution, an approach I apply regularly, is to convert raw scores to z scores. That lets me see exactly where each student's result falls relative to standard deviations from the mean of the group. Simply calculate the mean and standard deviation for the distribution, subtract the mean from each score to arrive at each person's deviation score, and then divide each deviation score by the standard deviation to arrive at each person's standard score (z). (Reminder: Microsoft® Excel makes these calculations easy, and also leaves you with a written record.) If you have a great number of students across several sections of the course you are teaching (even across school years), you can make a large distribution that increases the chances of your basing results on a population representative of a normal distribution. The z scores then should give a clear picture of where individual students lie relative to the population as a whole, and ultimately should help you develop a highly consistent system of awarding grades relative to merit.

The Multiple Choice Test

Multiple choice tests take quite a beating. A derisive description used by some is "multiple guess," suggesting that no great level of thought is expected. That is true only if the test is written poorly. Critics commonly submit as evidence of the format's inferiority such banal items as the one shown in Figure 7. Just as reckless people can reflect poorly on the group to which they belong, so can recklessly written multiple choice tests reflect poorly on the multiple-choice test format.

1. The capital of Japan is

    a. Berlin
    b. London
    c. Tokyo
    d. Paris

Figure 7. Banal Multiple Choice Item, a Fault of the
Test Writer Rather Than the Format

A multiple choice test handled well from inception through interpretation of results is in fact a powerful measurement tool with great potential for reliability and validity. It is also a powerful force for improving instruction. In this section, after acquainting you with common multiple choice terms, I will describe in detail how to create, use, and interpret a multiple choice test so it becomes a powerful tool for knowledge testing and learning.

Multiple Choice Terms

Each entry on a multiple choice test is referred to best as an *item* rather than as a question. That is because all items are not presented in the form of questions. A test having forty entries, then, would be described as a "forty-item" multiple choice test.

Multiple choice items begin with a partial statement needing to be completed by the choice of a response, or by a question needing to be answered by the choice of a response. That opening is called the *stem*. The stem is followed by a series of potential responses, typically identified by a letter. Each potential response is called an *option*. The option keyed as the *correct response* is called just that. The other options are called *distractors* or *foils*. I prefer the term *foil*, because it is more precise: the three incorrect options do more than distract test-takers; they present confounding information that foils attempts to succeed without knowing. That being said, I will go forward with *distractor,* because that is the more common term.

Be sure you are familiar with the terms introduced here. I will use them freely from this point on.

I will assume the tests you write for classroom use are to be taken by pencil-and-paper and scored by computers. If you score by hand, adjust your thinking accordingly as you read. Three paper components of a multiple choice test are the *test booklet*, which contains all the items in numerical order, the *response sheet* (bubble sheet) on which test-takers record responses, and the *key*. The key is simply a response (bubble) sheet on which you, the test-writer, fill in the correct responses to be read by the computer.

Types of Multiple Choice Items

The most straightforward type of multiple choice item requires test-takers to simply recognize the correct response by discriminating among pieces of information shown in the options. That type of item is a *discrimination item.* A more complex type of item requires test-takers to think with several pieces of information to reject distractors containing falsehoods; that is, identify the correct response indirectly by inference. That type of item is an *inference item.*

Figure 8 contains a pair of discrimination items. Figure 9 shows an inference item related to the discrimination items shown in Figure 8.

Mozart died in	Beethoven was born in
a. 1756	a. 1770
b. 1776	b. 1790
c. 1791	c. 1801
d. 1809	d. 1827

Figure 8. A Pair of Multiple Choice Discrimination Items

Which is most plausible?   Mozart's influence on the work of Beethoven was

    a. enhanced by Beethoven's admiration for Mozart during the short time they were composing concurrently.
    b. less than it would have been had Mozart lived during Beethoven's young adult life.
    c. enhanced by their long-standing relationship as contemporaries.
    d. powerful in relation to Beethoven's early works, despite the lapse of time between Mozart's death and Beethoven's first compositions.

Figure 9. An Inference Item Related to the Figure 8 Discrimination Items

To answer the two discrimination items shown in Figure 8, test-takers need to have simply memorized the birth and death dates of Mozart and Beethoven, a feat of short-term memory easily reversed by time. To answer the inference item shown in Figure 9, test-takers need to reject three distrators by thinking in ways similar to this:

> Option "a" looks plausible, but let me think through the others to be sure. Option "b" is wrong, because Mozart did live during Beethoven's young adult life. Option "c" is wrong, because Beethoven was only 21 the year Mozart died; that didn't give enough time for a long-standing relationship as contemporaries. Option "d" is wrong, because Beethoven composed prior to age 21. So option "a" has to be correct; they were composing concurrently for a short time, and Beethoven certainly admired Mozart's work. The correct response is "a."

When your students reach adulthood, they will not negotiate life's challenges simply by pulling facts out of a mental file cabinet—the task asked of them by the Figure 8 discrimination items. Most of life's challenges will require your students to think with multiple pieces of information, to mix in quantities of insight and reflection, and to "figure out" what they need to do. Those are the tasks asked of them by the Figure 9 inference item. So not only do inference items require more extensive knowledge of the subject matter, and an ability to think with that subject matter in ways that encourage retention (a fact evaporates more quickly and easily than does a network of thought), but inference items condition students to function at a higher intellectual level altogether—a level that will serve them well in everything they do, and for all time.

The high-level thought demanded by powerful multiple choice inference items contrasts not only with multiple choice discrimination items, but with essay test items that encourage simple regurgitation of short-term information. Powerful inference items, however, are a challenge to write. That may explain in part why so many multiple choice tests are loaded heavily with discrimination items, and why the multiple choice format has an undeserved reputation as a non-thinking approach to testing.

I should add here that a good multiple choice test will contain both discrimination items and inference items, probably in approximately equal number. That is because some recall of rote information is a legitimate part of learning. Facts learned by rote become part of the material for higher level thinking: no one can make a clay pot without clay. Your responsibility as a teacher and test-writer is to decide which straightforward information is worth reinforcing through discrimination items, and which concepts and thought patterns are so valuable that you want to force students to probe them through inference items.

General Advice: Constructing and Administering a Multiple Choice Test

Time and Approach. To write a good multiple choice test, plan to spend a great amount of time per item from the time you begin until you finish your final revisions and have the test ready to administer. You will write some discrimination items in final form in a short time, but you will rethink and revise some inference items multiple times over several days.

The first step to be taken is to match test content to course content. Once you have done that, write items with an eye toward having about half discrimination items and half inference items. Which of the content you cast as discrimination and which as inference will depend on the nature of the material and on what information, concepts, and understanding you want students to acquire.

For administration time, plan on one to one-and-a-half minutes per item. One minute per item is standard, but that seems short to me. You may want to give more time to accommodate thought-provoking inference items.

Number of Options. Probably you have taken enough multiple choice tests to observe that the number of options per item is generally four or five. As with rating scales, too few options or too many options will damage reliability. Five may be the ideal number of options, but four works well enough to have become the standard for classroom tests. Giving students one less option to read leaves time for a greater number of items, which is important where class schedules allow perhaps 40 to 50 minutes to administer the test.

If you are working with young children or learning-impaired children, you will want to reduce the number of options further. Probably three options present as much rigor for elementary students as four options do for secondary students. Primary-aged children probably can handle no more than two options: yes/no or true/false.

True/false tests, given commonly to students of all ages, are in effect a variation of the multiple choice test—a multiple choice test having only two options. Some content you test may lend itself to the true/false format, but you will want to use it infrequently. The amount of information a true/false item can contain is small, making the format inefficient for secondary or higher education students beyond its usefulness for quizzes. Also, the fifty percent chance of guessing correctly lowers reliability. To review more details about the true/false format, re-read pages 126–128.

Writing Multiple Choice Items

There is no better way for me to advise you about specific writing techniques than to give you examples. For item content I will use the content of this book. That will allow you to review previous information at the same time you acquire new information about how to write (and how not to write) multiple choice items. I will number the items as you would number items in a test, but then I will follow each item with three additional entries: *Comments* (pointing out flaws), *Improved Version* (one way to improve the item, with correct response shown), and *Explanation* (the thinking that the item requires of students).

1. A good test

    a. is more likely to be written by professionals than by a teacher.
    b. is one that can be given within a short period of time and yields a wide
       distribution of grades.
    c. is likely to reveal shortcomings in the work of the teacher.
    d. is to a great extent a matter of subjectivity.

Comments. When the stem of a multiple choice item is an incomplete statement to be completed by the correct response, it should contain the essence of the problem to be solved. That is, it should prompt the test-taker to have some tentative answer in mind before reading the options. "A good test" could be completed by "is difficult to write" or "is a joy forever," or by any of a thousand other general responses.

Improved Version of Number 1:

The primary purpose of achievement testing is most likely served by a test that

    a. has been written by professionals rather than by the teacher.
    b. can be given within a short period of time and yields a wide
       distribution of grades.
    ⓒ reveals shortcomings in the work of the teacher.
    d. is to a great extent a matter of subjectivity.

Explanation. Test-takers need to know the primary purpose of testing (improve instruction) to know that it will not be served by any of the distrators. Though the correct response to this item entails only one aspect of improving instruction, it is (as compared to the three distrators) "most likely" to improve instruction. Option "a" is untrue because the teacher, more so than any outside professional, is familiar with the course content, the course objectives, and the students—all keys to improving instruction. The "b" distrator sounds desirable, even though it contains pure nonsense. That kind of distractor tempts students who know least about the content involved. Students who know better reject it. If the "d" option were true, advice about test writing would be of little use.

2. A comparison of two distributions of scores is accomplished by
   a. the calculation of a validity coefficient.
   b. the calculation of a reliability coefficient.
   c. the calculation of a correlation coefficient.
   d. the calculation of an intercorrelation coefficient.

Comments. Avoid repeating material common to every option. The repeated words irritate and distract (there is a true distractor!) test takers. Put material common to all options in the stem unless it is needed to make the options read easily. Sometimes a repeated word or two at the beginning of options keeps them from reading awkwardly, but that is rare—and it is not the case here.

Improved Version of Number 2:

A comparison of two distributions of scores is accomplished by calculating
   a. a validity coefficient.
   b. a reliability coefficient.
   ⓒ a correlation coefficient.
   d. an intercorrelation coefficient.

Explanation. Test-takers need to recognize that the three distractors all represent specific uses of correlation that may be, but are not necessarily, the reason for comparing two distributions of scores. The generic stem needs to be paired with the generic response: a correlation coefficient. This is a good place for me to make a point that applies to all testing: while much of a test-taker's success will depend on effort and study time, general intelligence and ability to think will play a part—as in discerning the distinction in this item between specific and generic application. The edge that thinking power gives to some test-takers cannot be, nor should it be, factored out of a test. Instead, as a teacher you should recognize the value of thinking power and do all you can to foster it in children from a young age and reinforce it throughout the full range of education. One of the best venues you will have in which to reinforce thinking power is in the writing of your tests.

Notice that Item 3 varies from the improved version of Item 2 in a very subtle detail, but it is an important detail.

3. A comparison of two distributions of scores is accomplished by calculating a
   a. validity coefficient.
   b. reliability coefficient.
   c. correlation coefficient.
   d. intercorrelation coefficient.

Comments. The word at the end of the stem rules out the "d" option by grammatical incompatibility. "Intercorrelation" begins with a vowel, requiring "an" rather than "a." That makes this a three-option item. Damage could be even greater if such carelessness were applied on a larger scale. In the example below, the grammar faux pas virtually gives the correct response away.

Each of the statements following the stem of a multiple choice item is called an
   a. option.
   b. response.
   c. choice.
   d. distractor.

Improved Version of Number 3: same as the Improved Version of Number 2.

4. The term _____ refers to the dispersion of the
   scores of a distribution about the mean.
   a. central tendency
   b. variability
   c. normalcy
   d. correlation

Comments. Avoid any visually cumbersome arrangement of an item, as it will only steal time and concentration from the test-takers—time and concentration that they could apply to content. Rather than interrupt a stem, as in this item, make the correct response a completion of the stem. Other visually cumbersome arrangements to avoid are (1) embedding the options into the stem horizontally rather than stacking them vertically on lines of their own, and (2) arranging options in an illogical order (dates or values out of order). Do not give test-takers a job to do in addition to identifying the correct response.

Improved Version of Number 4:

The dispersion of scores about the mean of a distribution is referred to as that distribution's

    a. central tendency.
    b. variability.
    c. normalcy.
    d. correlation.

    Explanation. This is a straightforward discrimination item.

5. The most accurate description of the relationship between measurement and evaluation is that

    a. the application of measurement to pedagogically oriented circumstances attenuates prudence, whereas the application of evaluation does not.
    b. the epistemological indiscretions of the latter preclude its effective application in the absence of the former.
    c. formulae are an integral part of measurement, but are only a peripherally cogent aspect of evaluation.
    d. measurement may be addressed either as a precursor to or as a post hoc tool of evaluation, but evaluation is a less flexible, unidimensional factor.

    Comments. Pompous, unnecessarily complex language—as seen in this example—will obstruct your testing objective by turning an item into a test of vocabulary more so than a test of content knowledge. You will need to use mature, precise test language to close loopholes and to be sure you say exactly what you mean. For that reason, test language must be elevated above the slapdash language spoken on the street. Still, you should elevate your language only to the extent necessary to express yourself with complete precision and accuracy.

Improved Version of Number 5:

The most accurate description of the relationship between measurement and evaluation is that

    a. measurement may endanger educational processes, but evaluation will not.
    b. the validity of evaluation in education is generally increased by the concurrent use of measurement.
    c. formulas are very important to measurement, but are applied infrequently to evaluation.
    d. measurement may either precede or follow evaluation, but evaluation can be used in only one way.

Explanation. Option "a" is incorrect because measurement and evalation are both capable of either helping or endangering education, depending on how they are used. Option "c" implies that formulas are sometimes applied to evaluation. They are not. Evaluation is a matter of judgment. The last part of the "d" option is incorrect: evaluation may be based on measurement or may not, and it may apply to any of a host of circumstances. The power of measurement coupled with evaluation makes "b" the correct response.

    6. When writing a test, a teacher should always take precautions to

    a. have the test content parallel the class content.
    b. check the reliability of the test before administering it to students.
    c. avoid high intercorrelations with the tests of other teachers teaching the same subject.
    d. keep students from lapsing into a deep sleep.

Comments. If you write an option for comic relief, as is the case for "d," in essence you place a three-option item among the four-option items in your test. That will remove some power from your test. Although the loss is not great, you might want to either forego the comic relief or make the entire item a joke—then eliminate it from the scoring of the test.

Improved Version of Number 6:

When writing a new test, a teacher should always take precautions to

    a. have the test content parallel the class content.
    b. check the reliability of the test before administering it.
    c. avoid high intercorrelations with the tests of other teachers.
    d. check the mean to be sure it is neither too high nor too low.

Explanation. Options "b" and "d" are impossibilities, because only after students have taken a test will you have the data needed to check the reliability or the mean. Option "c" is impossible for the same reason, and besides, the notion of intercorrelations with tests of other teachers is pure nonsense. Option "a," the correct response, is an important tenet of test writing.

7. The best description of test reliability is

    a. a test that is always available.
    b. a test that yields expected grades.
    c. consistency on all tests for a given student.
    d. the extent to which students taking the test can be expected to maintain the same relative position in the distribution on repeated administrations.

Comments. A test-taker lost for an answer tends to be drawn to the longest option. You may lead students who do not know an answer to the correct response if you write it more elaborately than you write the distractors.

Improved Version of Number 7:

The best description of test reliability is

    a. a test that is always available.
    b. a test that yields expected grades.
    c. consistency on all tests for a given student.
    (d.)consistency among students given a retest.

Explanation. Option "a" might attract a student having no idea of the correct response. Option "b" might be chosen by a test-taker who fails to distinguish between test scores and grades. Option "c" implies that a single student's results can shed light on the reliability of the test as a whole. Only option "d" gets at the definition of a type of reliability measurement (test-retest).

8. The principal use of a reliability coefficient is to calculate the extent to which

    a. a given test is appropriate for a given population of students.
    b. parts of a test duplicate each other in function.
    c. a test can be relied upon to be consistent over time.
    d. a variety of professionals agree upon the quality of the test.

Comments. The correct response, the "c" option, has a clue embedded in it: the word "relied" hints at a direct relationships to the "reliability" mentioned in the stem. Avoid clues that might lead students who do not know the answer to find the correct response through detective work.

Improved Version of Number 8:

The principal use of a reliability coefficient is to calculate the extent to which

    a. a given test is appropriate for a given population of students.
    b. parts of a test duplicate each other in function.
    (c.)consistent results can be expected from a test over time.
    d. a variety of professional agree upon the quality of the test.

Explanation. Option "a" is a matter of validity, because a test must be valid for the group of students to whom it is administered. Neither the "b" option nor the "d" option relates to test reliability. Option "c" is the correct response because it is virtually a definition of test reliability.

9. The mean for the distribution described in the first item will be

    a. less than 110.
    b. less than 80.
    c. greater than 110.
    d. greater than 125.

Comments. (Note: the "first item" referred to in the stem is only hypothetical.) Avoid overlapping responses which, if one is correct another is also correct. Assuming that the correct response is "less than 110," a student who answers "b" can argue that anything less than 80 will necessarily be less than 110. Similarly, assuming that the correct response is "greater than 110," a student who answers "d" can argue that anything greater than 125 is necessarily greater than 110. Those are hair-splitting arguments that you can win, but you will save yourself trouble and appear more thorough and thoughtful to your students if you avoid the loopholes altogether.

Improved Version of Number 9:

The mean for the distribution described in the first item will be

    a. less than 80.
    b. between 81 and 110.
    c. between 111 and 125.
    d. greater than 125.

(No explanation is available, as the item refers to a hypothetical set of data.)

10. If you want to compare measurement and evaluation you will say

    a. measurement has no subjectivity to it, and evaluation does.
    b. one is used in math and the other in assessment.
    c. evaluation is more useful than measurement.
    d. there is no way to compare them because they are the same.

Comments. I apologize in advance for long-winded comments here, but this item demonstrates the most common and most damaging problem in the writing of multiple choice items: careless, imprecise use of language. The item is so full of holes as to be virtually unanswerable. The recklessly worded stem should read "compare measurement *to* (not *and*) evaluation." Further, it implies that anyone wanting to compare measurement to evaluation will be obligated to "say" that which appears in the correct response. That is nonsense born of a shallow, immature approach to language. A test-taker willing to overlook that reckless language is confronted with more confusion in the options. Option "a," intended as the correct response, is incorrect because of overstatement: measurement of human behavior can never be purged of all subjectivity. Option "b," intended as a distrator, is technically correct, because measurement is used in math and evaluation is used in assessment; the writer needed to write "only in math" and "only in assessment" to create the exclusionary circumstance intended but not written. Option "c," because it would be true for some circumstances and false for others, leaves test-takers wondering about what qualifications to infer. In option "d" the overstated term "no way" might tempt a student to think "there's still a way to compare them," and thus waste time looking for a loophole in what is merely a carelessly crafted option. **Without precise language, multiple choice items are virtually unusable.**

Improved Version of Number 10:

> The **most** accurate statement about the difference between measurement and evaluation is that
>
> a. measurement is objective and evaluation subjective.
> b. one is used only in math and the other only in testing.
> c. evaluation is useful to educators and measurement is not.
> d. educators generally perceive a difference, but in reality the two are interchangeable terms.

Explanation. The term "most accurate" in the stem allows the correct response to be less than 100% precise so long as it is clearly more accurate than any of the other three choices. Option "a" then becomes the correct response, even though neither measurement nor evaluation is purely objective or subjective. Option "b" is made false by the term "only," because measurement is used in both math and testing. Option "c" is false because both are useful to educators. Option "d" is false because the two terms are not interchangeable.

The stems of good multiple choice items sometimes contain such words as "all except" or "worst" or "least acceptable." The extent to which such qualifiers steer test-takers to the correct response lowers discrimination value (described later in this chapter) a bit, but that small technical sacrifice is well worth accepting in exchange for promoting learning. How do such qualifying words promote learning? When you force test takers to eliminate three correct responses, you force them to identify three truths. That amounts to a form of review and confirmation of learning. The test doubles as a teaching tool.

When you do use such qualifying terms, you should emphasize them by putting them in bold font to guard against test-takers misreading your intent: "Of the following, the **worst** advice for use of a rating scale is…." or "The grading of an essay item should entail all of the following **except**…."

When you write the stem of your multiple choice items, be sure to close all loopholes. If you were to write "the **worst** advice is" rather than "Of the following, the **worst** advice is," students could claim that none of the options contained the absolute worst advice. Students will use any technicality to argue that an item is unfair or misleading, and often they will be right.

That brings to mind a piece of general writing advice that seems particularly important to the writing of multiple choice items. Quintilian, a first century Roman, said "one should aim not at being possible to understand, but at being impossible to misunderstand" (Lederer, 1984, p. 221). If you fail to write precisely and clearly, your multiple choice tests will be flawed. If you have a friend who writes well, ask for proofreading and editing help. If you want to systematically improve your own writing, you might consider a book I published recently, titled *Write Well Now: Six Keys to Greater Clarity* (2008).

Notice that nearly all ten items I used above to show examples of potential test writing errors were inference items. That is because the danger of error is small in the writing of straightforward discrimination items. Do not take the proportion of discrimination items to inference items in those ten examples as a model for your tests. In your tests you are likely to need half of the items, or nearly so, to be discrimination items to cover the basic content that you expect students to learn by rote. An interesting challenge is to find ways to embed multiple pieces of basic knowledge into inference items, but in many cases you will find no substitute for testing plain facts.

Complex inference items increase the power of your tests, but they also increase the chances of your making a damaging mistake. You may write a distrator that can be construed as a correct response. You may make some other fine error that gives students a legitimate complaint. But when you write a complex inference item that is error-free, one that does the job you intended, its contribution to your test is well worth your having taken those risks. As odd as this sounds, **safety can pose a greater risk than danger. That is, if you avoid errors by writing safe, shallow test items, you will never develop an effective test. But if you make errors in the course of writing rich, thought-provoking items, in time you will find those errors and correct them—and produce highly effective test items that you can use over and over again for many years.**

An important advantage of the multiple choice format as compared to the essay format is the pure number and length of the items. That enables you to reuse items indefinitely as long as you never let students carry a test booklet out of your classroom. You can create banks of items, and select from them what you need to construct tests of specific content, difficulty, and length.

Thwarting the Games

As you write multiple choice items, probably you will find "c" the easiest placement for correct responses and "a" the most difficult. For that reason, conventional test-taking tips recommend that students use "c" when they need to guess. You can remove that advantage by distributing your correct responses evenly. Design your test to have about the same number of correct responses in each position: a, b, c, d. Each letter then will have approximately a 25 percent chance of being answered correctly by guessing.

Avoid predictable patterns. If students have found no correct responses in a particular position for several items, they will believe that particular response is due. If they have had three consecutive correct responses in the same position, they will believe the next correct response has to be something different. Be willing to leave one option unused for an extended number of items, or to use the same option for four or five consecutive items. Avoid predictability, and tell students ahead of time that you will avoid predictability—that test-taking games will not work on your tests. By doing so you will increase the chances that students will focus their responses on what they know or can figure out. That is exactly what you need for maximum validity.

Figure 10 is a summary of the preceding advice for writing multiple choice items. Refer to it periodically during your early experiences with the multiple choice format.

Item Analysis

No matter how carefully you monitor multiple choice items as you write them, you will have more to learn about each item after students have taken the test. Only then will you have the data you need to analyze each item for two important characteristics: difficulty and discrimination. These characteristics

1. Write the essence of the problem or question into the stem so test-takers can formulate some tentative answers before reading the options.

2. Avoid starting all the options with the same phrase if that phrase can be placed gracefully at the end of the stem. Test-takers should not be burdened with repetitious reading.

3. Make the stem match each option equally in terms of grammar and style; test-takers will assume that a poorly fitting option is a foil.

4. Stack options vertically beneath the stem as a completion of the stem, and arrange them according to any logic they present, e.g., chronological or numerical order. In short, avoid visual distractions that present a problem unrelated to content.

5. Avoid unnecessarily complex language that creates a test of vocabulary as an adjunct to the test of content.

6. If you write throw-away items for comic relief or some other reason, throw them away, i.e., do not key them into the test as part of the credit toward a score.

7. Keep options comparable in length. Particularly, do not make the correct response more elaborate than the foils; that will attract correct responses from test-takers who are making their best guess.

8. Be careful to not plant clues in the correct response, e.g., use wording that relates more directly to the stem than does the wording of the foils.

9. Write all options to be absolutely mutually exclusive; any overlap invites an argument in favor of a foil that overlaps the correct response.

10. Construct items with mature, precise, clear, grammatically correct, unambiguous language. Have a colleague proofread exams before you use them. If you write less than well, improve your writing. The ability to express oneself well on paper is profoundly important to a professional in any discipline, and particularly to a professional whose work is a model for students. One effective source for writing improvement is *Write Well Now: Six Keys to Greater Clarity* (Walters, 2008).

11. When you use important qualifying terms in the stem (worst, best, except, least acceptable, most likely), help the test-takers' comprehension by using bold font or underlines to call attention to the qualification.

12. Do all you can to thwart test-taking games that increase the power of guessing. Help students focus on content by telling them that you design your tests to be game-proof.

Figure 10. Principles of Writing Multiple Choice Items,
Based on This Chapter's Examples and Advice

are defined by test results. That is, the test-takers themselves—through the act of taking the test—create a body of information from which you will draw conclusions about individual test items.

Think back to the distinction between criterion-referenced tests and norm-referenced tests. *Item analysis*, because it is based on the reality of scores attained by a body of test-takers, is a norm-referenced process. The principal assumption is that the body of test-takers approximates a normal distribution. That becomes more likely as the number of test-takers increases, so initial statistics from a small sample will offer only a preliminary indication of the characteristics of the items. If you give a new test to only one small group of students, you will dare interpret statistics as only an indication of what might be. As the body of statistics grows in number, your confidence will grow that you are interpreting test results relative to a normal distribution.

Item Difficulty. This statistic for each item is a simple matter of the percentage of students who answered the item correctly. The formula used to calculate *item difficulty* is simply the number of correct responses the item drew from the body of test-takers divided by the number of total responses, as shown in Figure 11.

$$\text{Difficulty} = \frac{\text{No. of Correct Responses}}{\text{No. of Test-takers}}$$

Figure 11. Formula for Calculating the Difficulty of a Multiple Choice Item

An oddity of the difficulty statistic is that, being the proportion of students who answered the item correctly, it is more precisely a measure of easiness rather than of difficulty. For example, if 30 students were to answer an item, 10 correct answers would yield a difficulty of .33 (10/30), but 20 correct answers would yield a difficulty of .67 (20/30). For that reason, you need to think of a higher difficulty statistic (a higher proportion of correct answers) as an indication that the item is easier, and a lower difficulty statistic (a lower proportion of correct answers) as an indication that the item is more difficult.

What does the calculation of item difficulty mean to you as the writer of the test? You will want to balance the range of item difficulty of a test to approximate the shape of the standard normal curve. That is, you will want very few extremely difficult items and very few extremely easy items (representing the tails of the bell), a larger number of moderately difficult items and moderately easy items (representing the sides of the bell), and the largest number of items showing a difficulty near the mid-point of perhaps .40 to .60 (representing the crown of the bell). By keeping track of item difficulty over a period of time, and across hundreds of test-takers, you will be able to combine items into tests in a way that gives a roughly bell-shaped distribution of difficulty to individual tests.

When you assemble items into a test, you might begin with a moderately easy item to give students a relaxed start, and then mix more-difficult items and less-difficult items in a random-appearing way. That will allow students who have difficulty at any point to hope that an easier item will appear soon. Standardized tests sometimes have items arranged from easiest to most difficult, the thought being that most test-takers will not finish, and so will benefit from an early appearance of items they are most likely to answer correctly. By contrast, you intend for everyone (or nearly so) to finish classroom achievement tests. If you place items in order from easy to difficult, students having difficulty are likely to feel an ever-tightening vice that shuts them down before they have read all the items.

Item Discrimination. The overriding objective of a good test is to discriminate between students in terms of how much they know about the test content. An important characteristic of each item is the extent to which it contributes to the test's making that discrimination, i.e., its *item discrimination*, or *discrimination value*. Note the different use of the term *discrimination* here as compared to the description of a discrimination item. A discrimination item is one that asks the test-taker to discriminate among several straight-forward choices. The discrimination value of an item is the extent to which it helps the overall test discriminate between those who know most and those who know least. Do not confuse those two very different applications of the term.

A key question is "how can I as the test writer acquire a baseline that tells me who knows most and who knows least?" The best current indicator of knowledge will be the result of that overall test. So to calculate the discrimination value of any given item, you will compare results on that item with results on the overall test. If students who succeed most on the overall test also succeed most on the item whose discrimination power you are calculating, while students who succeed least on the overall test succeed least on that particular item, the item is said to be positively discriminating. In other words, that particular item is helping the test meet its objective. Conversely, if students who succeed least on the overall test succeed most on the item whose discrimination power you are calculating, while students who succeed most on the overall test succeed least on that particular item, the item is said to be negatively discriminating. In other words, that particular item is working at odds with the test's objective. Discrimination value is expressed as a **_discrimination coefficient_**. As with all coefficients, it can range from strong positive to strong negative, with 0 as the center point.

You are not likely to calculate discrimination values of multiple choice test items by hand, but you could do so as follows. Categorize each person's response for the item as coming from the upper half of the distribution (UH) or the lower half (LH). (In the case of an odd number of test takers, ignore the middle test for purposes of calculating discrimination values.) Then divide the difference between the number of UH persons who answered the item correctly and the number of LH persons who answered correctly by one half the total number of persons. The formula is shown in Figure 12.

$$\text{Discrimination} = \frac{\text{No. UH Correct Responses} - \text{No. LH Correct Responses}}{.5\,(N)}$$

Figure 12. Formula for Calculating the Discrimination Value
of a Multiple Choice Item

You can see that when the number of UH correct responses exceeds the number of LH correct responses the discrimination value of the item is positive, and when the reverse is true the discrimination value is negative. In Figure 13 you will see calculations for a fictitious Item 1 that is a *positively discriminating item*, and for a fictitious Item 2 that is a *negatively discriminating item*. In each case, a class of 20 students responded.

Item 1:
$$\frac{8 \text{ UH Correct} - 3 \text{ LH Correct}}{.5\,(20)} = \frac{5}{10} = .50$$

Item 2:
$$\frac{3 \text{ UH Correct} - 5 \text{ LH Correct}}{.5\,(20)} = \frac{-2}{10} = -.20$$

Figure 13. Calculation of Discrimination Value for
Two Fictitious Multiple Choice Items

I might summarize the findings shown in Figure 13 in this way: of the 20 students who took the fictitious test, 8 of the 10 most successful students answered Item 1 correctly, while only 3 of the least successful students answered Item 1 correctly. That means Item 1 is aligned with the test as a whole, i.e., Item 1 is helping the overall test to discriminate between those who know most and those who know least. Of those same 20 students, only 3 of the 10 most successful students answered Item 2 correctly, while 5 of the least successful students answered Item 2 correctly. That means Item 2 is not aligned with the test as a whole, i.e., Item 2 is working against the overall test objective of discriminating between those who know most and those who know least.

No matter how well you write a test, you are unlikely to avoid negatively discriminating items altogether. My experience is that a good test is likely to have 10% negatively discriminating items, and maybe more. (Some are well justified, as you will soon see.) That being said, you might use the guidelines shown in Figure 14 to interpret the extent to which test items of various discrimination levels are helping or hurting your testing objective. These are only guidelines, to be interpreted quite loosely.

> .40	very strong discrimination power
.20 – .39	enough discrimination power to be considered a solid contributor without revision
0 – .19	weak discrimination power; merits investigation for possible strengthening with revision
< 0	at odds with testing objectives; needs investigation for possible revision or elimination

Figure 14. Guidelines for Interpreting Discrimination Coefficients

One reason the guidelines in Figure 14 need to be interpreted loosely is that some items having weak discriminative power, and even some negatively discriminating items, are justifiable as they are. I will explain anomalies for weak items first, and then for negative items.

It is important for you to separate in your mind the difficulty statistic (a proportion having to do with the percentage of success on a given item) from the discrimination statistic (a coefficient having to do with congruence of a given item with the test as a whole). Discrimination coefficients have no direct relationship to difficulty. Having said that, I need to point out an indirect relationship between difficulty and discrimination.

Let us investigate the potential discrimination power for a very difficult or very easy item, an item answered correctly by only one person or incorrectly by only one person from our hypothetical class of 20. In either case, the discrimination power will necessarily be weak, as shown in Figure 15.

Discrimination coefficients are derived from comparisons of one category of student (high) with another category of student (low). When the two categories become very much alike (differing by only one student), the numerator in the formula necessarily becomes small, so the coefficient is destined to be small. All of this is a mathematical explanation for a principle to

Very Difficult Item:

$$\frac{1 \text{ UH Correct} - 0 \text{ LH Correct}}{.5 \, (20)} = \frac{1}{10} = .10$$

Very Easy Item:

$$\frac{10 \text{ UH Correct} - 9 \text{ LH Correct}}{.5 \, (20)} = \frac{1}{10} = .10$$

Figure 15. Calculation of Discrimination Values for Two
Fictitious Multiple Choice Items

keep in mind: as an item's difficulty statistic approaches an extreme—either very difficult or very easy—its potential for discrimination power is diminished. What that means in practical terms is that you need to accept weak discrimination coefficients for items that you have written to be very easy or very difficult. Realize that your greatest discrimination power will come from the many items that lie in the middle ground of difficulty, i.e., in your moderate items, and to some extent in your moderately difficult and moderately easy items. If you find a discrimination coefficient below .20 for an item of moderate difficulty, examine the item to see if you can make it more powerfully discriminating. If you find a discrimination coefficient below .20 for an item of extreme difficulty (or easiness), realize that the item is providing about all the discrimination power it can, and accept it for what it is.

Negatively discriminating items offer yet another challenge. Reasons for items showing negative discrimination vary. Some are unjustifiable, calling for removal or revision. Others require no change at all, unusual as that may seem on the surface. Just as the malfunction of an automobile engine prompts a mechanic to check a hierarchy of potential causes, from simple to complex, so a negatively discriminating test item should prompt you to check a hierarchy of potential causes. They are as follows:

1. Check the key to be sure you have not marked a distrator as the correct response.

2. Read carefully the distractor that top-scoring students tend to choose as correct to be sure you have not inadvertently written a subtle truth into it. That happens sometimes when you take the risk of writing a complex inference item.

3. Read the entire item as if you were a test-taker, looking for language that might confuse or deceive students.

4. Ask students in a class discussion how they reacted to the item and how they account for their answers.

During that fourth step, students may help you see a flaw that you could not see from your perspective. Or you may find during discussion that one of the top-scoring students either mis-keyed the answer or made an uncharacteristic mistake on impulse, while a couple of the low-scoring students made lucky guesses. Those events coinciding can flip a normally positive item to negative. That is particularly true in a small class, because each student represents a larger percentage of the whole. When that happens, you need to assume that the item itself is fine, and that over the long haul it will show itself to be positively discriminating.

I said earlier that you are unlikely to calculate discrimination coefficients by hand. That calculation is commonly made by a computer. Computer calculations are not only easier, but more precise. That is because a particular kind of correlation coefficient is calculated that differs fundamentally from the Pearson product moment correlation. You need not know how to calculate the new correlation coefficient, because the computer will do it for you, but it is called a ***point biserial correlation***, symbolized with r_{pbs}.

The point biserial process correlates a distribution of scores with a ***dichotomous*** (either/or) ***variable*** rather than with a second distribution of scores. In this case, the dichotomous variable is correct vs. incorrect. In other words, the discrimination power of a given item is calculated by correlating the distribution of scores (1–20 in our hypothetical class) with whether each person's response was correct or incorrect. The greater precision as compared to by-hand calculation comes from giving weight to each response according to its placement in the distribution rather by residence in the top half or bottom half of the distribution. Figure 16 is a visual depiction of the hand calculation of a discrimination coefficient; Figure 17 is a visual depiction of the computer calculation of a discrimination coefficient. In the hand calculation, dividing the difference between UH and LH by half the total yields a correlation between two dichotomous variables (UH/LH and correct/incorrect). In contrast, the computer calculates a correlation between the distribution of scores and a dichotomous variable (correct/incorrect).

You can see the logic in the greater precision of the computer calculation. The by-hand calculation places persons 1 and 10 in the same category, but persons 10 and 11 in different categories. Imprecision stems from the fact that persons 10 and 11 are much more alike in terms of influence on overall test data than are persons 1 and 10. Any time data are lumped into categories, some precision is lost. Think of the by-hand calculation as a macro approach to analyzing data, and the computer calculation as a micro approach—one that gives each score precisely the weight it deserves. The comparison is akin to using a sharp knife verses a dull knife to make a critical cut: the sharper instrument will deliver a more precise cut—or in this case, a more precise discrimination coefficient.

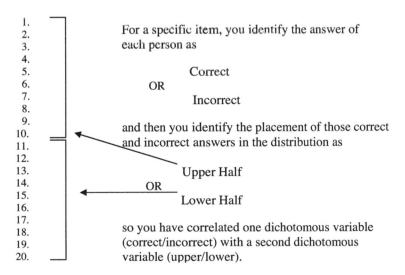

Figure 16. Visual Depiction of a Discrimination Coefficient Calculated by Hand

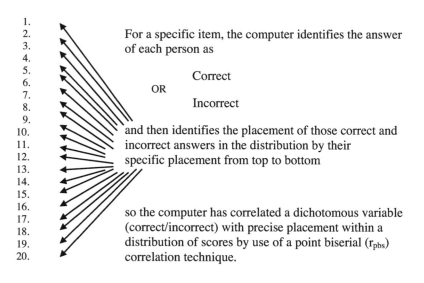

1.
2.
3.
4.
5.
6.
7.
8.
9.
10.
11.
12.
13.
14.
15.
16.
17.
18.
19.
20.

For a specific item, the computer identifies the answer of each person as

Correct

OR

Incorrect

and then identifies the placement of those correct and incorrect answers in the distribution by their specific placement from top to bottom

so the computer has correlated a dichotomous variable (correct/incorrect) with precise placement within a distribution of scores by use of a point biserial (r_{pbs}) correlation technique.

Figure 17. Visual Depiction of a Discrimination Coefficient
Calculated by Computer

Reliability

The two principal ways to estimate the reliability of a multiple choice test are by test-retest and split halves. Test-retest reliability (as mentioned in Chapter Four) is a simple matter of giving the same test to the same test-takers, and then calculating the correlation between the distribution created the first time and the distribution created the second time. The closer the subjects come to maintaining their same relative positions in the distribution from one testing session to the next (indicated by the strength of the correlation coefficient), the greater the consistency, i.e., reliability. The second administration of the test needs to be given distant enough in time from the first to minimize direct recall (about two days) and close enough in time that the two events can be considered concurrent (within about seven days). Because the coefficient indicates how stable the test results have remained from one test administration to the next, the correlation coefficient is sometimes called by an even more specific term than *"reliability coefficient."* That term is *"coefficient of stability."*

A more practical way to estimate test reliability, considering the extravagance of asking so much time of students, is the split halves method. Calculating **split halves reliability** is a matter of splitting the test items into two groups, each group simulating a test one-half the length of the original. Then the full, original test is administered just one time. The predetermined split is used to estimate reliability by comparing the results of one half of the test with results of the other half of the test for consistency. Because the coefficient indicates how consistent the test is within itself, this correlation coefficient is also sometimes called by a more specific term than "reliability coefficient." That term is *"coefficient of internal consistency."*

The obvious problem to be overcome within the split halves method of estimating reliability is to make the two halves comparable in terms of both difficulty and content. That challenge has been removed by a computer calculation known as the **Kuder-Richardson Formula 20 (KR 20)**, now the most common expression of test reliability for a multiple choice test. The Kuder-Richardson calculation, by computing every possible combination of splits (for a 40-item test, 780 calculations) and then delivering a coefficient that amounts to the mean of all the possibilities, eliminates the need to match test halves.

The KR 20 reliability coefficient does need an adjustment, however. Remember that a greater number of items increases the reliability of a test. Because of the splitting process, the KR 20 coefficient applied to a 40-item test yields a reliability estimate for a 20-item test. The question then becomes, "if the reliability of this test calculated as a 20-item test is X, what is its true reliability—considering that it is actually a 40-item test?" A formula known as the **Spearman/Brown Prophesy Formula** is applied to the KR 20 to adjust the coefficient for test length. It is called a prophesy formula because it prophesizes what the reliability coefficient would become if the test length were doubled (which, in reality, it is). The calculation is a simple matter of multiplying the KR 20 coefficient by 2, and then dividing that value by 1 plus the KR 20 coefficient, i.e., $2r/1+r$. For example, if the KR 20 coefficient were .68, the estimated reliability for the full test (double the length) would be 1.36/1.68, or .81. While all these inner workings of the computer calculations are interesting, all you need to know is this: when the computer printout gives you a KR 20 coefficient, it has been calculated on the basis of all possible split halves and has automatically been adjusted for length by use of the Spearman/ Brown formula. All you have to do is look at it and decide what you think of it. What a convenient age we live in!

How high should a reliability coefficient be, whether a coefficient of stability (test-retest) or a coefficient of internal consistency (split halves or KR 20)? Nailing down a consistent benchmark for a reliability coefficient is impossible because of the number of variables at work. A longer test should produce a higher reliability than a shorter test, and a larger group of test-takers should produce a higher reliability than a smaller group of test-takers. And to add to the complication, a small number of test-takers creates a volatility that on occasion—by pure chance—spikes the reliability coefficient. In general, with some allowances made for circumstances, test writers want to see reliability higher than .70, and feel comfortable when it exceeds .80.

Validity

As was true for performance tests, validity needs to be considered both objectively and subjectively. As a teacher and writer of classroom tests, you will control test validity almost wholly with subjective tools. That being said, I want to give you some information first about objective validity so you understand how it is estimated. Then I will give specific advice for improving the subjective validity of your tests.

Objective validity. Objective validity is calculated mathematically. Remember that validity is defined as the extent to which a test accomplishes what it is intended to accomplish. The first step in estimating validity objectively, then, is to decide exactly what the test is designed to measure. The next step is to identify another measurement or measurements whose scores should correlate highly with the test scores if the test is indeed measuring what it should measure. Because the measure used for comparison becomes the criterion by which we judge the validity of the test, it is called the ***criterion measure***. Test-takers generate scores on the test, and also on the criterion measure, and the two distributions are correlated to estimate the validity of the test.

Let me give a concrete (though hypothetical) example. I have a music ensemble of 80 students, and I want an objective measure of the level of musicianship of each member of the ensemble. I have each student play or sing a prepared piece for me. I give each a lesson, during which we play or sing duets. I have each of them sight read. I form small ensembles that rehearse multiple times, then record ensemble performances that allow me to score the work of each person by use of rating scales. After hundreds of hours of work over a period of a school year, I have individual musicianship scores that I believe are valid because of the rigor I invested.

I do not want to invest that amount of time in subsequent years, nor do I believe other music teachers want to invest that amount of time—though they would be interested in the results. I use my insight to develop a 30-minute General Test of Musicianship (GTM) that can be administered to all 80 students at one time by use of a recording to which the students respond with pencil and paper on a sheet to be graded by computer. If I give that test to the students with whom I have spent those hundreds of hours, and if I find a high correlation between the rigorously obtained results (criterion measure) and results of my recorded test, I can claim that my GTM shows high objective validity. (Common sense tells us that such a test as the GTM would almost surely show a very low relationship to the criterion measure. Musicianship is too complex a characteristic to be measured by a non-performance test.) By checking documentation for such evidence of validity before using a test, you can guard against using an invalid test and then believing in the results.

Less is expected of validity coefficients than of reliability coefficients, because validity is derived from a comparison of separate measures—as compared to reliability being derived from comparison of a single measure with itself. Validity coefficients in the .40s or .50s make a test look good.

An important condition for calculating objective validity is that the criterion measure and the test being validated be administered within the same time frame. That is important because people change over time—learning and forgetting at varying rates—and the sets of scores correlated need to belong to essentially unchanged people. Because the testing is all done within the same general time frame, i.e., concurrently, the coefficient obtained through this measure of objective validity is called a measure of the test's ***concurrent validity***.

You can see from the rigor involved that concurrent validity is calculated almost exclusively by test manufacturers, who can afford to invest the time and money required. You are unlikely to calculate concurrent validity for a test unless you engage in research, perhaps as a graduate student. By knowing what concurrent validity is, however, you can read test manuals more thoroughly and more intelligently than when descriptions of those criterion measures and coefficients were a mystery to you.

Subjective Validity. Two other names for subjective validity might be *judgment validity* or *common sense validity*. You will improve the subjective validity of your test simply by thinking about what conditions you need to take care of to be sure the test measures exactly what it is designed to measure. Let me offer some examples.

The most obvious need, as introduced in Chapter Four, is for content validity. Your judgment is the only source of regulating a test to measure what you taught, and to emphasize content in proportion to the emphasis you gave to it. Before writing a test, prepare a sketch of the course content—a kind of taxonomy of what you taught. Refer to that list as you write test items, and check off content you have used until you have included everything you consider important. You will keep the test length manageable by constructing some complex inference items that require students to know several pieces of important information to avoid all the distractors and identify the correct response. Write those items first, because to add discrimination items that pick up facts yet to be included is relatively quick and easy. By that method you will guarantee content validity and have a test with a good mixture of discrimination items and inference items.

A many-faceted aspect of subjective validity, also introduced in Chapter Four, is process validity. Whereas content validity guards against testing content not taught (or skipping content that was taught), process validity guards against testing test-takers' ability to overcome hurdles placed between them and the content itself. I touched on some issues of process validity with the poorly written sample items and with my comments about them, but I want to be explicit and thorough about process validity here.

You place hurdles between the test-takers and your test content when you write items poorly: poor grammar, incorrect punctuation, redundancy, self-contradiction, vague terms, inconsistent terms, imprecise terms, misleading terms, non-parallel terms, non-parallel construction, or any of the many writing faux pas that burden test-takers with challenges beyond the challenge of identifying the correct response. If you do not write well in general, you will not write tests well. That is a simple, inescapable truth.

You will impose hurdles on test-takers also if you ask them to take a test in a room that is noisy, or extreme in temperature, or distracting in any other way. You will impose hurdles if you ask test-takers to use equipment, perhaps computers, with which some students are familiar and others are not. In short, the process of taking the test should be as free as possible from disruptions.

I think of process validity as common sense validity, because so much of what you need to do as a teacher to guard against poor process validity is a matter of common sense. For example, assume that you are giving a multiple choice test that involves students listening to musical examples and then responding on the basis of what they have heard. Here are a few threats to process validity that amount to violations of common sense—with a major problem being that test scores will not be affected uniformly from one student to another.

1. Poor sound reproduction will dampen everyone's ability to hear precisely what is there, but some students will be more able than others to overcome the difficulties.

2. Weak speakers placed in the front of the room will give front-row students a keen hearing as compared to the muddle heard by students in the back. Differences in acuity of individual hearing may magnify the discrepancies.

3. Playing the example before giving students a chance to read the item, with all of its options, will force them to listen with no context in mind.

Some will be more facile than others at retaining what they heard while simultaneously reading the item. Ask students to read each item thoroughly before you play the corresponding example.

These are just a few examples of the "common sense" behind process validity. The list of potential disruptions to good testing processes is endless.

To summarize, process validity (as the name implies) is a matter of interruptions in the process of taking the test. It is damaged by anything that requires test-takers to respond to something other than content. If test scores ultimately measure students' abilities to interpret your poor writing, or their ability to ignore distractions, or their ability to overcome anything other than the challenge of the content, the test will not have measured precisely what it was designed to measure, e.g., it will lack validity.

Matters of subjective validity—content and process—are completely within your control as the teacher. The responsibility is all yours. Failure to be conscientious about matters of content validity and process validity when writing and administering tests amounts to educational malpractice.

Interpreting Results With the Help of Theoretical Constructs

As was true in your interpretation of performance tests, you will need some benchmarks against which to compare the results of your multiple choice tests. As with performance tests, those benchmarks are the theoretical constructs (theoretical mean and theoretical standard deviation) of the test, derived from the theory of the standard normal curve.

The theoretical mean and theoretical standard deviation for rating scales remain constant from one scale to another, assuming that all scales span 5 points. Multiple choice tests, by contrast, vary in the number of items they contain. It is the number of items that serves as the basis for calculating the theoretical constructs.

The first statistic to be calculated is the *chance score*. You know from experience that all correct responses made in the taking of a multiple choice test are not based on knowledge: sometimes a test-taker guesses correctly. The chance of that happening is related directly to the number of options within each item. For a four-option item, the test-taker has one chance in four of guessing correctly. Statistically, then, a person who knows nothing—perhaps marks responses without even reading the options—will answer correctly one-fourth of the time. That occurrence, known as chance score, has to be taken into account in the calculation of theoretical constructs. The formula for chance score is shown in Figure 18. In the case of a 40-item, 4-option multiple choice test, the chance score would be calculated as 40 divided by 4, which equals 10.

$$\text{Chance} = \frac{\text{No. of Items}}{\text{No. of Options}}$$

Figure 18. Formula for Calculating the Chance Score of a
Multiple Choice Test

Assuming that test-takers can attain the chance score without knowing anything, the remainder of the items becomes the statistical meat of the test for the purpose of calculating theoretical constructs. The theoretical mean, for example, will not be the mid-point (remember that mean and median coincide in the standard normal curve) of the whole test, but rather of what is left after the chance score is removed. Because the chance score is assumed to be a part of everyone's score, the chance score is then added back on to arrive at the total number of correct responses representing the theoretical mean. The formula for the theoretical mean of a multiple choice test is shown in Figure 19. In the case of a 40-item, 4-option multiple choice test, the theoretical mean would be calculated as 40 − 10, divided by 2, plus 10, which is 25. Beginning on page 180 you will read about a philosophy of testing that explains why this theoretical mean is much lower than those attained on the typical school test.

$$\overline{X}_{\text{THEO}} = \frac{\text{No. Items} - \text{Chance}}{2} + \text{Chance}$$

Figure 19. Formula for Calculating the Theoretical Mean of a
Multiple Choice Test

The theoretical mean of a multiple choice test allows you to see if your obtained mean is somewhere "in the ball park." An obtained mean much higher than the theoretical mean may indicate that you have written a test too easy to discriminate well between those who know the course content and those who do not. In that case you will have risked having an undifferentiated crowd at the top (ceiling effect), a sign that the test has not discriminated among students sufficiently to separate them. An obtained mean much lower than the theoretical mean may indicate that you have written a test too difficult to discriminate well between those who know the course content and those who do not. In that case you will have risked having an undifferentiated crowd at the bottom, also a sign that the test has not discriminated among students sufficiently to separate them.

Even if your obtained mean is somewhat disparate from the theoretical mean for one small group of test-takers, your test may be of an appropriate difficulty: the group that produced the aberrant mean may have been exceptionally gifted, or the reverse, as compared to the larger population for whom you designed the test.

Another significant theoretical construct to be calculated for comparison is the theoretical standard deviation. Remember that the standard normal distribution assumes three standard deviations between the mean and the highest possible score. The theoretical standard deviation, therefore, will be one-third of the distance between the theoretical mean and the top. The formula for the theoretical standard deviation of a multiple choice test is shown in Figure 20. For a 40-item, 4-option multiple choice test, the theoretical standard deviation will be 40 minus 25, divided by 3, which is 5.

$$SD_{THEO} = \frac{\text{No. Items} - \overline{X}_{THEO}}{3}$$

Figure 20. Formula for Calculating the Theoretical Standard
Deviation of a Multiple Choice Test

The theoretical standard deviation of a multiple choice test allows you to see if your obtained standard deviation is somewhere "in the ball park." A smaller-than-expected standard deviation may be the product of a test that bunches students artificially by being extremely easy or extremely difficult. Or an obtained standard deviation may be disparate from the theoretical standard deviation through no fault of the test itself. An obtained standard deviation much higher than the theoretical standard deviation may indicate that you have a wildly divergent class, and a standard deviation much lower than the theoretical standard deviation may indicate that you have an oddly homogeneous class. Every group of students will not conform to the bell curve. Groups showing a great amount of variability (large standard deviation) will be more difficult to teach than classes in which students are less divergent. The larger body of students over time should show a standard deviation somewhere near the theoretical standard deviation.

To help you visualize the theoretical constructs of a multiple choice test, I have drawn a rectangle in Figure 21 that represents a 40-item test. Superimposed on that rectangle are indications of where the various theoretical constructs fall.

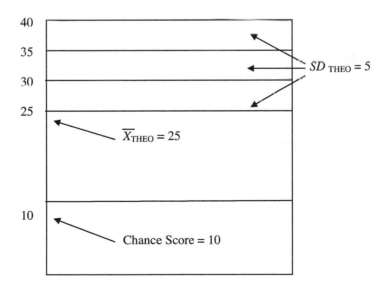

Figure 21. Depiction of a 40-Item Multiple Choice Test,
With Theoretical Constructs Shown

Reading a Computer Printout

Your school system, intermediate school district, regional school district, or university is likely to have a testing service that allows you to use computer-prepared answer sheets for multiple choice tests. Students register their responses by filling in bubbles with a pencil, choosing a, b, c, or d for each item—something you have done yourself many times. As test-writer, you will fill bubbles on an answer sheet to show all the correct responses, and mark that sheet KEY for use by the testing service. Personnel at the testing service then analyze results by use of a computer program containing the KR 20 Formula and the Spearman/Brown Prophesy Formula, and return a printout to you that shows summary test results for the overall test and an item analysis that reveals difficulty and discrimination information for each item. An actual test-result summary page from Temple University is shown in Figure 22. Your measurement center will generate something different, but much of the same information will be shown.

The first time you look at a summary sheet you will feel disoriented. To save you the trouble of poking through the numbers and trying to figure out what everything means, I will guide you through each part of the summary sheet shown in Figure 22. Notice in the upper left that the number of students taking the test is 11, an atypically small group. I chose this summary sheet nonetheless, because it and the item analysis sheet that corresponds to it (Figure 23) show a helpful cross-section of features. Listed below the line showing number of students is an indication that the test contained 34 items. That is a moderate-sized test, given during a 50-minute period. It was designed to give students approximately one and one-half minutes per item.

Completing the upper left quadrant of information are measures of central tendency (mean, median, mode) and an indication of the highest and lowest scores attained (31 and 13). In the upper right quadrant is information about variability (standard deviation and range) and shape (skewness and kurtosis, as described on pages 26–28). If you want to calculate the theoretical mean and standard deviation of this 34-item, 4-option multiple choice test, do so now before reading the answers in the next couple sentences. The chance score is 34 divided by 4; that amounts to 8.5. The theoretical mean is 34 minus

SUMMARY STATISTICS

TOTAL TEST STATISTICS – TEST DISTRIBUTION

NUMBER OF STUDENTS TAKING TEST = 11
NUMBER OF ITEMS IN TEST = 34

MEAN TEST SCORE = 22.27	STANDARD DEVIATION = 4.49
MEDIAN = 22	SKEWNESS = - 0.04
MODE = 20	KURTOSIS = 0.13
MAXIMUM = 31	RANGE = 18
MINIMUM = 13	

RELIABILITY ESTIMATES – BASED ON 29 ITEMS

KUDER-RICHARDSON 20 (KR 20) = 0.780
STANDARD ERROR OF MEASUREMENT = 2.109

PERCENT CORRECT DISTRIBUTION			POINT BISERIAL DISTRIBUTION		
BASED ON 34 ITEMS			BASED ON 29 ITEMS		
RANGE	NUMBER OF ITEMS	PERCENTAGE OF ITEMS	RANGE	NUMBER OF ITEMS	PERCENTAGE OF ITEMS
.81-1.00	16	47	81-1.00	0	0
.61-.80	5	15	.61-.80	3	10
.41-.60	2	6	.41-.60	10	34
.21-.40	10	29	.21-.40	3	10
.00-.20	1	3	.00-.20	8	28
			BELOW .00	5	17

MEAN PERCENT CORRECT = .655

Figure 22. A Sample Summary Sheet for a 34-item Multiple Choice Test

Reprinted with permission of Dr. David D S Poor, MeadowBrook Industries, Ltd.
And the Measurement and Research Center, Temple University.

8.5, divided by 2, with the chance score added back on, that amounts to 21.25. The theoretical standard deviation is 34 minus 21.25, divided by 3, that amounts to 4.25. Having identified the theoretical constructs as a mean of 21.25 and a standard deviation of 4.25, you can now compare those figures with the obtained mean and standard deviation. The obtained mean of 22.27 is approximately one raw score (one item) higher than the theoretical mean of 21.25, so the central tendency of the distribution is close to the value expected for a test that functions well. The obtained standard deviation of 4.49 is also very close to its theoretical counterpart, a theoretical standard deviation of 4.25.

Skewness is near 0, so apparently there are no outliers pulling the mean far from the median. You can see verification of that in the accounts of central tendency, which show a median of 22 as compared to a mean of 22.27. Nor is the shape of the distribution particularly peaked or flat, judging by a kurtosis statistic that also approximates 0. The measures of skewness and kurtosis together tell us that the shape of the distribution approximates normality.

The KR 20 statistic, located in the center of the printout, is .78. That is high enough for us to have faith that the test is operating with a healthy degree of consistency. But notice just above that statistic that reliability is based on 29 items. Why would that be, if the test contains 34 items? The answer is that for five of the items, all students answered correctly or all students answered incorrectly. The dichotomous variable of correct/incorrect requires some variability in response for that item to be entered into the calculation. The other statistic shown in the center of the summary sheet, standard error of measurement, shows the amount of latitude needed in passing judgment on a particular student's score. That is, taking testing error into consideration, you can be quite confident that the knowledge base of a student who scores 20 (barring extreme illness or some other extraordinary circumstance) lies somewhere between about 18 and 22.

The lower left quadrant is a summary of item difficulty, and the lower right quadrant is a summary of item discrimination. Notice that difficulty coefficients are based on all 34 items, because difficulty can still be calculated even if all students answer an item correctly or incorrectly. Discrimination coefficients, by contrast, are based on the same 29 items that were the basis for the reliability estimate. That is because when all students are on the same side of the correct/incorrect dichotomy for a given item, that item by definition shows no discrimination between test-takers. Therefore, no discrimination coefficient can be calculated.

The item difficulty information tells you that 16 of the 34 items were answered correctly by 81 to 100 percent of the class. That may seem like a large number of easy items, but the difficulty analysis usually is loaded heavily on the easy end. That is because the difficulty statistic is a function of all correct responses given, including responses made correctly by chance, i.e., the chance score. Looking further, you will see that only one item was so difficult that fewer than 20 percent of the students answered it correctly. The column titled "percentage of items" simply shows the percentage of the test accounted for by a particular number of items. For example, the 10 items answered correctly by 21 to 40 percent of the class amount to 29 percent of the 34 items in the test.

SUMMARY STATISTICS

TOTAL TEST STATISTICS – TEST DISTRIBUTION

NUMBER OF STUDENTS TAKING TEST = 11
NUMBER OF ITEMS IN TEST = 34

MEAN TEST SCORE = 22.27	STANDARD DEVIATION = 4.49
MEDIAN = 22	SKEWNESS = − 0.04
MODE = 20	KURTOSIS = 0.13
MAXIMUM = 31	RANGE = 18
MINIMUM = 13	

RELIABILITY ESTIMATES – BASED ON 29 ITEMS

KUDER-RICHARDSON 20 (KR 20) = 0.780
STANDARD ERROR OF MEASUREMENT = 2.109

PERCENT CORRECT DISTRIBUTION   POINT BISERIAL DISTRIBUTION

BASED ON 34 ITEMS   BASED ON 29 ITEMS

RANGE	NUMBER OF ITEMS	PERCENTAGE OF ITEMS	RANGE	NUMBER OF ITEMS	PERCENTAGE OF ITEMS
.81–1.00	16	47	81–1.00	0	0
.61–.80	5	15	.61–.80	3	10
.41–.60	2	6	.41–.60	10	34
.21–.40	10	29	.21–.40	3	10
.00–.20	1	3	.00–.20	8	28
			BELOW .00	5	17

MEAN PERCENT CORRECT = .655

Figure 22 Repeated for Convenient Comparison with Narrative Information

The item discrimination statistics in the lower right quadrant show that 16 items (3+10+3) had acceptable to strong discrimination power, i.e., greater than .20. The eight items showing a discrimination power between 0 and .20 included one very difficult item, one moderately difficult item, and six easy or moderately easy items—some answered incorrectly by only one person. The low potential for discrimination power among items extreme in difficulty or easiness explains the low coefficients, so there is no reason to believe they need revision. Still, I studied them and made an adjustment to one item.

The five negatively discriminating items represent 17 percent of the test, a slightly greater portion than I like to see. The small number of test-takers (11) accounts for three of those negatively discriminating items—answered incorrectly by a high-scoring student and correctly by a low-scoring student (perhaps by chance). If the number of test-takers were large, one or two students could not flip an item so easily. In this case, one student represents nearly 10 percent of the class; a lucky guess here and an uncharacteristically poor response there can affect discrimination statistics markedly.

Of the other two negatively discriminating items, one was worded in a way easily misinterpreted (process), and the other was taught less well than it should have been (content). It is those kinds of discoveries, stemming from warning signs in the computer printout, that enable a test writer to improve both instruction and test items. This test had been revised many times, which accounts for the obtained mean and standard deviation being close to theoretical constructs and the reliability coefficient being moderately high.

Another important part of the computer printout from a multiple choice test is the page containing item analysis data, shown in Figure 23. Interpret headings as follows:

ITEM MSG This infrequently used column flags items with such messages as <10%, meaning that fewer than 10% of the students answered the item correctly.

ITEM NUM This column shown item numbers.

PT BISERIAL This column shows point biserial (r_{pbs}) discrimination coefficients.

PHI COEFF This column gives an alternate type of coefficient, valid only for large numbers of test-takers, i. e., more than about 100. For our purposes, ignore this column.

SIG	This column is related to the level of confidence in the Phi coefficient. For our purposes, ignore this column.
PERCENT RESPONSES	Each option has a column showing the percentage of test-takers who chose that option as the correct response. A pair of asterisks (**) indicates the correct response. BLNK shows the percentage of responses left blank, and ERR the percentage of responses marked in an invalid way.

ITEM MSG	ITEM NUM	PT BISERIAL	PHI COEFF	SIG	A	B	C	D	E	BLNK	ERR
							PERCENT RESPONSES				
	1	.613	.354	N.S.	9	0	0	91**	0	0	0
	2	NO ITEM VARIANCE			0	0	100**	0	0	0	0
	3	.092	−.167	N.S.	0	45	27**	27	0	0	0
	4	.613	.354	N.S.	0	9	91**	0	0	0	0
	5	NO ITEM VARIANCE			0	100**	0	0	0	0	0
	6	−.115	.000	N.S.	0	9	91**	0	0	0	0
	7	.000	.091	N.S.	27**	27	36	9	0	0	0
	8	.469	.750	.02	0	27	9	64**	0	0	0
	9	−.352	−.417	.20	18	27	36**	18	0	0	0
	10	.144	.417	.20	0	36	0	55**	0	0	0
	11	.562	.750	.02	9	18	73**	0	0	0	0
	12	.219	.548	.10	82**	9	0	9	0	0	0
	13	.529	.730	.02	73	0	27**	0	0	0	0
	14	.605	.548	.10	0	18	0	82**	0	0	0
	15	.101	.091	N.S.	36**	18	27	18	0	0	0
	16	.429	.417	.20	27**	45	27	0	0	0	0
	17	NO ITEM VARIANCE			100**	0	0	0	0	0	0
	18	NO ITEM VARIANCE			0	0	100**	0	0	0	0
	19	NO ITEM VARIANCE			0	100**	0	0	0	0	0
	20	−.045	.000	N.S.	0	91**	0	9	0	0	0
	21	.376	.354	N.S.	82**	9	9	0	0	0	0
	22	.562	.750	.02	9	0	18	73**	0	0	0
	23	.196	.548	.10	0	36	64**	0	0	0	0
	24	.516	.730	.02	18	45**	27	9	0	0	0
	25	.368	.417	.20	36	36**	27	0	0	0	0
	26	.196	.167	N.S.	0	18	64**	18	0	0	0
	27	.701	****	.001	36**	0	55	9	0	0	0
	28	.580	.730	.02	9	18	45	27**	0	0	0
	29	.605	.548	.10	0	82**	18	0	0	0	0
	30	.097	.354	N.S.	0	91**	9	0	0	0	0
<10%	31	.201	.471	.20	64	9**	27	0	0	0	0
	32	.412	.417	.30	55**	18	27	0	0	0	0
MULT*	33	−.115	.000	N.S.	0	55**	9	36**	0	0	0
	34	−.115	.000	N.S.	0	91**	0	9	0	0	0

Figure 23. Item Analysis Sheet for the 34-item Multiple Choice Test
Summarized in Figure 22

The term NO ITEM VARIANCE in place of a coefficient marks items that everyone answered in the same way, either all correct or all incorrect. Easy and difficult items are easy to spot by looking at the columns under PERCENT RESPONSES. All the items having NO ITEM VARIANCE in place of a discrimination coefficient have a designation of 100**, indicating that those items were answered correctly by all test-takers. Those, of course, judging by the results of this particular test administration, are the easiest items; items having a 91 percent designation are the next easiest, having been answered correctly by all but one test-taker (in the case of this small class, 9% of the class is one person).

Sometimes an item marked NO ITEM VARIANCE will be answered correctly by none of the students. If there were such an item on this printout, you would see 0** in the correct response column. In that case, the "ITEM MSG" column would have the same entry shown for Item 31: <10%, meaning fewer than 10 percent of the students answered the item correctly. The other message entry on the Figure 20 sheet, the MULT* entered for Item 33, means that the test-writer keyed in multiple correct responses. Notice that options B and D are both starred as correct. In this case, as students were taking the test I discovered an error that made a second option technically correct. To avoid having to make score adjustments after receiving results, I entered multiple correct responses on the key.

This item analysis sheet also lets you see which distractors are being used. For example, Item 28 looks rich. All four options were used, several test-takers chose the correct response, and—judging by the powerful (.58) discrimination coefficient—those who answered correctly were at or near the top of the distribution. The distractors in this item provide rich fodder for class discussion, as all were found believable by someone. Items 6 and 34 look weak. Only two options were used, and—judging by the negative discrimination coefficient—the incorrect option in each case was chosen by someone near the top of the distribution of test scores. Remember, though, that the small number of test-takers makes those statistics volatile. If you give a test to multiple sections of students, you can check the statistics relative to a larger number of test-takers. Then if you find a foil left unchosen by hundreds of students over time, you may want to reevaluate it. A distractor that lies dormant, never contributing to the power of the test, in effect leaves you with a three-option item.

ITEM MSG	ITEM NUM	PT BISERIAL	PHI COEFF	SIG	PERCENT RESPONSES						
					A	B	C	D	E	BLNK	ERR
	1	.613	.354	N.S.	9	0	0	91**	0	0	0
	2	NO ITEM VARIANCE			0	0	100**	0	0	0	0
	3	.092	–.167	N.S.	0	45	27**	27	0	0	0
	4	.613	.354	N.S.	0	9	91**	0	0	0	0
	5	NO ITEM VARIANCE			0	100**	0	0	0	0	0
	6	–.115	.000	N.S.	0	9	91**	0	0	0	0
	7	.000	.091	N.S.	27**	27	36	9	0	0	0
	8	.469	.750	.02	0	27	9	64**	0	0	0
	9	–.352	–.417	.20	18	27	36**	18	0	0	0
	10	.144	.417	.20	0	36	0	55**	0	0	0
	11	.562	.750	.02	9	18	73**	0	0	0	0
	12	.219	.548	.10	82**	9	0	9	0	0	0
	13	.529	.730	.02	73	0	27**	0	0	0	0
	14	.605	.548	.10	0	18	0	82**	0	0	0
	15	.101	.091	N.S.	36**	18	27	18	0	0	0
	16	.429	.417	.20	27**	45	27	0	0	0	0
	17	NO ITEM VARIANCE			100**	0	0	0	0	0	0
	18	NO ITEM VARIANCE			0	0	100**	0	0	0	0
	19	NO ITEM VARIANCE			0	100**	0	0	0	0	0
	20	–.045	.000	N.S.	0	91**	0	9	0	0	0
	21	.376	.354	N.S.	82**	9	9	0	0	0	0
	22	.562	.750	.02	9	0	18	73**	0	0	0
	23	.196	.548	.10	0	36	64**	0	0	0	0
	24	.516	.730	.02	18	45**	27	9	0	0	0
	25	.368	.417	.20	36	36**	27	0	0	0	0
	26	.196	.167	N.S.	0	18	64**	18	0	0	0
	27	.701	****	.001	36**	0	55	9	0	0	0
	28	.580	.730	.02	9	18	45	27**	0	0	0
	29	.605	.548	.10	0	82**	18	0	0	0	0
	30	.097	.354	N.S.	0	91**	9	0	0	0	0
<10%	31	.201	.471	.20	64	9**	27	0	0	0	0
	32	.412	.417	.30	55**	18	27	0	0	0	0
MULT*	33	–.115	.000	N.S.	0	55**	9	36**	0	0	0
	34	–.115	.000	N.S.	0	91**	0	9	0	0	0

Figure 23 Repeated for Convenient Comparison with Narrative Information

Finally, Item 9 looks highly controversial. All four options were used, only about one-third of the students answered correctly, and the strong negative discrimination coefficient indicates that the correct answers came from students in the lower part of the distribution more so than from students in the upper part of the distribution. That item bears scrutiny from the test-writer/teacher, followed by class discussion.

Understanding the Power of Highly Discriminating Tests

If you are acclimated to criterion-referenced testing—to having top students answer 100 percent of the test questions correctly, with 92 percent considered the threshold between A and B—the approaches to knowledge testing shown here may be difficult for you to accept. You may wonder what highly discriminating tests accomplish. "If my goal is to teach," you might ask, "do I not want to see every student succeed at the highest possible level on every test? Is there something wrong with rooting for large numbers of students to score 100%?" Now that you are familiar with the details of this chapter, you will benefit from an exploration of the philosophical foundation behind the details.

If 20 students take a test, and if 8 of those students attain the exact same score (100%), what are the chances that all 8 understand the material to the exact same depth? If the material has some range to it—if it is more than a matter of memorizing facts—the answer is zero. There is virtually no chance that those eight students are equal in their understanding of the subject. Eight students scoring 100 percent means only that scores do not reflect reality. Among those 8 may be one or two who could break free from the pack dramatically, but they have no place to go other than to the general category of 100 percent correct on an exam that under uses their potential. The truth has been hidden. The test was insufficient to detect the actual differences in knowledge and understanding among the eight. As a tool of assessment, the test is dull rather than sharp. It gives approximations rather than measurements. Its discriminative powers are weak.

At best, failure to discriminate among students will leave the brightest and most capable students unchallenged. At worst, it will bore them, and give them the message that school is just a series of games to play until freed by graduation—not a place to learn and stretch and grow to maximum potential.

As schools proceeded down the road of criterion-referenced testing over the last half century, probably it was bright students' reactions to being stifled that prompted the creation of programs for gifted students. But if teachers were to use highly discriminating exams and a norm-referenced approach to educational assessment, all students could have an opportunity to show what they can do—with no ceilings in place. The sociological impediment to the approach is this: a system that exposes fine gradations of accomplishment among the best students also exposes fine gradations of accomplishment among the poorest students. There is no way to leave the lower tail of the curve undefined while illuminating the upper tail.

What highly discriminating tests do is expose where students lie on the continuum of learning, and that enables teachers to diagnose strengths and weaknesses in detail. Teachers and students, working in partnership with test results as a guide, can see clear evidence of improvement, understand potential, and together design instruction to match what is needed. By having a clear view of where they are, students can see more clearly where to go next and how to get there.

Whatever problems highly discriminating tests pose, grading is not a part of that problem. Once a test is used to measure learning, a teacher is free to assign any grade to any given score. That evaluation is purely subjective. If rampant grade inflation is the norm, and if a teacher wants half of the students to receive a grade of A on a test for which the student at the median answered only 60 percent of the items correctly, every student who answered more than 60 percent of the items correctly can be awarded a grade of A.

The real problem seems to be a much-nurtured addiction to answering a large percentage of test items correctly. Students need to be oriented to the premise that their aim should be to learn as much as possible, not to achieve a high raw score on tests. Students need to understand that answering 30 of 34 items correctly on an exam that only one student has completed perfectly in a year or two is a greater accomplishment than answering 34 of 34 items correctly on an exam that several students out of every class complete perfectly.

These thoughts return me to the theory of the standard normal curve. You might ask, "how do we protect the self-esteem of students who score low?" I suggest being honest with students. Ask "Do you think you scored low on this test because you cannot do better, or because you need to be more conscientious?" If the answer is the latter, we have unmasked the sloth so it can be taken care of. If the answer is the former, students need to know that everyone is not equally capable of everything. Then the search can begin for that student's greatest capabilities and greatest interests. Self-esteem will come in spades when the student finds those capabilities and interests and begins to build on them. And it will be a more genuine self-esteem than any that can be had from test scores, particularly on a test in which crowds of others have done as well or better.

Involving Students for Your Edification and Theirs

Probably you have taken many tests after which you were hurried on to the next unit of study with little or no discussion of the test results. You may have had questions to ask about some of your answers. You may have had questions to ask about some of the items themselves—about either content or process. You may have wondered where your score fell relative to the rest of the class. But once the test was completed and the grade recorded, the teacher was ready to move on and leave it in the past. A teacher who follows that practice misses a golden learning opportunity for both students and teacher.

I believe firmly that the next class meeting after a test has been graded should be devoted to a class discussion of the test. Preparing for and carrying out such a discussion is more involved for a multiple choice test than for an essay test, but essay test discussions should not be ignored. I will offer advice for both. Discussion of tests given in simpler formats is straightforward.

Discussing the Essay Test

To begin discussion of an essay test, remind students of the scoring process you used, including the measures you took to make the scoring impartial and reliable. Then show the distribution of scores and basic statistics (enlighten them about means, and maybe even standard deviations), and discuss the overall test—strengths and weaknesses—before giving individual results. You might use Microsoft® PowerPoint to display the distribution and statistics, similar to the example shown in Figure 24 (p. 185) relative to a 34-Item Multiple Choice Test. Your willingness to discuss thoroughly and openly the results of your work as the writer and scorer of the test will make students more receptive to discussing their work as takers of the test. Let students know that you see their role and yours as a partnership for learning.

After you have talked about the test in general terms, hand the individual tests back to students. Have their scores written somewhere on the second page so each person has the option of keeping the information confidential. Give students some time to look over the first item and formulate questions, and then open discussion by asking about their initial reaction to the item. Knowing how it struck them will give you some insight into possible problems of content and process. Then invite students to offer their opinions about the information a response should contain, including questions about their responses and your reaction to them. That will open opportunities for you to reinforce important material and debunk misconceptions. Some questions about your scoring may arise. If a legitimate question is asked, one that is on the mind of a large number of students, answer the question and put it to rest if you can. If students have a legitimate point, admit it and make an adjustment (though this should be extremely rare if you have been thorough in your work). If students begin to nitpick about issues not worth class time, ask them to see you privately afterward.

When you have exhausted discussion of the first item, or feel you have given it all the time you can afford, move on to the second item and follow the same steps. After you have discussed the full exam in this way, students will know immeasurably more about the subject matter than if you had not held the discussion. Point out to them that their grades reflect what they knew at the time of the exam—and rightfully so—and that they now know much more. Encourage them to value the learning. Encourage them to invest themselves as thoroughly in class discussions not related to test results, because that will prepare them to be more successful with the next test.

The students will not be the only learners. You will learn much from the discussion. What you learn about their reaction to your test items, and to the responses you expected of them, will help you write ever better tests and templates. You will also learn something about the students themselves—about their thought processes, their attitudes, and their potential. When you encourage them to become diligent about improving their results the next time around, let them know that you will also take what you have learned from the discussion and improve your work—teaching and testing—on their behalf.

You can use essay-test discussions also to reward and motivate good work. Find a few elegant and insightful sentences—the passages that gave you a lift when you were grading the items—and read those passages to the class. Not only will those readings give students well-earned public recognition for good work, but they will give samples of good work to other students and motivate some of them to work at matching those samples. The reading of passages will be particularly rich if you teach a course in which the quality of writing is an integral part of the test.

Discussing the Multiple Choice Test

Unlike essay tests, multiple choice tests leave no room for scoring controversies (unless you have mis-keyed an item). There will be much about the inner-workings of your multiple choice test, however, that students will want to ask about. How did the class do, and where do I fit into that? How do we know the test was fair? What were you trying to accomplish when you wrote the correct response to Item X? How did you come to write the distractors as you did, particularly those that students found most attractive—and exactly what makes them wrong?

Student questions will lead to your telling them about your content taxonomy, your intent for specific items, and other inside information that reveals the thoroughness and thoughtfulness behind the test. If you can open up the test as a whole to students in that way—remove that feeling of a barrier between them and the process—you are likely to dispel misgivings they have and get them focused on the learning itself.

Start by showing and discussing basic information about testing in general and about the test they have just taken. Students will appreciate learning about the standard normal curve, means and standard deviations (theoretical and actual), and even reliability coefficients if you take time to teach how those statistics relate to testing. Not only will you give students passage to important information from which they have felt excluded, but you will show that you are willing to account for your work as test-writer. Figure 24 shows a PowerPoint slide that I used to reveal basic information to students after a test. For students below the college level, the KR 20 reliability coefficient may be more than you want to explain, but I believe students of all ages above the primary grades can understand and appreciate knowing the average score (mean), and secondary school students might be interested in the average difference from the average (standard deviation). Results shown in Figure 24 are from a 34-item test taken by 17 students.

Test Results				
	X	f	Mean	
A	30	1	Theoretical	21.25
	28	1	Obtained	21.71
	26	1		
	25	1	Standard Deviation	
A −	24	2		
	23	2	Theoretical	4.25
B	22	3	Obtained	4.62
	21	2		
C −	16	1	KR Formula 20	.73
D	14	3		

Figure 24. Results for a Multiple Choice Test Having 34, 4-Option Items

When you share such extensive information about tests with students, they appreciate your openness. In teaching college classes, I even distribute copies of the summary sheet from the testing center so they know that nothing is hidden. Over time they develop trust in your commitment to fairness and to their well-being. All of that helps to build a learning partnership between you and them.

After discussing the test in general terms, return the test booklets to students in preparation for discussing each item. I need to digress for a moment here to describe how you might advise students, at the time they take the test, to prepare those test booklets for this discussion. Tell them just before they take the test to put their names on the test booklet, and to indicate on the booklet the responses they have chosen. Suggest that they take the test by circling the letters of the correct responses on the test booklet itself, and then carefully transfer those responses to the bubble sheet. Urge them also to jot down any questions they have about an item while taking the test. Tell them you will return these very test booklets to them when time comes to discuss the test, and you want them to have all the information they need to make the most of the discussion. (You might dispense this information in writing at test time rather than verbally. That will allow students to take in the information quickly and get on with the test whenever they are ready.)

Before the test discussion, prepare student test booklets by writing the score for each test somewhere on the second page. That will allow students to keep their scores confidential if they choose. You will also need to prepare your master copy of the test booklet so all the information you need is readily available. What I do is this: I write the r_{pbs} discrimination coefficient next to each item number, I write the number of students who chose each option next to that option, and I circle the number next to the correct response. Then the items on my master test booklet, as prepared for discussion, look basically like the items shown in Figure 25. Some items will contain elaboration beyond what you see in Figure 25, because I also make notes to prepare myself for potential controversies. The master test booklet becomes my lifeline for test discussion. I write rationale for difficult distractors, arguments for correct responses—anything that might prepare me to handle the discussion well.

For item-by-item discussion with the students, I place the option letters (a, b, c, d) vertically on the board. As we discuss each item, I write the number of students who chose each response and circle the number corresponding to the correct response. Then I proceed, with a combination of lecture and discussion, to reveal fully why each distractor that someone chose is not a viable choice as compared to the correct response. Some items generate discussion. Sometimes during discussion I make notes on my master copy about an improved wording for a stem or an option. The newer the exam, the more likely I am to capitulate and give credit for an item because of a weakness in the test. Still, that is rare in even the newest of tests, and almost unheard of once I have improved a test over several semesters.

.267 1. The principal use of a reliability coefficient by educators is to calculate

   2   a. the appropriateness of a given test for a given population of students.
       b. the extent to which parts of a test duplicate each other in function.
   ⑨   c. the extent to which consistent results can be expected from a test over time.
   5   d. the extent to which a variety of professional agree upon the quality of the test.

−.146 2. The most accurate description of the relationship between measurement and evaluation is that

   1   a. measurement may endanger educational processes, but evaluation will not.
   ⑩   b. the validity of evaluation in education is generally increased by the concurrent use of measurement.
   4   c. formulac are very important to measurement but only marginally important to evaluation.
   1   d. measurement may either precede or follow evaluation, but evaluation can be used in only one way.

Figure 25. The Look of Items in a Master Test Booklet
Prepared for Discussion

The gains to be had from discussing multiple choice test results with students in this way are numerous and powerful:

1. Students leave that class session knowing the correct response to every test item, and knowing why incorrect responses are incorrect. That is, students know everything you would have wanted them to know to score 100%.

2. Students know that in addition to examining their knowledge, you have examined your teaching and the test itself. That sense of fair play nourishes both their attitude and their motivation.

3. Students improve their thinking skills by having been taken through your thought processes as the teacher.

4. You learn what content needs to be taught better and which test items need revision. That enables you to constantly improve both your teaching and your test writing.

5. A spirit of cooperation grows between you and the students—a sense that you and they are engaged in a partnership for learning, and that they are the recipients.

I have come to see test discussion as indispensable. Those class sessions, without question, have been the richest learning experiences the students and I have had together. I give my final exams on the last day of class and reserve the scheduled exam time for discussion. Students never have to walk away from an exam with unanswered questions. (Note: Be sure no one walks away with the exam booklet. Unless you retrieve all the exams after the discussion, the items you worked so diligently to construct will become public domain!)

Despite these gains, you may think of such an open test discussion with students as risky and harrowing. It can be; outstanding gains usually entail an element of risk. Still, you will gain more respect from students by admitting you are fallible than by pretending you are not. More important, your willingness to subject yourself, your tests, and your teaching to such scrutiny the first year will improve your teaching and testing the second—and still more the third, etc. If you are serious about your profession, you will not want to pass up an opportunity to climb that ladder. Finally, the ultimate payoff comes a few years down the road, after your experiences at teaching, test-writing, and test discussions have elevated your overall proficiency and confidence to such a level that you look forward to test discussions and enjoy them. By then you will have built a window through which you can see your own work clearly—a window that cannot be built without the help of student insight over time.

Two Parting Thoughts About Knowledge Testing

Using Parts to Make a Whole

Assume that for a given class you administer a mid-term exam and a final exam using essay format, multiple choice format, or one of each. Assume that you have crafted and administered those exams so that they are high in content validity and process validity, you have honed them to the point that each yields a high reliability coefficient, your item difficulty is well distributed, your array of discrimination coefficients is strong, and your discussions of exam results with students have shown the tests to be valuable learning tools. Assume also that you administer four to eight quizzes along the way, using any combination of short answer, matching, and true/false formats. Each of those quizzes is likely to be low in reliability as compared to the exams, due in part to their being short and in part to your having designed them more as information inventories than as carefully crafted exams.

If you combine the results of all the quizzes into one composite distribution of scores, however, that composite distribution is likely to show much higher reliability than will a score distribution from any one individual quiz. A general explanation is that the mass of the whole, being four to eight times greater than any individual quiz, raises reliability. A more specific explanation for the salubrious effect of that mass is that it cancels out some of the random weaknesses inherent in the individual quizzes. Those weaknesses may have played out in some students' favor with one quiz and other students' favor with another quiz. The distribution of chance occurrences along the lines of the standard normal curve tends to wash out such advantages and dis-advantages. By thus using the parts to make a whole, you can create an additional distribution of grades whose reliability is likely to approach that of your mid-term and final exams.

Keeping Your Eye on the Prize

The ultimate prize in your sights should be success at fulfilling your overarching responsibility as a teacher: to help students prepare themselves for life as adults. They will not solve adult problems with scattered facts. They will be required to think. As a teacher, you should do all you can to convince your students that thinking their way through life is important, and you should reinforce that principle by presenting them with circumstances that require them to exercise and improve thinking skills. The tests you give can be a powerful tool by which to accomplish that. Test students in a way that encourages them to use more than short-term, memorized facts. Once they can memorize, push them to recognize (examine a range of familiar possibilities and decide which is the best means of solving a problem). Once they can recognize, push them to identify (compare and contrast the unfamiliar with the familiar as a way of "figuring out" what the unfamiliar is and how it might be used). In short, prompt them to rummage through their mental reservoirs of information, insight, and experiences in search of food for thought. As adults they will be required to do exactly that to thrive. Embrace testing for its potential to help you prepare them for that transition.

Terms Important to This Chapter

shortcut (121): an appropriate way to think of a test, because the information any test is designed to probe is greater than it can probe comprehensively.

short answer format (123): a testing format that has students either complete or respond to a statement by writing a word or a few words in a designated space.

matching format (124): a testing format that has students pair items to show recognition of a logical basis for association.

true/false format (126): a testing format that, in its pure form, has students simply identify statements as either true or false.

true/false alternative response (127): a variation on the pure true/false format that gives students such enhanced tasks as identifying the reasoning behind a true statement or repairing a false statement.

pure essay format (129): an essay test for which the test-taker is expected to write narrative responses, using complete sentences and paragraphs.

constructed response format (129): a content-centered variation of the essay test that gives test-takers greater freedom of response, e.g., the writing of outlines, lists, etc.

extended response item (129): an essay item that solicits a broad survey of thought.

restricted response item (129): an essay item that solicits specific, content-related information.

grading on the curve (136): assigning grades not on the basis of percentage correct, but by taking into account obtained grades, i.e., responding to the reality of the standard normal curve.

item (138): the term applied to each entry in a test, particularly a multiple choice test.

stem (138): the opening partial statement or question of a multiple choice item.

option (138): each of the four or five potential responses that follows the stem of a multiple choice item.

correct response (138): the option keyed by the test writer as correct in a multiple choice test.

distractor or foil (138): an option not keyed by the test writer as correct in a multiple choice test.

test booklet (138): the complete collection of multiple choice test items used by test-takers.

response sheet (138): the sheet on which multiple choice test-takers indicate their responses, generally by filling in a "bubble" with a pencil.

key (138): a response sheet on which the multiple choice test-writer indicates all correct responses; the response sheet against which student sheets are compared during the scoring process.

discrimination item (138): a multiple choice test item requiring test-takers to use low levels of thought to indicate their acquisition of a piece of information by discriminating among the pieces of information shown in the options.

inference item (138): a multiple choice test item requiring test-takers to apply high levels of thought, using combinations of information and insight to identify, by inference, the option that is the strongest response. (Ironically, the greater complexity makes inference items more discriminating than discrimination items.)

item analysis (154): analysis of individual items within a multiple choice test after it has been given, the purpose being to learn each item's level of difficulty and power to discriminate between students who know most and students who know least.

item difficulty (154): one of the two components of item analysis; a simple calculation of the percentage of students who answered a given item correctly, actually making the value obtained an indication of item easiness rather than item difficulty.

item discrimination (155): one of the two components of item analysis; a calculation of the relationship between student success for a given item and student success for the test as a whole, showing the extent to which the item analyzed contributes to the objective of the test, i.e., to discriminating between students who know most and students who know least.

discrimination value (155): a term that refers to an item's discrimination power, as expressed by a discrimination coefficient.

discrimination coefficient (156): a term that refers to the coefficient yielded by analysis of an item's discrimination power.

positively discriminating item (157): a multiple choice test item for which correct responses come more from students who do well on the overall test than from students who do poorly on the overall test.

negatively discriminating item (157): a multiple choice test item for which correct responses come more from students who do poorly on the overall test than from students who do well on the overall test.

point biserial correlation (160): a type of correlation procedure that estimates the relationship between a dichotomous variable and a distribution of scores.

dichotomous variable (160): an either/or variable, having only two possible values, e.g., male/female, correct/incorrect.

reliability coefficient (162): any correlation coefficient calculated as an estimate of reliability.

coefficient of stability (162): specific name used to describe a reliability coefficient estimated by comparing a first administration with a second administration of the same test.

split halves reliability (163): an alternative to test-retest reliability, whereby the test is given only one time and its reliability is estimated by comparing results from one half of the test with results from the other half.

coefficient of internal consistency (163): specific name used to describe a reliability coefficient estimated by use of the split halves process.

Kuder-Richardson Formula 20, or KR 20 (163): a computer formula that avoids the split halves problem of balancing for difficulty and content by calculating all possible split halves combinations and yielding an average.

Spearman/Brown Prophesy Formula (163): a computer formula applied to the KR 20 result to correct it for length, i.e., return the number of items to the reality of the test after having reduced that number by half to calculate internal consistency.

criterion measure (164): a benchmark that represents comprehensively the achievement a test is designed to measure, and therefore is worthy of serving as a standard against which test results can be compared.

concurrent validity (166): test validity estimated objectively by comparison with a criterion measure, providing that the test and the criterion measure were administered within a close enough time frame to consider the two events concurrent, and the subjects therefore essentially unchanged.

chance score (168): the score that one can statistically be expected to score on a multiple choice test through guessing alone.

References

Gordon, Edwin E. (1965). *Musical Aptitude Profile.* Boston: Houghton Mifflin.

——— (1979). *Primary Measures of Music Audiation.* Chicago, GIA Publications.

——— (1982). *Intermediate Measures of Music Audiation.* Chicago, GIA Publications.

——— (1986). *The Nature, Description, Measurement, and Evaluation of Music Aptitudes.* Chicago: GIA Publications.

——— (1989). *Advanced Measures of Music Audiation.* Chicago, GIA Publications.

——— (1989). *Audie.* Chicago, GIA Publications.

Lederer, Richard (1991). *The Miracle of Language.* New York: Pocket Books

McLeish, John (1972). *Seventh Mental Measurements Yearbook*, Vol.1, ed. Oscar Buros. Highland Park, NJ: Gryphon Press.

Seashore, Carl E. (1919). *Seashore Measures of Musical Talent.* New York: Columbia Phonograph Company.

Walters, Darrel (1991). "Edwin Gordon's Music Aptitude Work." *The Quarterly* Vol. II, Nos. 1 & 2. Greeley, Colorado: School of Music of the University of Northern Colorado.

——— (2010). *Write Well Now: Six Keys to Greater Clarity, 2nd Edition..* Ft. Washington, PA: Revisionary, Inc.

Glossary

additive rating scale (79): a five-point check list used to measure a dimension of performance not suited to a continuous rating scale; the score is expressed simply as the number of criteria satisfied by the performance.

analytic rubric (102): a rating-scale-based tool used to measure separate dimensions of a performance, but not necessarily through separate observations—as with the traditional rating scale approach.

assessment (3): the attaching of a value to something by use of measurement, evaluation, or both.

asymmetrical (26): a general term to describe any distribution whose shape is not symmetrical.

bi-modal (30): a term that describes the shape of a distribution as having dual points at which the frequency of scores tends to peak.

case (24): any particular score within a distribution of scores.

central tendency (28): one of the three principal ways to describe a distribution of scores (the others being shape and variability); central tendency, which answers the question "on the whole, how did they score?" describes the distribution's typicality mathematically by use of the mean (arithmetic average), or relatively by use of the median (central score) or the mode (most frequently occurring score). The mean, as the staple of central tendency, is entered into further calculations

chance score (168): the score that one can statistically be expected to score on a multiple choice test through guessing alone.

checklist (71): a list of criteria for performance that can be answered by "yes" or "no; during assessment, the criteria met are checked and the criteria unmet are left blank.

coefficient of determination (49): a value equal to the correlation coefficient squared (r^2), and representing the percentage of common ground between the correlated variables. Another perspective on r^2 is to think of it as the percentage of one variable that can be explained by the presence of the other.

coefficient of internal consistency (163): specific name used to describe a reliability coefficient estimated by use of the split halves process.

coefficient of stability (162): specific name used to describe a reliability coefficient estimated by comparing a first administration with a second administration of the same test.

concurrent validity (166): test validity estimated objectively by comparison with a criterion measure, providing that the test and the criterion measure were administered within a close enough time frame to consider the two events concurrent, and the subjects therefore essentially unchanged.

constructed response format (129): a content-centered variation of the essay test that gives test takers greater freedom of response, e.g., the writing of outlines, lists, etc.

content validity (12): a subset of subjective validity; the extent to which the content of a test is congruent with the content taught, and in proportion to the emphasis given to one part of the content over another.

continuous rating scale (75): a specific type of rating scale designed as a continuum of achievement that requires students to pass through lower levels on their way to achieving higher levels, with the level achieved constituting the score.

correct response (138): the option keyed by the test-writer as correct in a multiple choice test.

correlation (42): the type (positive or negative) and degree of relationship between two variables.

correlation coefficient (44): the number that identifies numerically the correlation (relationship) between two variables, expressed as a coefficient that varies from –1.00 (a perfect negative relationship) to 1.00 (a perfect positive relationship), with a mid-point of 0 (no relationship).

criteria (71): standards against which something being judged is compared.

criterion (71): singular form of the term *criteria*.

criterion measure (164): a benchmark that represents comprehensively the achievement a test is designed to measure, and therefore is worthy of serving as a standard against which test results can be compared.

criterion-referenced (13): a test whose results are interpreted relative to the number of test items answered correctly, without reference to the success of other test-takers.

curvilinear relationship (49): a relationship that conforms to (moves in, describes) a curved line, e.g., the relationship between time and physical development for living things, which evolve from weak to strong to weak.

deviation score (32): a given score minus the mean of the distribution within which it lies, causing the deviation score for each person who scores above the mean to be a positive number and the deviation score for each person who scores below the mean to be a negative number.

dichotomous variable (160): an either/or variable, having only two possible values, e.g., male/female, correct/incorrect.

dimension (74): a category of achievement measured by use of a list of criteria; a dimension might be rhythm accuracy, pitch accuracy, tone quality, intonation, expressiveness, etc.

discrimination coefficient (156): a term that refers to the coefficient yielded by analysis of an item's discrimination power.

discrimination item (138): a multiple choice test item requiring test-takers to use low levels of thought to indicate their acquisition of a piece of information by discriminating among the pieces of information shown in the options.

discrimination value (155): a term that refers to an item's discrimination power, as expressed by a discrimination coefficient.

distractor or *foil (138):* an option not keyed by the test-writer as correct in a multiple choice test.

distribution (24): a term used to describe an array of scores obtained from testing a group of persons, the logic being that an array of scores can be thought of as being "distributed" from highest to lowest, or "distributed" around a central point (mean).

essay format, pure (129): an essay test for which the test-taker is expected to write narrative responses, using complete sentences and paragraphs.

evaluation (3): a subjective process that yields a judgment, as in deciding what grade to award or who should sit ahead of whom in an ensemble; evaluation gains effectiveness when based on information generated by a reliable, valid measurement tool.

extended response item (129): an essay item that solicits a broad survey of thought.

extreme score (27): a score so unusually high or unusually low as compared with the body of scores that it skews the distribution in its direction.

foil or *distractor (138):* an option not keyed by the test writer as correct in a multiple choice test.

formative evaluation (4): evaluation aimed at guiding the next instructional step, i.e., contributing to the formative process by which one improves musicianship.

frequency distribution (25): a method of displaying a distribution of scores compactly by showing the number of times each repeated score appears rather than listing every individual case regardless of repetitions.

frequency polygon (27): a graph created by placing frequencies on the vertical axis and scores on the horizontal axis, and then placing a point at each intersection of score with frequency to create a graph that shows the shape of the distribution.

Gaussian distribution (22): a synonym for "standard normal distribution," so named because of its association with nineteenth-century mathematician Carl Frederick Gauss.

grading on the curve (136): assigning grades not on the basis of percentage correct, but by taking into account obtained grades, i.e., responding to the reality of the standard normal curve.

halo effect (87): the effect that knowledge of a person's previous achievement has in biasing one's assessment of current achievement.

holistic rubric (102): a rubric in which levels are collapsed, allowing the assessor to ignore the assessment of separate dimensions in favor of quickly producing a single value that represents the quality of the overall performance.

inference item (138): a multiple choice test item requiring test-takers to apply high levels of thought, using combinations of information and insight to identify, by inference, the option that is the strongest response. (Ironically, the greater complexity makes inference items more discriminating than discrimination items.)

instruction (2): a term used in this book to represent a process that encompasses both teaching and learning.

intercorrelations (91): correlations between the dimensions of a multi-dimensional rating scale used to assess performance skills of a given set of students.

inter-quartile range (31): an infrequently used statistic showing the range of the two middle quartiles of a distribution, designed specifically to blunt the effect of extreme scores that can make the range of a distribution a volatile statistic.

inter-rater reliability (99): an estimate of the reliability of a measurement instrument made by calculating the correlation between the ratings of two persons who used the same rating scale independently to rate the same set of performances.

item (138): the term applied to each entry in a test, particularly a multiple choice test.

item analysis (154): analysis of individual items within a multiple choice test after it has been given, the purpose being to learn each item's level of difficulty and power to discriminate between students who know most and students who know least.

item difficulty (154): one of the two components of item analysis; a simple calculation of the percentage of students who answered a given item correctly, actually making the value obtained an indication of item easiness rather than item difficulty.

item discrimination (155): one of the two components of item analysis; a calculation of the relationship between student success for a given item and student success for the test as a whole, showing the extent to which the item analyzed contributes to the objective of the test, i.e., to discriminating between students who know most and students who know least.

key (138): a response sheet on which the multiple choice test-writer indicates all correct responses; the response sheet against which student sheets are compared during the scoring process.

knowledge tests (17): tests designed to measure what a person knows and understands (described fully in Chapter Six).

Kuder-Richardson Formula 20, or *KR 20 (163):* a computer formula that avoids the split halves problem of balancing for difficulty and content by calculating all possible split halves combinations and yielding an average.

kurtosis (27): a measure of the relative peakedness or flatness of the curve described by a distribution of scores.

leptokurtic (27): label given the shape of a distribution whose kurtosis has it stretched vertically, producing a peaked shape as compared to that of the standard normal distribution (less-than-normal variability).

Likert scale (72): a response scale used commonly in survey research to solicit levels of agreement or disagreement.

linear relationship (48): a relationship that conforms to (moves in, describes) a straight line, e.g., the relationship between speed and distance of a moving body.

matching format (124): a testing format that has students pair items to show recognition of a logical basis for association.

McCall T (41): the transformed standard score most widely used, particularly in norms tables of standardized tests; based on a mean of 50 and a standard deviation of 10.

mean (29): the arithmetic average of a distribution of scores, which theoretically coincides with the crown of the bell curve; the point around which frequencies tend to gather in large numbers, and away from which frequencies tend to diminish with greater distance in either direction.

measurement (3): an objective process that yields specific information, as in the measurement of a room; educational measurement, accomplished through testing, is necessarily less precise than physical measurement because of the unpredictability of human behavior and the imprecision of even well-constructed tests as compared to physical devises such as tape measures.

median (29): the mid-point of a distribution of scores, without regard for arithmetic value; the median thus eludes the influence of extreme scores.

mesokurtic (27): label given the shape of a distribution whose kurtosis has it approximate the kurtosis of the standard normal distribution.

mode (30): the most frequently occurring score in a distribution.

music achievement (5): the music learning that one can demonstrate as having been acquired.

music aptitude (5): one's potential to learn music; music aptitude is to music learning as IQ is to academic learning.

negatively discriminating item (157): a multiple choice test item for which correct responses come more from students who do poorly on the overall test than from students who do well on the overall test.

normal distribution (28): a nickname used commonly to describe a distribution that approximates the standard normal distribution, a.k.a. bell curve.

norm-referenced (13): a test whose results are interpreted relative to the success rate of other test-takers, without reference to the number of test items answered correctly.

objective validity (12): process for estimating the validity of a test by administering it and a criterion measure (a more comprehensive and trustworthy measure of the same trait the test measures) to the same population, and then calculating the relationship between the test and the criterion measure; used primarily to validate published, standardized tests.

one-dimensional rating scale (75): a rating scale designed to measure only one dimension of achievement, as compared to a multi-dimensional rating scale that might be designed to measure two, three, or more dimensions of achievement.

option (138): each of the four or five potential responses that follows the stem of a multiple choice item.

outlier (27): a term used commonly as a synonym for *extreme score*.

Pearson product moment correlation, Pearson correlation, Pearson r (48): several labels for the most common among several types of correlation statistics, used to estimate the relationship between two distributions of scores.

percentage correct (35): the percentage of the measurement tool's items that a given person answered correctly, e.g., 90 percent 86 percent.

percentile rank (36): the percentage of the larger population of scores (perhaps national norms) that are equal to or lesser than a given person's score, e.g., "her score is at the 74th percentile rank."

performance tests (17): tests designed to measure what a person can do(described fully in Chapters Four and Five).

pilot study (76): use of a measurement tool such as a rating scale with a test group to identify strengths and weaknesses of the tool, revise it as needed, and establish guidelines for its use.

platykurtic (27): label given the shape of a distribution whose kurtosis has it stretched horizontally, producing a flat shape as compared to that of the standard normal distribution (greater-than-normal variability).

point biserial correlation (160): a type of correlation procedure that estimates the relationship between a dichotomous variable and a distribution of scores.

positively discriminating item (157): a multiple choice test item for which correct responses come more from students who do well on the overall test than from students who do poorly on the overall test.

predict (43): this very common word is included here for an opportunity to emphasize the power of a strong correlation; the stronger the relationship (correlation) between two variables, the greater is the power to predict one from knowing the other.

process validity (13): a subset of subjective validity; the extent to which hurdles have been removed from the administration of the test so that students are being tested on content alone rather than on extraneous challenges such as interpreting poorly written items, losing a visual or aural advantage due to placement in the room, suffering distraction due to conditions in or around the testing area, or any other irregularities that might affect the test's outcome beyond knowledge of content.

quasi-validity (99): a term sometimes applied to inter-rater reliability, because agreement between two persons increases the chance that the scale is measuring what it was intended to measure.

range (31): the span of scores in a distribution from highest to lowest.

rank (35): placement of a given person's score relative to the scores of others in a particular group measured by the same measurement tool, e.g., first, second, etc.

rate-rerate reliability (88): a term that describes more accurately (as compared to *test-retest*) the process of estimating reliability for a rating scale, because the two measurements correlated are not of separate events, but rather two independent ratings of the same event by the same person.

rating scale (73): a scale consisting of a list of criteria that describe in a concise, specific way the levels of achievement a teacher might identify in a performance.

raw score (35): simply the number of items from a measurement tool that a given person answered correctly.

reliability (9): the consistency with which something is accomplished; dependability.

reliability coefficient (162): any correlation coefficient calculated as an estimate of reliability.

renegade score (27): a term used less commonly as a synonym for *extreme score.*

response sheet (138): the sheet on which multiple choice test-takers indicate their responses, generally by filling in a "bubble" with a pencil.

restricted response item (129): an essay item that solicits specific, content-related information.

rubric (100): a term adopted by educators to describe an assessment tool based on rating scale principles and used to measure degrees of performance quality (see also *analytic rubric* and *holistic rubric*).

scattergram, scatterplot (47): a graphic illustration of the relationship between two variables, generally shown with values from one variable displayed on the vertical axis and values from the other variable displayed on the horizontal axis. If values are omitted, showing only a visual representation of the relationship, the term *scatterplot* is more precise than the term *scattergram*

shape (26): one of the three principal ways to describe a distribution of scores (the others being central tendency and variability); the symmetrical, bell-shaped standard normal distribution is the standard against which other shapes are compared.

short answer format (123): a testing format that has students either complete or respond to a statement by writing a word or a few words in a designated space.

shortcut (121): an appropriate way to think of a test, because the information any test is designed to probe is greater than it can probe comprehensively.

shortcut assessment (70): assessment by a process lacking the thoroughness of systematic assessment, but justifiable in many circumstances; quality is heavily dependent on the assessor's teaching experience and previous experience with systematic assessment.

skewed (26): pulled out of shape; the property of a distribution that is asymmetrical.

skewed to the left, or *negatively skewed (26):* the specific description of a distribution whose asymmetrical shape is caused by extreme scores at the low end of the distribution pulling the mean (arithmetic average) below the median (mid-point) of the distribution.

skewed to the right, or *positively skewed (26):* the specific description of a distribution whose asymmetrical shape is caused by extreme scores at the high end of the distribution pulling the mean (arithmetic average) above the median (mid-point) of the distribution.

Spearman/Brown Prophesy Formula (163): a computer formula applied to the KR 20 result to correct it for length, i.e., return the number of items to the reality of the test after having reduced that number by half to calculate internal consistency.

split halves reliability (163): an alternative to test-retest reliability, whereby the test is given only one time and its reliability is estimated by comparing results from one half of the test with results from the other half.

standard deviation (32): the average distance (roughly speaking, though not precisely so mathematically) that cases within a distribution of scores vary from the mean; a key benchmark within the theory of the standard normal distribution.

standard normal distribution (bell curve) (21): a model that shows the way in which variables of all kinds—animate and inanimate, human and non-human, physical and behavioral—tend to be distributed from one extreme to another, with a gathering of greatest frequencies around the center point.

standard score (39): an expression of an individual score relative to the standard normal curve.

stem (138): the opening partial statement or question of a multiple choice item.

subjective validity (12): process for increasing the validity of a test by making sound judgments about its content and the process for administering it, thus keeping test-takers free of impediments other than those related to content; involves no statistical value.

summative evaluation (4): evaluation aimed at summarizing a segment of achievement, i.e., generating a grade or some other symbol of what has been accomplished.

symmetrical (26): the shape of a distribution whose mean, median, and mode coincide, and whose upper half (distribution of scores above the mean) is a mirror image of its lower half (distribution of scores below the mean).

systematic assessment (70): assessment using a planned, practiced, systematic approach that produces a written record and is high in subjective validity (content and process) and reliability.

systematic observation (74): a key tool of systematic assessment.

tally sheet (88): a form designed to hold results of an assessment and its subsequent statistics for convenient referral.

test booklet (138): the complete collection of multiple choice test items used by test-takers.

test-retest reliability (11): process of administering a test twice within a short period of time (2–7 days), and then estimating reliability by calculating the correlation between the two distributions of scores (first and second administration); as applied to performance testing, the process is one of rate-rerate, with the same rater generating two ratings of the same performance and calculating the correlation between the two resulting distributions.

theoretical constructs (94): theoretical benchmarks of a measurement tool based on the theory of the standard normal curve, benchmarks that can be compared to obtained statistics to judge the typicality of those obtained statistics.

theoretical mean (94): a benchmark mean, which will be approximated by administering a well-designed, well-administered measurement tool to a normally distributed sample.

theoretical standard deviation (94): a benchmark standard deviation, which will be approximated by administering a well-designed, well-administered measurement tool to a normally distributed sample.

transformed z score (40): a standard score transformed from the z value to a more readable form whose values are all positive by inserting the standard deviation and mean of choice into this transformation formula $z' = z\,(\overline{SD}) + X$.

true/false format (126): a testing format that, in its pure form, has students simply identify statements as either true or false.

true/false alternative response (127): a variation on the pure true/false format that gives students such enhanced tasks as identifying the reasoning behind a true statement or repairing a false statement.

validity (9): the extent to which something is accomplished as intended; accuracy.

variable (42): anything that can be measured and is subject to change from one group of subjects to another or from one time to another; the opposite of a constant.

variability (31): one of the three principal ways to describe a distribution of scores (the others being shape and mean); variability, which answers the question "how wide are the differences among the scores?" is described by the range (top score minus bottom score), the inter-quartile range (not practical for you as a teacher), or the standard deviation (roughly, the average number of score points away from the mean). The standard deviation, as the staple of variability, is entered into further calculations. (Another expression of variability, the variance—standard deviation squared—is also impractical for you as a teacher.)

z score (39): the most basic of standard scores, corresponding directly to the standard deviation units of the standard normal curve, with a mean of 0 and a standard deviation of 1.

Appendix A:

A Collection of the Formulas Presented in This Book

Many of these formulas can be written in alternate ways. Use whatever symbols are comfortable for you so long as the result is the same.

Chapter Two

Mean of a Distribution of Scores, p. 29

$$\bar{X} = \frac{\sum X}{N}$$

Standard Deviation of a Distribution of Scores, p. 33

$$SD = \sqrt{\frac{\sum (X-\bar{X})^2}{N-1}}$$

Percentile Rank of a Score Within a Distribution of Scores, p. 36

$$PR = \frac{N<X + .5(N \text{ at } X)}{N} \ (\text{x } 100)$$

Standard Score (z), p. 39.

$$z = \frac{X-\bar{X}}{SD}$$

Transformed Standard Score, p. 40

$$z' = z\,(SD) + \bar{X}$$

Correlation Coefficient, p. 44

$$r = \frac{[\sum (X-\bar{X})\,(Y-\bar{Y})]}{\sqrt{\sum (X-\bar{X})^2 * \sum (Y-\bar{Y})^2}}$$

Chapter Four

Theoretical Mean of a Five-Point Rating Scale, p. 95.

$$\bar{X}_{THEO} = \frac{\sum \text{Potential Ratings}}{N \text{ Potential Ratings}}$$

Theoretical Standard Deviation of a Five-Point Rating Scale, p. 96.

$$SD_{THEO} = \frac{\text{Top Score} - \bar{X}_{THEO}}{3}$$

Chapter Six

Difficulty of a Multiple Choice Item, p. 154.

$$\text{Difficulty} = \frac{\text{No. of Correct Responses}}{\text{No. of Test-takers}}$$

Discrimination Value of a Multiple Choice Item, p. 156.

$$\text{Discrimination} = \frac{\text{No. UH Correct Responses} - \text{No. LH Correct Responses}}{.5\,(N)}$$

Chance Score of a Multiple Choice Test, p. 169.

$$\text{Chance} = \frac{\text{No. of Items}}{\text{No. of Options}}$$

Theoretical Mean of a Multiple Choice Test, p. 169.

$$\overline{X}_{\text{THEO}} = \frac{\text{No. Items} - \text{Chance}}{2} + \text{Chance}$$

Theoretical Standard Deviation of a Multiple Choice Test, p. 170.

$$SD_{\text{THEO}} = \frac{\text{No. Items} - \overline{X}_{\text{THEO}}}{3}$$

Appendix B:

PowerPoint Narrations

To Users of This Text and CD

Inside the back cover of this book is a CD that contains PowerPoint sessions related to specific pages of the book. This appendix contains a series of narratives meant to help you get the most from viewing those PowerPoint sessions.

These narratives contain roughly the information you are likely to have heard from your instructor at the time the PowerPoint slides were shown to you as part of a class lecture. You may find that you can review some of the PowerPoint sessions efficiently without narrative help, either because you recall with some precision what your instructor said, or because the PowerPoint is self-explanatory. When that is not the case—when a particular PowerPoint session presents details and complexities that you need explained—turn in this appendix to the narrative for that presentation and follow it as you advance the slides.

Note: dots (•) indicate slide advance.

---

1. Music Aptitude, Chapter 1, pages 5-9

The primary aim of this course is to prepare you to assess your students' achievement, but it's also important for you to know something about their potential to learn. • That's where measures of music aptitude come in. • You'll find this information elaborated on in Chapter One of the textbook, on pages 5 through 9.•

The principal writer of music aptitude tests recognized as valid today is Edwin Gordon. Gordon published • the Musical Aptitude Profile (MAP) • in 1965 for students in grades • 4 through 12. He tried to get reliability with MAP for younger children, but couldn't. Eventually he formed his theory of stabilized and developmental aptitude, MAP being a measure of stabilized aptitude. • He theorized that the potential to learn is still being formed during the early years of a child's life. It's volatile, meaning that it can be influenced by instruction and other musical experiences. • In 1979 • he published the Primary Measures of Music Audiation (PMMA) • for children in grades • kindergarten through third. After several users of PMMA took children's strengths and weaknesses into account in their music instruction in response to PMMA scores, the volatility of developmental aptitude showed itself in improved scores on subsequent testing. When it became apparent that children from rich musical environments would blow the top off from the PMMA well before they reached grade three, Gordon wrote a more rigorous version of the test. He published that version • as the Intermediate Measures of Music Audiation • in 1982, and normed it for children in Grades • one through four.

• At this point, let's take a closer look at the period of a child's life during which • Gordon theorizes that aptitude is still developing. From conception • to birth • some level of music aptitude is developing in the fetus, • a level that varies genetically from one person to another. The theory says that from the moment of birth, aptitude naturally begins to decline to the extent that it's not reinforced by rich musical experiences. In other words, music aptitude, if the child is left to his own resources, will not hold up over the years at the level seen at birth, • as pictured here. Instead, • as the years go by, aptitude will need to be propped up by rich musical experiences. According to Gordon, we have about nine years • during which we can influence the level at which aptitude will stabilize. • And the richest time for us to do that work is the time closest to birth. As the window closes • the influence we have lessens until it disappears altogether. What's left after that is a container for music achievement that's set to a particular size, and the larger the container the easier and faster the learning. Theoretically, no one will be able to retain 100% of the inborn potential • but rather the amount retained will depend on the richness of the musical environment. A rich musical environment may allow this much • to be retained, a less-enriched environment this much • and a relatively impoverished musical environment only this much.. • That makes early music experiences very important.

• Seeing the importance of an early assessment of a child's potential to learn music, in 1989 Gordon developed an aptitude measure for young children. • *Audie* is given aurally to young children individually, • • and takes just a few minutes. That same year, Gordon expanded the age level of his music aptitude tests the other direction • with the *Advanced Measures of Music Audiation* for • • post–high-school students.

• Let's think for a minute about how aptitude tests and achievement tests relate to each other. • A music aptitude test • • is designed to measure potential for learning music. • A music achievement test • • is designed to measure what has been learned. How do you suppose scores on the two would relate? You'd expect the two to be related, but how strong will the relationship be? Because you use the aptitude test to get baseline information, and then use achievement tests at intervals during instruction, • • time is going to elapse between the two tests. What effect will that have? • Intervening factors are going to affect individual students in different ways. They'll differ in • their musical environments, • in the music instruction they receive, and • in personal ways that include the extent of their interest in music. • All these intervening factors • will make the relationship between aptitude scores and achievement scores a bit less predictable than you might expect. After you've learned about specific statistical processes used to analyze relationships, you'll see how that predictability can be quantified. •

2. Reliability and Validity, Chapter 1, pages 9-13

So now that we've defined reliability and validity, • let's take a graphic look at how they relate. • You'll find this information elaborated on in Chapter One of the textbook, on pages 9 through 13. • We'll use three targets • • • to make a physical depiction of reliability and validity. These six shots aimed at the first target • • • • • • show consistency, which we said is the definition of reliability. This shooting is reliable • because we can rely on the person doing the shooting to put the shots consistently in one particular place. Assuming that the goal is to hit the bulls eye, though, the shooting isn't accurate. Since accuracy—doing something as it's intended to be done—is the definition of validity, we need the shooting you see in the second target • • • • • • to achieve validity. • What do we have in the second target along with validity? Reliability, • because validity isn't possible in the absence of reliability. If the shots were sprayed around the target • • • • • • without the consistency you see in the first two targets, • you'd have neither reliability nor validity. This physical example of reliability and validity will transfer well to our later conversations about reliability and validity relative to test results. •

3. The Standard Normal Curve, Chapter 2, pages 21-24

The best answer to the question "What is normal?" • is given by the theory of the Standard Normal Curve • described in the textbook on pages 21 through 24. • What's been discovered over time is that for any variable we measure, • whether it's a physical variable like rainfall or crop growth, or a human variable like aptitude or achievement, the results across the larger population are distributed symmetrically • according to the proportions of a bell-shaped curve called the Standard Normal Curve. Whatever the collection of quantities is, it has a mathematical average called the "mean." • That's represented on the curve by a zero, because we'll be thinking of variability above the mean as positive and below the mean as negative. It also has a standard deviation, which we'll learn more about very soon. For now, think of the standard deviation as roughly the average distance from the mean among all the quantities measured. • The numbers along the base of the curve show the distance in standard deviation units that a particular score might lie away from the mean. • Notice that they also run to the negative side to accommodate scores that lie below the mean. • If I segment the curve at the standard deviation points • • • • I can show you the theory of the curve, which is that whatever variable is measured among a whole population, • about 34% of the population will fall between the mean and one standard deviation above the mean, • about 34% between the mean and one standard deviation below, • about 13.5% between one and two standard deviations above, • about 13.5% between one and two standard deviations below, • about 2% between two and three standard deviations above, • and about 2% between two and three standard deviations below. In other words, we live in a symmetrical world, with the greatest number of occurrences gathered around the mean and with the decrease of numbers away from the mean occurring symmetrically in both directions. Now, • what percentage of the population do you see represented there between three standard deviations each side of the mean? • (99%). So for whatever we measure among a large population of occurrences, we can expect 99% of the cases to fall within three standard deviations of the mean either direction. Where is the other 1%? • They're the exceptional cases that lie beyond three standard deviation units either direction. • Up here we have Einstein's IQ and Mozart's music aptitude. • Down here we have persons so mentally impaired that they have to be institutionalized. Within that 99%, • • 95% will fall within two standard deviation of the mean either direction, • • and 68% will fall within one standard deviation either direction. These percentages are worth memorizing because of the fundamental importance of the bell curve to measurement. •

4. Describing Distributions, Chapter 2, pages 24-34

• The next three sessions, beginning with this one, will amount to a mini-statistics course. Think of these statistics sessions as filling a toolbox with tools that you'll need for the rest of the semester.

Whenever you measure learning for a group of students you'll end up with a list of scores from highest to lowest. • In this session we'll be exploring ways to make sense of that list of scores — ways to describe it. • You'll find this information elaborated on in Chapter Two of the textbook, on pages 24 through 34.

• Here's a list of students who took a test. • In statistical terms, each of them is called a case. • Here are their scores. This set of scores is called a distribution of scores, because they're distributed from highest to lowest. They're also said to be distributed around the mean. We need to give each distribution a name so we can refer to it. • So we'll call this distribution X. • let's also put up a distribution Y • so we have two distributions to work with. These distributions are purposely small to make them easier to use, but you're more likely to have 25 or 30 cases, and sometimes a lot more.

Long distributions are cumbersome to list as individual cases, • so sometimes scores are put into a frequency distribution. • There's a column for the individual scores without showing repeated scores, • • another column that shows how many times each score appears in the distribution, • —the f represents *frequency*— • • a column for cumulative frequency, and • • a column for cumulative percentage. Let's look at the score of 6, for example. This frequency distribution tells us that two persons scored a six, that the number of persons at or below a score of 6 was 8, and that those 8 constitute 89 percent of the total cases. •

So the list of scores and the frequency distribution amount to two ways we can display a distribution of scores. Next we need to explore ways to describe a distribution of scores beyond simply looking at the list of values it contains. • One way to describe a distribution of scores is by its shape. • If we were to create a graph that shows the scores along the horizontal axis and the frequencies along the vertical axis, and if we were to plot the points at which the scores and the frequencies intersect, the X distribution would create a graph like this one. The score of 7 • appears once, the score of 6 • appears twice, the score of 5 • appears three times, the score of 4 • appears twice, and the score of 3 • appears once. If we were to connect these points, we'd see that the shape of the X distribution is perfectly symmetrical. • If you were to draw a line down the center, the right half and left half would be mirror images, just as with the standard normal curve.

Now, let's do the same thing for the Y distribution. • The score of 10 • appears one time, the score of 8 • appears one time, the score of 5 • appears one time, the score of 4 • appears twice, the score of 3 • appears three times, and the score of 2 • appears once. We can see that the shape of the Y distribution is asymmetrical. • Another name for that is skewed. • This is very important: which end of the scoring is causing distribution Y to be skewed: the high end or the low end? The high end. The extreme scores • — called outliers— • are at the top of the distribution. When the outliers are at the top of the distribution, the shape of the distribution is said to be skewed to the right • or positively skewed. • It's easy to see the bulk of the scores piled up at the left, and think of the distribution as skewed to the left, or negatively skewed. Don't let that misperception creep into your thinking. Here's how to remember the type of skew you're seeing. The outliers form a tail, and the tail pulls the mathematical average, the mean score, in the direction of those outliers—makes it artificially high as compared to the group as a whole. That means that the skew is in the direction of the outliers. When you describe the shape of a skewed distribution, remember that the tail tells the tale.

To talk about the shape of a distribution is to describe that distribution in only a general way. • To become specific in our description of a distribution, we need to describe some quantities, • beginning with those in a category known as central tendency. The central tendency of a distribution is a mathematical description that answers this question: on the average, how did they do? When you think of average, what comes to mind? Add the scores • • and then divide by the number of cases. • • Generally we call that the average score, but there are other ways of thinking about the term "average," so we give the mathematical average a specific name • the mean. • This formula reads simply "the sum of the scores divided by the number of cases," with the upper-case sigma sign meaning sum of, the X representing the scores, and the N representing the number of cases. In the case of the X distribution • • we have 45 divided by 9, which is 5. • The statistical symbol for mean is the symbol for score with a bar over it. • Sometimes people even refer to the mean as X-bar. • Now we can do the same thing with the Y distribution. • • • • And we see that the answer to the question "on the average, how did they do?" is that they did a little less well on Test Y than they did on Test X.

So, do you think the mean is a reliable gauge of how a distribution of cases fared on a particular measure? Generally, yes—but not always. When extreme outliers are causing the mean to give us a false picture of the typicality of the distribution, we can eyeball the distribution's central tendency by using another statistic • the median. The median is simply the midpoint of the distribution, the score equidistant from the top and the bottom. What is the median for distribution X? • 5. For distribution Y? • 4. Now, there's still one more way to answer the central tendency question, and that's something called the mode. • The mode is simply the most frequently occurring score. What would that be for X? • 5. For Y? • 3. You need to realize an important truth about the relationship between the central tendency of a distribution and its shape. Look at the measures of central tendency for the X distribution. • • • What was the shape of the X distribution? Symmetrical. The closer a distribution is to symmetrical, the closer the three measures of central tendency will be to each other. If a distribution is perfectly symmetrical, the mean, median, and mode will be identical. That's the case here with the X distribution. Which of these three measures of central tendency is most fundamental? The mean. Only the mean weighs each score of the distribution in exact proportion to its value, so only the mean can be entered into calculations. • The mean is the bread-and-butter statistic of central tendency. Now, let's assume that you have two distributions of scores that are identical in mean, median, and mode. Picture those distributions a minute, and tell me if you think of them as similar. They may be similar, but in fact they may be very dissimilar. • Let's look at two very small distributions, the heights of two groups of four men each. • • • • The mean, median, and mode for both distributions is exactly 6 feet. But look what happens when we fill out the rest of the distributions. • • • • The four guys from the X distribution could walk down the street and draw little notice. The four from the Y distribution couldn't. What's the difference? • A final characteristic for us to consider when we describe a distribution of scores is variability. • • Central tendency answered the question, "on the average, how did they do?" Variability answers the question "on the average, how much did they vary from the average?" • The range gives a general feel for the variability of a distribution, range being simply the difference between the highest score and the lowest score. • The range of distribution X is 4. • The range of distribution Y is 8. That's quite a difference. We can see on the surface that if X and Y represent two tests taken by this group of students, the students were much more alike in what they knew about the content of Test X than they were in what they knew about the content of Test Y. That gives you a peek at how statistics can be valuable to you as a teacher. Knowing how much the students in your class vary in their understanding of what you're teaching will help you tremendously in crafting lesson plans that make sense.

Unfortunately, range isn't a very useful statistic. If Bert and Ophelia had done poorly on Test Y, for example, the range would have been 3 rather than 8. Range is too volatile a statistic—too easily influenced by outliers—to be mathematically useful. The most useful statistic of variability for test analysis is a statistic called the standard deviation. • Think of it roughly as the average number of points that the scores vary from the mean, though technically it's a bit different from that. First I'll show you how to calculate the standard deviation, then I'll show you how to interpret it. • We'll create a column here that shows the difference between each score and the mean. Remember that the mean of the X distribution is 5, so the values are as follows. • • These values go by the name deviation scores. They simply show the extent to which each score deviates from the mean. • • Now we'll create another column that shows those values multiplied by themselves. • • These values we'll call squared deviation scores. Remember those terms, because I'll be using them as if you're familiar with them: deviation scores and squared deviation scores. •

The first calculation we do is to add the column of squared deviation scores. • • That's called the sum of the squared deviation scores, and it's entered into the formula like this. • Then we divide the sum of the squared deviation scores • by the number of cases, minus 1, and take the square root of that value. • That formula will give us the standard deviation. For the X distribution, • that's the square root of 12 divided by eight. Do you see why we use a 12 and an 8? • When we work that out • we end up with a standard deviation of 1.22.

• The formula for the standard deviation of the Y distribution could be written specifically like this. What do we need first? • The Y deviation scores. What's the mean of the Y distribution? 4.67. So for practice, see if you can come up with Bert's deviation score. It's 5.33. • Here are the Y deviation scores. What do we need next? The squared deviation scores. • What will that be for Bert? 28.40. • Here are squared deviation scores for Y. Then what do we do? Sum the squared deviation scores. • • So if we work it out according to the formula, • we get this: • • The standard deviation for the X distribution • is 1.22, and the standard deviation for the Y distribution • is 2.65. So what does that mean? It means that on Test X this group varied from the mean by an average of about one and a quarter points, but on Test Y they varied from the mean by an average of more than two-and-one-half points. As the range hinted to us, they were somewhat alike in what they knew about the content of Test X, but they were very different from each other in what they knew about the content of Test Y. That's the kind of valuable, specific information you can get from test statistics. One last note about standard deviation: • the standard deviation is the bread-and-butter statistic of variability, just as the mean is the bread-and-butter statistic of central tendency. It's the statistic that we can enter into formulas for further calculations. • Finally, • the statistics we're working with here are called descriptive statistics. They're called descriptive statistics because they're used to describe tangible quantitative information that we have available. Test results are a perfect example of tangible quantitative information. The symbols used are • X bar for the mean and • SD for standard deviation. There's another branch of statistics used to make estimates and predictions—the kind of statistics that tell us we have, for example, 2.3 children per household, and the kind that predict who will be the next president. Those are called inferential statistics • and the symbols used there are mu • for mean and lower case sigma • for standard deviation.•

Work the practice calculations on page 54. Be careful not to look ahead to the next page. That will ruin your chance to check yourself on what you understand.

5. Describing Individual Scores, Chapter 2, pages 34-41

•   This is the second of the three sessions that constitute a mini-statistics course. In the first session we explored ways to describe and make sense of distributions of scores. We ignored individual scores completely except to the extent that we needed their information to learn something about the distribution. • In this session we'll explore ways to describe individual scores within a distribution. • You'll find this information elaborated on in Chapter Two of the textbook, on pages 34 through 41.

• • First, though, we should review a few terms from last time. • • • What would you call these lists of test scores? • These are distributions of scores, distributed from high to low and distributed around their means. What's the most fundamental way to describe a distribution of scores? • Its shape. And what shapes do you see in these three distributions? Look them over, and see if you can identify a particular shape to any of them. The first • is nearly symmetrical; the second has outliers at the bottom, • so it's negatively skewed; the last has outliers at the top, • so it's positively skewed.

What's another way to describe a distribution of scores besides its shape? • By its central tendency, answering the question "on the average, how did they do?" What statistics are used within the description of central tendency? • Mean, • median, • and mode.

And what's a third way to describe a distribution of scores? • By its variability, which answers the question "on the average, how much did they deviate from the average?" What gives a general clue about variability? • The range. And what gives valuable, specific information about variability? • The standard deviation. What did we call the bread-and-butter statistic of central tendency? • The mean. And for variability? • The standard deviation. So, those are all important basic terms that you'll want to be ready to use as fluently as you use the names of people you know.

• Now, moving on to the description of individual scores. The most common way for teachers to interpret a test score is as a percentage of the test. If these distributions came from ten-item quizzes, the typical teacher would say that Bert scored 70% on Test X, and 100% on Test Y. A traditional awarding of grades according to percentage correct would generate poor grades for nearly everyone in these two distributions. The teacher who wrote and administered these quizzes could write easier quizzes to make the criterion-referencing work. Or that teacher could let Bert be the star, and let Ophelia show remarkable progress from Test X to Test Y. In other words, the teacher could keep this highly discriminating test in place and use the results as information about how truly different some students are from others, and about what to teach to whom—that is, compare students to each other (norm-referenced) rather than to the number of test items answered correctly (criterion-referenced).

• Let's examine one norm-referenced approach called the percentile rank. Percentile rank compares a given score with the scores of other test-takers in the population rather than with the test. In other words, percentile rank is a norm-referenced statistic rather than a criterion-referenced statistic. A percentile rank shows the percentage of the population scoring at or below each score in the distribution. Of course the size of the population needs to be at least 100 for percentile rank to stay within the realm of descriptive statistics. And generally the statistic is applied to large populations. For example, percentile ranks are used to report results of nationally administered standardized tests. You may have brought information home as a student saying that your verbal skills were at the 87th percentile and your math skills at the 70th. Those were percentile ranks. That means your verbal skills are equal to or better than 87 percent of the population, and your math skills are equal to or better than 70 percent of the population. Percentile ranks are not particularly appropriate for populations smaller than 100, but we could calculate them for any sized population with a formula that lets us infer where missing cases might fall in a population of fewer than 100. Actually, small numbers of cases can be instructive for learning the principle of percentile ranks, so let's learn how to calculate percentile ranks for very small populations as an illustration of how the principle works.

• Here is a ridiculously small distribution of scores. Each of these five cases would have to represent a potential twenty cases if we were to calculate percentile ranks. • So what would common sense tell you the percentile rank is for the score of 4? You might think the 80th percentile on first thought, • but the first case has to accommodate the top 20th percentile, • and the second case the next 20th percentile. A best estimate then, to accommodate the missing cases, would be that a score of 4 is at the 70th percentile rank. Let's look at the formula for percentile rank, and take it from there. • The numerator reads "the number of cases scoring lower than the score in question, plus one-half the number of cases at the score in question." • The number of cases scoring lower than 4 is three. • one-half the number of cases scoring at the score of 4 is one-half. • That puts 3.5 in the numerator. • If we divide that by the five cases, we get the proportion .70, • • which becomes the 70th percentile rank. • I have to emphasize that this exercise is artificial. It just shows graphically how the percentile rank formula uses data from actual cases to accommodate the possibility of an unlimited number of additional cases from the population.

• Let's look at another small distribution, but with a case added to make the answer less predictable by eye. • How many cases have scored lower than the case in question? • Again, the answer is three. Be sure you are thinking in terms of "lower in value," not simply located lower on the page. How many at the case in question? Two, • so one-half of that is one, • for a numerator of

4. • Divide that by the six cases, • to get .66. • That gives us a percentile rank, rounded off, of 67. •

• Now. let's get a little practice at using this formula. Choose any case in the X distribution (more than one if you like), calculate the percentile rank, and when you're through, advance the slide to reveal the answers. •

• Let's try another one, using distribution Y. (Make calculations) •

• The validity of the percentile rank depends on your having administered the test to a normal distribution of cases, which generally requires a greater number of cases than in these distributions. • Let's review for a minute the answer to the question, "What is normal?" • Remember the normal distribution? Let's take another look at it with the percentile rank in mind. • First, notice that I've now added the inferential symbol, mu, for the mean. • And I've added the inferential symbol, lower case sigma, for the standard deviations. • Those symbols reinforce that the standard normal curve is theoretical. • • • • Now let's get a feel for where percentages of the populations would fall relative to a couple specific variables. • Assume these to be the mean and standard deviation for men's height among a particular population. • With the mean at the center, we'll insert the heights that would fall at the various standard deviation points. • • • • • • Let's do the same thing for IQ: • • • The mean and standard deviations shown here are from the Wechsler Intelligence Scale for Children, commonly used in schools. • Here's the mean, • and scores at the standard deviation points. • • • • • • You might recognize that Wechsler score of 130 as the cut off point for gifted programs in some schools. The Standard Normal Curve is applied to more real-life situations than you might think.

Now suppose we were to account for the population that falls within a particular linear distance along the base of the curve. • If we were to take that linear distance near the mean, we'd encompass a large portion of the population. • If we were to take that linear distance near one of the tails, we'd encompass a small portion of the population. That means that the linear distance covered, for example, between the 10 th and 20th percentile rank is much greater than the linear distance covered between the 50th and 60th percentile rank. • Said another way, percentile rank does not have a constant relationship to raw score. • • Let's look at Lenyatta's numbers as an example. Lenyatta's raw score is half of Rhonda's, • but his percentile rank is much less than half of Rhonda's. • What that means is that we can't multiply and divide percentile ranks and make any sense of the results. • You'll remember that we've encountered other statistics that aren't mathematically usable—the median and mode for central tendency, and the range for variability. We have to use the mean to represent central tendency in formulas, and we have to use the standard deviation to represent variability. The percentile rank is another of those mathematically unusable statistics because of its not having a constant relationship to raw score. What we need is a statistic for individual scores that, like the mean and standard deviation, is mathematical usability. We have one. • It's called a standard score. The standard score is a simple, logical operation that's very easy to use. To express a person's score as a standard score, divide the person's deviation score • by the whole distribution's deviation, • • in other words, by the standard deviation. It's as simple as that. • The result is called a z score.

• Now. let's get a little practice at using this formula. • Choose any case in the X distribution (more than one if you like), calculate the z score, and when you're through, advance the slide to reveal the answers—but first. • you'll need to remember a couple other statistics. • • the mean and standard deviation of the X distribution. (Make the z calculations for the X distribution, and then • to reveal answers). • Let's try another one, using distribution Y. • • Here are the mean and standard deviation you need. •

• When I insert z scores into the Standard Normal Curve • • you can see that they have a mean of 0 and a standard deviation of 1. • • • • • • • That means z scores have a one-to-one relationship with standard deviations. When you convert student scores to z scores you see exactly where in the distribution each score falls. A z of 1.5 is one-and-one-half standard deviations above the mean, a z of −.5 is half a standard deviation below the mean, etc. •

The only problem with z scores is that they're awkward to report, especially for the general public to interpret. No one wants to hear that his daughter is a –.4.

• z scores sometimes are transformed into more palatable numbers. It's a bit like translating English into Spanish to make the message easier for someone to receive. • Here's a formula transforming a z score. Multiply the z by the new standard deviation, and then add the new mean. In the 1920s, William McCall proposed a transformed standard score that he named the T score. • Though McCall's mathematical rationale is much more complex than we can explore here, • his standard deviation of 10 and mean of 50 is something you'll see commonly in test manuals. As a sample. if you were to convert this z of 1.26 to a McCall T, what would it be? • How about this z of –.63? • (The answers are 62.6 and 43.7) •

• • Let's put the McCall T scores into the Standard Normal Curve. • • • • • • • When you look at the norm tables in the manual of a standardized test and see numbers concentrated in the 30s, 40s, 50, and 60s, you'll know the norms are reported as standard scores, and that McCall's T is being used instead of the z.

• You might be interested to see one more transformed standard score. • Do these numbers look familiar to you? • SAT scores are nothing more than transformed z scores. The mean of 500 and the standard deviation of 100 • • gives us this. • • • • • • • You'll recall that the highest score on a portion of the SAT is 800. Also, you've heard that "you get 200 points for just putting your name on the paper." That sounds as if you're getting something free, but you're not. The bottom score is 200 rather than 0 because of a phenomenon called chance score, which you'll learn about later in some detail. What it amounts to is that statistically, pure guessing will get you 200 points. Actually, zero would be as difficult to score as 800, because you'd have to know all the correct answers to avoid choosing one by chance. •

Work the practice calculations on page 55. Be careful not to look ahead to the next page. That will ruin your chance to check yourself on what you understand.

6. Describing Relationships, Chapter 2, pages 41-49

• This is the third of the three class sessions that constitute our mini-statistics course. In the first session we explored ways to describe and make sense of distributions of scores, and in our second we explored ways to describe individual scores within a distribution. • Today we'll learn how to describe the relationship between two distributions of scores. • You'll find this information elaborated on in Chapter Two of the textbook, on pages 41 through 49.

• The statistical operation used to estimate a relationship between two variables is called correlation. Whether we're talking about a relationship between the X and Y distributions we've been working with, or any other pair of variables that we might name X and Y for convenience, • if one variable tends to increase as the other increases, the correlation between the two • is positive. • If one variable tends to decrease as the other decreases, that correlation is • also positive. In short, if you can say "as goes X, so goes Y," the two are positively correlated. • It's when the two variables tend to change in opposing directions • that the correlation is negative • • And if information from one variable gives no clue about predicting the other • • the correlation is zero. There is no relationship.

• Here's a matrix of figures that should look familiar to you from the work with standard deviations. Now it's time to learn to calculate something called a correlation coefficient, a number that will give information about the relationship between the X distribution and the Y distribution. The formula might look intimidating at first sight, so we'll build it as we go—out of mostly familiar pieces. • The symbol for correlation is r, which stands for "relationship." • • You know the square root sign, • and the summation sign, • and you're familiar with the sum of the squared X deviation scores. • That value goes right here. • • Then we multiply that • • by the sum of the squared Y deviation scores., • • a value that goes right here. • • • So now • we have this: • • • • • •

Maybe you've noticed that all the calculations we've done have involved the X distribution and the Y distribution independently. It stands to reason that at some point we need an operation that will intermix the two if we're going to end up with a value that tells us something about their relationship to each other. That's where the numerator of this formula comes into play. The numerator is the sum of the deviation score products. It looks like this. • • We'll put the column for deviation score products over here. • This next operation will look a bit tedious, but experience shows this to be the best way to avoid confusion.

• If you multiply Bert's X deviation score by Bert's Y deviation score, • and put the product of the two here, • you've begun to build the column of deviations score products. Now we'll continue to calculate deviation score products for each case, like this. (*Eight sets of three slide changes will take you to the bottom of the columns.*) Remember your old math rules that 0 time anything is 0, and a negative times a negative is a positive, and when you get to the bottom of the column, you simply add what you have • • and you find that the numerator for the formula is 23. • • Now we'll move that value into the formula we've built, • and we're ready to finish working our way to the correlation coefficient. (*Click repeatedly until showing the coefficient .89.*)

• So now we have a correlation coefficient that carries information about the relationship between distribution X and distribution Y. The next step is to learn what it means—in other words, how to interpret it. •

• • • Correlation coefficients revolve around a 0 point. To the positive side, • • they range to a perfect positive correlation of one. To the negative side, • • they range to a perfect negative correlation of negative one. • • As correlations approach 0, they're considered weak. • • As they approach the end points, they're considered strong. • • And the stronger a correlation between two variables, the more confidently we can predict one from knowing the other. • What can we say about our .89 coefficient? It's a strong positive correlation. (Remember this: the sign indicates the direction of the correlation, and the absolute number indicates its strength. For example, a –.75 correlation coefficient gives more predicting power than a coefficient of .70.)

There's a tendency to perceive a .89 correlation coefficient as an indication that the two variables have 89% common ground. • That's not the case. • • • Here's an array of correlation coefficients. The nice, neat whole numbers will make the math easier to see. • If we were to square these coefficients, we would see the amount of common ground between whatever two variables have been correlated. • • These squared correlation coefficients • • • are called coefficients of determination, because they determine the amount of common ground that the corresponding coefficient indicates.

• • If two variables overlap to this extent, • the correlation might be about • .80, which would indicate that the amount of common ground is • 64%. • • If two variables overlap to this extent, • the correlation might be about • .60, which would indicate that the amount of common ground is • 36%.• • If two variables overlap to this extent, • the correlation might be about • .30, which would indicate that the amount of common ground is • 9%.

7. Checklists (and an Introduction to Rating Scales), Chapter 4, pages 71- 73

• The checklist is a simple device for assessing either a performance or a product of some kind. • Checklists are elaborated on in Chapter Four of the textbook, on pages 71 through 73. • (Advance slides eight times while delivering this): Here's a list of eight accomplishments you might be looking for in a beginning instrumentalist. We'll call these criteria. They have to be written to accommodate a "yes" or "no" answer. • Where the answer is "yes, I observe this," the blank preceding that criterion gets a mark. Where the answer is "no, I do not observe this," the corresponding blank is left empty. This assessment device is a simple checklist. • After you've used it, you know what's present and what's not, but you have no idea of the degree, from most desirable to least desirable.

• A tool designed to show degrees is the Likert scale. • It has a baseline along which the degrees of accomplishment or agreement run. • It has vertical lines to show five categories of response, and descriptions of the responses. • • • • • The Likert scale is used most commonly to collect opinions, but it could be customized to be used as an assessment tool.

• Some teachers use a numbered scale to show degrees of accomplishment. Typically, it shows general statements something like these, • • • • • and each general description is associated with a number: • • • • • The problem with this scale is that it gives no information about what makes the perform-ance, for example, average as compare to good. So there are no clues about how to teach for improvement. Remember, the purpose of assessment is to improve instruction. For an assessment tool to help us do that, it needs to tell us in more specific terms the level of accomplishment.

• We can get that kind of information from a good rating scale. We'll be delving deeply into rating scales beginning with the next session. For now, we'll just take a surface look at a rating scale to give a starting point for next time. • First, a good, diagnostic rating scale is aimed at one particular dimension of the performance, because no one is average, good, or outstanding in every respect. • • The dimension shown in this first sample rating scale is tone quality. • Next, a good rating scale has some form of rating for the assessor to use. • • • • • In this case, we have a top rating of five and a bottom rating of one. • And finally, a rating scale has criteria that the assessor is listening for. • In this case, the best tone quality that might be heard among the performers being assessed is described in this way. • The worst tone quality that might be heard among the performers being assessed is described in this way. • This scale covers too wide a span to be practical for any one, cohesive group, but it could apply to secondary school instrumentalist in general. Some have a tone quality that would fit anywhere if they had the technique and musicianship to go with it, and some have such undeveloped sounds as to leave question about exactly what's being heard. Now let's fill in the other criteria. • • • This is a specific kind of rating scale. We have a lot to learn about it. We'll get into details next time.•

8. Rating Scales, Chapter 4, pages 74-85

• Rating scales are the bedrock of performance assessment. Rubrics, the most visible performance assessment tool in today's schools, are just a variation of the basic rating scale. That makes what you learn about rating scales fundamental to all other performance assessment. • Basic information about rating scales is found in Chapter Four of the textbook, on pages 74-85, with guidance for using rating scales continuing to page 92.•

This is the rating scale introduced at the end of the last session. • What's this called? • • The dimension. Because nothing is one dimensional, nothing can be assessed thoroughly by examining only one dimension. A thorough performance assessment will involve examining multiple dimensions, tone quality being only one. What do we call the list of qualities we have here as a guide? • Criteria, each one individually being called a criterion. And the numbers? • Ratings. This kind of rating scale has a specific name. • This is a continuous rating scale, because the criteria progress up a continuum. • • That is, 1 logically precedes 2, 2 logically precedes 3, etc. And because the top rating is a 5, it's called even more specifically • a five-point continuous rating scale. This is the Cadillac of performance assessment tools.

• If I were to list these five items • • • • • and then put blanks by them, •
what would I have? • A checklist. And because I've limited it to only five items, • we might call it a five-point checklist. Then if I were to add a dimension name, • call these items criteria, • and call the blanks ratings, • I'd have a lot of the characteristics we just saw in the rating scale. • If we were to call this a kind of rating scale, we'd have to distinguish it from the continuous rating scale. Why? Because the criteria aren't arranged on a continuum. Rather than progress from the bottom to the top, performers might achieve any number of these criteria in unpredictable order. The rating awarded, instead of the number reached, will be the number of check marks

achieved. Because we're adding the number of criteria achieved to get a rating, • this is sometimes called an additive rating scale. Specifically, • it's called a five-point additive rating scale. You can mix the rating scale and checklist approach by having some continuous and some additive dimensions, the purposes being to (1) accommodate dimensions that don't operate continuously, and (2) maintain ratings of 1-5 for all dimensions, giving continuity to the thinking of the assessor and cohesiveness to the statistical analysis.

This general performance scale will require you to decide ahead of time how accurate rhythms or pitches must be to achieve a check mark. This is a kind of big-picture scale, which you'll want in some circumstances, but additive scales can be written more specifically if you want to focus in more tightly on a specific criterion. • For example, we could take the criterion "expressive performance" from this general scale, and make it the dimension for a new, more specific scale. • The new scale might be either continuous or additive, depending on its nature. • • • We'll make this one additive so you can see a more specific approach to additive scales. • • The ratings will be blanks to be checked. • The criteria will need to be specific and concise, and written in parallel structure. • • • • •

• To finish, let's double back to the continuous scale, the more difficult to write of the two kinds of rating scales. • Let's look at a supposed continuous scale that's problematic. (*A series of 9 slide changes builds the scale.*) I'll build the scale here, which consists of parts that are all recognizable to you now, and you see if you can tell me what problems it presents. This scale is likely to not operate continuously. What rating would you give if a performer achieved criteria 3 and 4, but not criterion 2? You don't want to ever put yourself into that position. A good continuous rating scale is a powerful assessment tool, but a good additive scale is superior to a problematic continuous scale.

• To finish on a positive note, • let's take a look at a continuous scale that works well. • This was written to measure the ability of primary-aged children to synchronize movement with musical examples at a variety of tempos. • •

The ratings show it to be continuous. • Let's evaluate the criteria for their ability to function continuously. • • • • •

One last point to be made about rating scales is that the result of writing a good scale and using it well is likely to conform roughly to the standard normal curve. • Think of the base of the curve turned 90°. Then if you draw in the bell, • • you'll see that ratings of 1 and 5 fall in the tails. That is, they should be rare events, as compared to the other ratings that fall in the large part of the bell.

• Finally, let's review rating scale concepts with a hypothetical assessment of fifth grade instrumental performances. What will we use for the assessment? • A rating scale. • Why not just count the number of errors? Because we need some specific information if we expect to improve instruction. We'll organize our rating scale into large units called what? • Dimensions. Will we use more than one dimension? • • • We will if it's an assessment circumstance that calls for us to be thorough. (All circumstances don't call for that. We'll talk about shortcut assessments later.) • Why multiple dimensions? Performances are by nature multi-dimensional, so a thorough assessment should be multi-dimensional. What will we have within each dimension? • Criteria to guide the assessment. • • • And ratings from which to choose. • Why two kinds of ratings? Because every dimension of a performance doesn't operate continuously. It's the same reason we have hammers and screwdrivers: a single tool can't do every job well. • Why five? Experience shows that five criteria yield the highest reliability for continuous scales. • • Why the same number? It makes assessment thinking more consistent and statistical analysis more cohesive. •

9. Theoretical Constructs of a Five-Point Rating Scale, Chapter 4, pages 92-97

After you've written a rating scale and used it to assess a group of performances, you'll have a distribution of scores. What would you learn about the central tendency and variability of that distribution by calculating a mean and a standard deviation? In other words, what's a "good" mean or a "good" standard deviation? You need some kind of benchmarks with which to compare your results. • Those benchmarks are the theoretical constructs of a five-point rating scale. • You'll find this information elaborated on in Chapter Four of the textbook, on pages 92 through 97.

• The theoretical mean of a five-point rating scale is based on what we should expect if the distribution of scores conforms to the theory of the standard normal curve. • That is, the mean, theoretically, is expected to fall at the mid-point of the distribution, with the scores above and below the mean roughly mirroring each other. For something as simple as a five-point scale, you'd think you could find that midpoint easily enough just by looking at the scale. • The midpoint is obviously a 3. • • We can confirm that by applying the formula for the theoretical mean: the sum of the potential ratings divided by the number of the potential ratings. • The ratings add to 15, • which we then divide by the number of ratings, 5: • • That gives us the theoretical mean that we expected when we just eye-balled the scale: 3. There's one small technical problem, though. • It's possible for a student to do nothing, or do something that fails to reach even the criterion described as a 1. That means we have six potential ratings, • • which changes the theoretical mean to 2.5. • • • Because the 0 is less likely than any of the other responses, you might want to think of the theoretical mean, sometimes called the expected mean, as floating somewhere between 2.5 and 3, but for calculations, we'll use the 2.5. •

Do you have any thoughts about how we might arrive at a theoretical standard deviation? • How many standard deviations should we expect between the theoretical mean and the top? 3. • So if we were to put into the numerator figures that would give us the distance between the mean and the top, • • then all we'd have to do is divide that by 3 • to find the expected size of the standard deviation for an ideal rating scale, like this: (***Click repeatedly to show the working out of the calculations.***) •

10. Review of the Uses of Correlation with Rating Scales, Chapter 4, page 98

• This is just an overview of the ways we've used the correlation statistic to gain insight into our rating scale process. • This information is shown in the textbook in Chapter Four, on page 98. • We've calculated correlation coefficients for three distinct purposes: to estimate • the extent of our own consistency or reliability, • the extent to which our ratings are consistent with those of someone else, • and the extent to which our dimensions appear to operate independently.

• • • In all three cases, we compare an X distribution with a Y distribution. • When we estimate our own consistency—our internal, or intra-judge reliability—the X distribution is the distribution we create with our first rating and the Y distribution is the distribution we create when we re-rate the performances after letting a little time pass. • When we estimate our consistency with another rater, the X distribution is the distribution we create and the Y distribution is the distribution the other person creates. • When we estimate intercorrelations, the X distribution is the set of ratings we create when we rate one particular dimension, and the Y distribution is the set of ratings we create when we rate a second dimension.

A few important thoughts. (1) The only purpose in your making a second rating is to create data for calculation of your reliability within yourself. For all other correlations, pretend that second rating doesn't exist: use only your first ratings. (2) Your expectations should be different for each type of calculation. You should be able to achieve reliability with yourself above .80, and likely above .90. Your reliability with another person will be lower, but should reach .70 and is likely to be above .80. Your intercorrelations should not be nearly as high as either reliability correlation, because the intercorrelations show the degree of independence between dimensions. Intercorrelations for a rating scale with truly independent dimensions are likely to range from about .40 to .60, and should not approach the figure reached for reliability. •

11. Multiple Choice Terms, Chapter 6, page 138

• You need to be familiar with a few standard terms related to multiple choice tests. • This information is shown in the textbook in Chapter Six, on page 138.

• • The entries in a multiple choice test aren't referred to as questions, because all of them aren't phrased as questions. More common are statements that need to be completed. • So each of the entries is called an item. • This is not question number one, but item number one. • The fragment following the item number is called the stem, • • and the choices that follow it • are called options. • • The correct response, • oddly enough, goes by the name • • "correct response." And the three responses that are not correct • are called foils • • or distractors.

The items that students read from when they take the test need to be legible and easy to use. That may require quite a few pages, creating a packet that's sometimes called • the test booklet. If you have students record their responses on a bubble sheet, that's called • a response sheet, and the response sheet on which you record the correct responses for scoring is called • the key. •

12. Writing Multiple Choice Items, Chapter 6, pages 140-151

(Note: This series of multiple choice items and suggested revisions is taken directly from the textbook. You may find simply studying those pages of the book the most efficient way to review. If you do want to use the slides, open the book to the appropriate pages and read the advice that accompanies each example as you progress through the slides.)

13. Multiple Choice Analysis of Items, Chapter 6, pages 152-162

The quality of a test depends on the quality of its individual items. • There are ways to analyze the items in a multiple choice test to learn specifically how they're contributing to the overall effect of the test. That gives you confidence in the items that are working well, and it gives you a chance to repair or remove weak items. • You'll find this information elaborated on in Chapter Six of the textbook, on pages 152 through 162. •

The two characteristics of the items that you'll be checking are difficulty— • measured by the percentage of correct responses—and discrimination.• Keep in mind all this time that everything we're talking about applies to a particular individual test item, not to the test as a whole. •

• Item difficulty is a simple matter of finding the percentage of the test-takers who answered the item correctly, which is a matter of dividing • the number of correct responses by • • the number of test-takers. Here are a few examples. (*Advance a series of three calculations, each with four slide changes.*) • Which of these items is most difficult? • The last, because it was answered correctly by the smallest percentage of students.

• Item discrimination is a measure of how well an item discriminates between those who know most and those who know least, which, of course, is what a test is designed to do. Scores on the test as a whole are used as the measure of who knows most. • What's desirable is to have positively discriminating items, items that are answered correctly by the most successful students more so than by the least successful students. • Where you see the red flags are for items that act in the opposite way.

• Here's a way to analyze by hand the discrimination power of an item. • You separate the tests into two halves, the top-scoring half and the bottom-scoring half. (If you have an odd number, set the middle score aside and don't use it.) The discrimination power of the item then is indicated by • subtracting the number of correct answers given by the least successful half of the class from the number of correct answers given by the most successful half of the class, and • • then dividing that value by one-half the number of students. Here are two examples. (*Advance through a pair of calculations, each with eight slide changes.*) •

The next step after obtaining a discrimination coefficient is to know what it means. Here are some very general ways you might think of discrimination coefficients. • • • • You need to know, though, that weak discrimination coefficients don't always signify that an item needs revision. Calculation of discrimination power by the formula we're using depends on our identifying two groups of students fundamentally different from one another. The more those groups become like each other, the less potential there is for an item to discriminate between them. • Let's look at the discrimination analysis for a very easy item. • The easiness leaves a difference of only one student between the two groups. • • When we divide that by half the number of students, • • • • we end up with so small a numerator • that a small coefficient is pre-ordained.

• The same is true for a very difficult item. (*Advance calculations through a series of slide changes.*) What all this means is that for items at either extreme of difficulty, you have to lower your expectations for a strong discrimination coefficient. Why? • Because the two groups that supposedly act differently act very much alike if the item is very easy • or if it's very difficult, •

• • • Now let's consider the negatively discriminating items. Consider a negative coefficient a red flag that alerts you to examine the item to see if it needs to be revised or removed. You'll never eliminate all negatively discriminating items, and some will pass the test when you check them out. In a small class, particularly, a careless error or two from top students combined with a lucky guess or two from bottom students can flip a perfectly good item from positive to negative.

• What we've been talking about up to this point is by-hand calculation of discrimination coefficients, a skill that you might need to exercise in isolated circumstances. • • Usually, though, the calculation of discrimination coefficients is done by computer. • • Let's contrast discrimination analysis by hand with discrimination analysis by computer. The latter gives not only quicker results, but more precise results. (*Advance through 28 slide changes to build the complete figure. Consult the textbook for clarifying details.*) •

14. Estimating the Reliability of a Multiple Choice Test, Chapter 6, pages 162-164

A theme that's run throughout this course is that reliability is essential if a test is to be valid. • Let's look at ways that a multiple choice test can be checked for reliability. • You'll find this information elaborated on in Chapter Six of the textbook, on pages 162 through 164. • Along the way we'll review some of our previous methods of estimating reliability for performance tests.

• A basic method of estimating reliability • is by test-retest. That amounts to administering the test, readministering the test, and then calculating a coefficient between the first and second distributions of scores. • In general terms, the coefficient yielded is a Pearson correlation, in more specific terms, a reliability coefficient, • • and in most specific terms a coefficient of stability. Let's think about which factors hold constant • and which are variable. • For the two testings, • the items and the subjects are the same. • All that changes is the time. • • • •

A major drawback to the test-retest approach is that it requires a lot of time from students, time that's difficult to justify. • The antidote to that is another method of checking reliability, in which a distribution consisting of one-half of the test items is correlated with a second distribution consisting of the other half. The reliability coefficient yielded by the split halves method is called the coefficient of internal consistency. • The constants are subjects and time; • the variable is the items. •

• A third method is a matter of making multiple forms of a test and then checking them against each other to be sure they equate. This is used, for example, for civil service exams given to rooms full of people who are kept from cheating by having different forms of the same test. • The reliability coefficient yielded by the parallel forms method is called the coefficient of equivalence. • The constants and variables are the same as for the split halves method. • • You're not likely to make use of the parallel forms method for classroom testing. • • •

Let's reinforce the terms used for each of these methods. Test retest yields a • coefficient of stability, split halves yields a • coefficient of internal consistency, and parallel forms yields a • coefficient of equivalence. Of course all of them, in more general terms, are reliability coefficients.

• Let's review some of the reliability testing we talked about for performance tests. • • When you used a rating scale twice to check your own consistency over time, you used a variation of the test-retest method, • which I refer to as rate-rerate, • or intrajudge reliability. • • Here are the constants and the variable. When you and a partner used the same rating scale, • you got a measure of interjudge reliability, • • with these as the constants and this as the variable.

We talked a short while ago about the challenges involved in the split halves approach to estimating reliability. What if, instead of having to make all those decision about the nature of the split, we were to calculate every possible split and take an average of the results? For a 40-item test, that would require 780 correlation calculations (N x N–1 over 2, = 40 x 39 over 2) That would be daunting to do by hand, but the computer age has ushered in • the Kuder-Richardson Formula 20 (KR 20) that does just that. • • technically, the constants and the variable are the same as for the split halves technique, • but in reality, the problem of item differences has been washed out, • making the items functional as a constant. • The only problem with KR-20 is that the coefficient it yields is for a test half the length of the original. • To compensate for that problem of test length, we need another formula applied to give us the reliability estimate for a test of our original length. • That formula is the Spearman/Brown formula. • It's a matter of • doubling the KR reliability estimate, and then dividing it by one plus the KR reliability. • For example, if the KR figure were .68, • and we applied the Spearman/Brown formula, • we'd find that the true reliability of our test is not • .68, but rather .81. • •

15. Theoretical Constructs of a Multiple Choice Test, Chapter 6, pages 168-171

After you've written a multiple choice test and used it to assess the learning of a group of students, you'll have a distribution of scores. What would you learn about the central tendency and variability of that distribution by calculating a mean and a standard deviation? What's a "good" mean or a "good" standard deviation? You need some kind of benchmarks with which to compare your results. • Those benchmarks are the theoretical constructs of a multiple choice test. • You'll find this information elaborated on in Chapter Six of the textbook, on pages 168 through 171. First we'll look at the formulas and think through the reasoning for the formulas, and then we'll look at a specific application of those formulas.

The theoretical constructs of a multiple choice test, unlike those of a rating scale, vary from one test to another. That is, they're influenced by the number of items in the test and by the number options for each item. • Test-takers will mark correct responses for some items through pure chance. The first step to calculating the theoretical constructs of a multiple choice test is to calculate the chance score, • the score that statistical probability would give to a person who marked answers without even reading them. • The chance score is simply the number of items in the test, • • divided by the number of options for each item. Statistically, for a test having four options per item, one could expect to answer one in four items correctly while knowing nothing.

• The theoretical mean would not be the middle score, because chance score has to be accounted for. The first step to calculating the theoretical mean, then, is to find the midpoint of what remains after chance score is removed. • To do that, we subtract the chance score from the number of items • • divide that by 2 to find its midpoint, • • and then add the chance score back on. •

• How many standard deviations do we expect between the theoretical mean and a perfect score? 3. • So to calculate the theoretical standard deviation, • • we have to subtract the theoretical mean from the number of items, • and then divide that value by 3. •

• • Let's assume we want to find the theoretical constructs for a 40-item multiple choice test having four options per item. • We'll let this rectangle symbolize the whole test. • At the top is a perfect score, • and at the bottom is 0. How many items will be answered correctly by chance? Ten, because 40 items divided by 4 options equals 10. • • So that's the chance score.

• How do we calculate the theoretical mean? We subtract the chance score from the total number of items to find the number of items in the meat of the test, and find that to be 30. Then we divide that 30 in half to get 15. But 15 isn't the answer, because we've set aside the chance score of 10 that we assume everyone will get. So we add that 10 back onto the 15, • • and arrive at a theoretical mean of 25.

Now how do we calculate the theoretical standard deviation? We expect how many standard deviations between the theoretical mean and the top? 3. • Because the space in which those three reside is 40 minus 25, or 15, we find the theoretical standard deviation to be one-third of 15, which is 5. • • From there we can easily find the score points • • • • • at which all of the standard deviations theoretically fall.•

Index